Notes

On the dynamics of man

Organization theory * Philosophy * Politics * Religion

BY *ROBERT MERCER-NAIRNE*

POETRY

Mercer-Nairne in Malta
Illustrated by Marisa Attard

On Fire
Illustrated by Marisa Attard

NOVELS

The Letter Writer
Like No Other
Warlord

NON-FICTION

***Notes** on the dynamics of man*

Notes

On the dynamics of man

By

Robert Mercer-Nairne

GRITPOUL INC. * WASHINGTON

First Edition 2010

Mercer-Nairne, Robert.
Notes : on the dynamics of man : organization theory, philosophy, politics, religion / by Robert Mercer-Nairne.
p. cm.
Includes bibliographical references and index.
LCCN 2009929518
ISBN-13: 978-0-9748141-4-8
ISBN-10: 0-9748141-4-8

1. Organizational sociology--Philosophy. 2. System theory--Philosophy. I. Title. II. Title: On the dynamics of man.

HM786.M47 2010 302.3'5
QBI09-600159

Published in the United States of America by Gritpoul Inc.,
601 Union Street, Suite 4900, Seattle, WA 98001-3906.
Published in the European Union by Gritpoul,
Meikleour House, Meikleour, Perth PH2 6EA, Scotland.

www.gritpoul.com

Interior Design and Typesetting: Publishing Professionals, Port Richey, FL.
Author photograph: RPM Limited, 24-40 Goodwin Road, London W12 9JW.
Cover Design: Larry Rostant.

Printed in Canada by Friesens Corporation.

Organization Theory — Philosophy — Politics — Religion.

10 9 8 7 6 5 4 3 2 1

The paper used in this publication meets the minimum requirements of the American National Standard for Information Sciences — Permanence of Paper for Printed Library Materials, ANSI Z39.48-1984.

For

Borje O. Saxberg

CONTENTS

Confessions, Acknowledgments and Thanks

THIS SECTION IS longer than is customary and more far-ranging. The reason is that lately I have been spotting the Reaper out of the corner of my eye, standing in the shadows, running a thumb across the blade of his scythe as he eyes me up. And although he seems a kindly gentleman, not the grim one of repute, I believe he is telling me I should get my thanks out while I can. So that is what I will do.

But first, the confession. Since I started writing in earnest, some ten years ago, I have published my own work. This is not a course I would recommend, as writing engagingly is hard enough without adding to it the burden of publishing and self-promotion. In my case, I had spent time running several small businesses before writing, so it seemed a natural thing to do and besides, it allowed me to develop in my own way. However, let me offer a warning to anyone contemplating a similar path. Writing, most of us can do. Getting a book printed is easy. But to get accepted as a writer, formidable barriers must be overcome. I will illustrate with a true story.

When my first novel, *The Letter Writer*, came out, my publicist secured an interview with a lady whose book show is quite widely syndicated. Now whatever you do, this publicist told me, don't tell her your book is self-published. Excited, and rather nervous, I went to the studio she used in a suburb of Los Angeles. After a momentary hiatus, just before I was due to go 'on air', when the lady's assistant thrust a document in front of me to sign, giving her boss all rights to what was about to transpire, the camera rolled and the interview began. She had obviously enjoyed the book and our conversation went well. So a day or two later I invited her and her husband to dinner. While my wife was talking to her husband and the wine and atmosphere were working their wonders, I felt an overpowering urge to confess and let slip that my book was self-published. It was as if I had taken out a gun and pulled the trigger. I thought my guest was going to choke on her confit de canard. The evening went rapidly downhill after that, and she has never dealt with me since, which is a pity, as I liked her and think she liked my book.

The book world is a mesh of interlocking hierarchies from distributors to publishers, agents and literary reviewers awash with titles and subject to brutal competition from other forms of media entertainment. It is a citadel under siege. The pipe that feeds information about books to the public is becoming ever narrower, and ever more pervasive, so that greater volumes of fewer titles must be marketed to the greatest number of people. This is not all bad, just as supermarkets are not all bad. But the homogenization of ideas, or, indeed, of any range of products, carries risks, as I hope this book will make clear. So rather than being thought of as a no-hoper who has resorted to 'vanity publishing', or as an arrogant s.o.b. who has sought to circumvent the book world's priesthood, I would rather you thought of me as a specialty-store offering something a little different. Who knows, one day I might even become mainstream.

* * * *

When it comes to acknowledgments, it is hard to know where to begin. Each of us owes so much to those whose ideas and personality we have encountered in books, on the stage, in films, on television, during our upbringing and education, and in our work. Later, you will see that I call this the *cerebral structure* we are part of. Our thoughts are the thoughts of others rearranged like china in a china cabinet to suit our own taste. Originality is a rare thing, and even it is only an alchemy applied to the labors of others. So my acknowledgments and thanks will merge into one.

When I asked Alastair Chirnside if he would edit my book he said he would be delighted, but was worried that he did not have the right expertise, and this from a man with a double first from Merton College, Oxford. I chose Alastair not only because of his formidable brain, but because he gave up a lucrative career in finance to become a teacher. I told him he had just the right expertise — he is also a classicist — as I was more interested in flow of argument and moral content than in getting bogged down in the nitty-gritty of the various fields I sped through. There are times for the particular and times for the general. ***Notes*** is about the general, and Alastair worked tirelessly to make my ideas more coherent and accessible. I am also grateful to Alastair's two colleagues, Percy Harrison and Justin Nolan for looking at specific chapters. Their help, generously given, steered me clear of many mantraps. Responsibility for the errors and omissions that remain is mine.

* * * *

When we start out on our journey through life, we do not have the slightest idea where it will take us. But as we look back, most of us can point to a few people who have nudged us this way or that and made a difference to the direction we took. I think I must have had a rather unruly childhood. My aristocratic father was a politician and my parents were away a good deal on official business of one sort or another. I dare say I was on the way to becoming an archetypal spoiled brat. Only once was I reigned in, in a serious way, when I was about ten, and that was by a Scottish gentleman, in the true sense of the word, who was my father's head keeper (the head of a team of men who looked after the game on the estate where I roamed). I cannot remember the exact circumstances, although am sure I had been behaving in an arrogant and thoughtless fashion, but can still feel the rebuke Archie Findlay gave me. No raised words. No anger. Just his sense of sorrow as he reflected back to me my own folly. Years later, my American grandfather would perform the same trick, and I loved them both dearly.

I was a late developer, academically, as mild dyslexia kept me near the bottom of every class. At the first boarding school I attended — you were sent away at 8 in those days — I had to carry a little book around, to be signed at the end of each class. A tick would mean the teacher thought I had tried. A cross would mean he thought I had not. As I kept jumbling up letters and words the crosses predominated, and after three had accumulated I had to take the book to the headmaster and receive a beating. This corpulent, chain-smoking man, who was very diligent with the flat side of a large clothes brush, died while I was there, and I remember feeling delighted, until I discovered his replacement was even worse.

Things were not much better at the next school I was sent to, although I was, largely, left to my own devices. However one man, Ian Lawson, realized I wanted to go to university and didn't stand a chance if I stayed. So thanks to him I was sent to a place of forced learning where I eventually met a remarkable man called George Campbell. He was very awkward, very shy and very private and must have seen something of himself in me, and we clicked. Thanks to him I did get into a university — although then found love and almost blew it. I squeaked out with an indifferent degree in economics, and the realization that I was going to have to try a good deal harder. That was the turning point.

Over the next forty years I moved between the academic world and the business world, all the time with a growing curiosity about how human systems work. On two occasions the University of Washington, in Seattle, has nurtured me and I owe it a great debt. I may not have followed a conventional path, but the freedom that university gave me to be unconventional is something I treasure deeply. Whether I am able to repay my debt will depend upon the extent to which what I argue in this book inspires young women and young men to develop human thought, just as others have inspired me. Here I want to thank Terry Mitchell, Tom Lee, Jody Fry, Denis Strong, Dick Peterson and, especially, Borje Saxberg, to whom this book is dedicated, for giving me the freedom to think, and the guidance to think with more clarity than I would have managed for myself.

* * * *

As I have increasingly turned, in recent years, to exploring the foothills of the mind, I have felt like one of those adventurers whose only link to the world of people is occasional radio contact. Three ladies of great (and I hasten to add, good) character have always bucked me up no end whenever I have spoken to them: my cousin Ginny Vanocur and friends Vicki Reed and Marie Mifsud. So, too has my sister, Georgina. When our parents' marriage was sinking into diabolical confusion, threatening to take us down with it, we hung on to each other like survivors from a shipwreck. Out of habit, we are still holding on, but now from the safety of dry land.

* * * *

Writers habitually thank their families, and for good reason. Their members are often the only people scribblers see, for months on end, when they emerge, periodically, from their labors, to blink at the sunlight. I have learned far more from my three children, all now adults, than I am sure they ever learned from me. And now I am learning from my grandchildren too, not least how precious the young are. And as for my wife, Jane, who believes men should be men, that women should be women and that children need both parents, what can I say? Well, she lets me ramble on about this and that, and we have been best friends now for over 35 years. To say that things have always been easy for us would be a lie, but as Winston Churchill did with his wife, whenever a bad stretch comes our way we just repeat to each other the initials K.B.O. (Keep Buggering On), and that seems to get us through. So, if none of my book makes sense to you, at least remember that —

K.B.O.

1

Introduction

SEVERAL YEARS AGO I wrote a poem and it went like this:

> I watched a blind cord
> Flapping in the wind,
> Clack, clack-clack,
> Twisting wildly,
> Full of life.
> To think it is a ripple
> From that primal cauldron
> That blew its energy into all things
> And gave *us* life,
> Is strange.[1]

The thought that something as simple as a length of thin rope, moving in front of an open window, could tie us to the start of our universe intrigued me. If its freedom was illusory, was mine? Or was there something in the unfolding of the universe, which embraces you, me, the blind cord and everything else, that is both constrained and unconstrained? And is the tension between these two extremes the dynamic that drives evolution, that drives life itself? If so, as I believe it is, then thinking about the dynamics of man requires us to think about

1. *Blind cord* included in *On Fire*, published by Gritpoul in 2004.

the full evolutionary process we are part of, and this raises the question — what do we mean by evolution?

Traditionally, the term has been applied to the process whereby organic life has developed from primitive organisms into the structures we see today, including ourselves. For my purpose, however, this is too narrow a use of the term. When I speak of evolution I am referring to the entire process of transformation that has characterized our universe from its beginning, as we understand it, to the present, and that includes, of course, organic elaboration.

We live in an age of increasing specialization. Scientific disciplines are now so focused and concentrated, even to the extent of having their own language, that it takes a great investment of time and energy to become an expert in almost any field. The generalist — which is what I consider myself to be — is often hard-pressed to see the wood for the trees. But hard-pressed does not mean incapable, even if I must ask all those specialists, whose territory I invade, for leniency.

As others have noted, it is difficult to escape the conclusion that all knowledge is contextual. I call context an explanatory story. Just play this simple game and you will see what I mean. Have someone write down a list of characteristics of two people, one whom you know and one whom you do not, using the same headings (age, height, weight, sex, eye color — a few simple things). Before being told which relates to the person you know, study the lists. The information — this knowledge — really won't mean much to you. But as soon as you are told which relates to your friend, all manner of thoughts will occur to you (*Goodness, he's put on weight!; No, her eyes aren't green!; etc.*).

Security services face this problem all the time. Huge amounts of information are gathered, although for it to mean anything their operatives have to know what they are looking for. But whenever you prejudge information, there is a risk that you will find what you are looking for, even when it is not there. Search for faces amongst some random patterns on the bathroom floor and you will probably discover them. The Christian religion invented the Devil and having done so, found Satan's evil ways — everywhere! Science is not immune from this problem. A scientific hypothesis is merely a special kind of question. In asking it, you have already formulated its answer.[2]

Context is the domain of the generalist. Every so often, we need to ask ourselves if we are looking at the world in the right way. And I hasten to add that the right way is not a fixed point, but merely a progression towards greater understanding. In this book I want to shift the context — to alter the way we look at ourselves — because I believe that sufficient knowledge has now accumulated to justify this and because I hope that doing so will improve the human lot.

But before I take you on this journey, I must tell you how we will approach it and what the key ideas are. In ***Part 1*** I lay out a framework showing how I believe the universe works and suggest that it is within this context that our considerable knowledge should be deployed. However, it needs to be recognized, perhaps more than it is, that whenever you codify something (using anything from a simple diagram to a complex algorithm) you gain in precision but lose in meaning. There is nothing wrong with precision, and much that is good about it, just so long as its limitations are recognized. In large part, these ***Notes*** are about the reason behind precision's limitations.

In ***Part 2***, I do great injustice to the history profession by trying to outline our past in under one hundred pages. Even Norman Davies, in his remarkable one volume history of Europe, needed over 1,384 of them. But my goal was more modest. I wanted to paint an admittedly selective and not always chronological picture that highlighted some of the ways in which our human structures have evolved. Naturally, my purpose in doing this was to illustrate the arguments I am developing, and so the history I present is not proof but judicious evidence, more akin to that which an advocate for the prosecution would advance in a court of law. In short, it is skewed in my favor, but isn't history, like knowledge generally, always hostage to its context?

---

2. That is to say, you have established the parameters within which the answer must fall. It leaves no scope for someone to say, now hold on a minute: that's the wrong question!

In ***Part 3***, I look at aspects of ourselves, in ascending order if you will, from the human brain to the individual, on through the various collective arrangements or structures, both informal and formal, that so influence our everyday actions. Having had a foot in both the scientific and the literary camps, I have come to the conclusion that we live within stories (a concept I discuss in ***Part 1***) and that politics, or how we attempt to rationalize change, is the process whereby these stories are built, maintained and amended. The fault-line is still between Plato's republic, governed by wise men but prone to authoritarian dictatorship, and the Periclean democracy of involved citizens, itself prey to mindless anarchy. In Part 4 I discuss how we might better reconcile these two positions.

Notes, however, is not primarily a how-to manual, but more of a mind-shift incitement, although I do suggest ways in which our political structures might be changed in light of the evolutionary processes I believe we are subject to. If some of what I say strikes a chord, others, I hope, will work on the details and develop further the implications.

My arguments are essentially these: that we are part of the universe and so must see ourselves in the context of the universe overall and as being subject to the same drivers; that evolution is not just a biological process but a universal one which mutates through a hierarchy of arrangements each subject to specific rules; that our future lies in leaving biology behind, while remembering always that feeling alone ties us to the universe we are part of; that much of what we have done, and still do, is biologically driven; that a new level of matter is evolving which I call cerebral structure and which entails expanding awareness; that the creative nature of the universe means that moral intent is the only reliable yardstick we can use; that the structures we build to regulate our individual and collective actions must be thought of in moral and not just functional terms; and that if we do not imbue them with structural integrity, our biological drivers, which are blind to individual well-being, will fill the inevitable gaps.

I have tried to use examples wherever possible, but hope I will be forgiven for not including a list of references. This is not intended to be an academic work (although I hope academics will read it) but a book for the general reader. The facts that I have used to build my arguments can easily be checked and are not original to me. Complex as some of the issues undoubtedly are, the overall vision I am trying to promote (the story I am telling, to use my own language) is straightforward enough. American spelling is used throughout.

Part 1

I AM ALWAYS skeptical when I hear the physics profession (or, as is more often the case, its journalistic advocates) talk about a theory of everything, so please forgive the hubris I displayed in the introduction, when I said that in ***Part 1*** I would lay out a framework showing how I believed the universe works. What I meant by that was no more (and no less) than saying to someone who has never seen an automobile before that it has four wheels and can carry people backwards or forwards under its own power. What I have tried to do in ***Part 1*** of ***Notes*** is to outline the basic dynamics I believe we are subject to. It is for others to inspect the chassis, kick the wheels and peer under the hood.

As I said in the introduction, precision has its downside. But we can't do without it. What we can do, however, is recognize that it is either a type of shorthand used to describe things that we only partly understand, or describes just one small part of a much larger process. In my case, it is a bit of both. I am trying to outline, in the most general terms, the essential dynamics I feel we should endeavor to understand. The model I am proposing in ***Part 1*** needs to be seen in that light.

The principal processes I believe we should concentrate on are eightfold. First, I think we need to keep reminding ourselves that we are part of a dynamic whole and that that whole is the universe (or multiverse) itself. At the very least, this might encourage us to be more humble than we are and more inclusive than is often our nature! Second, I believe we must have some sense about what drives the universe, and so us. Third, I propose that the universe has been and is evolving by establishing a hierarchy of structures defined by boundary conditions.

Fourth, I suggest that this evolutionary process unfolds not just horizontally (as through species differentiation) but vertically through what I call system states, such as the quantum state (the initial transformation of energy into structured matter including electrons, neutrinos and photons), the atomic state (when hydrogen and helium atoms formed and photons broke free[1]), the galactic state (when gravity pulled gasses into stars that created moons, planets and chemical compounds), and the biological state (when organic matter elaborated into plants, insects and animals), with each building on the other but subject to its own particular rules.

Fifth, I talk about the tension matrix which is the framework within which the elements of a system state express their dynamic and, within the human sphere, largely decide our actions. Sixth, I suggest that we need stories to make sense of the tension matrices we live within. Seventh, and possibly most controversially, I am drawn to the conclusion that a new system state is forming, which I call the cerebral state and that, eighth, the universe is a creative enterprise of opportunistic trial and error that embodies moral purpose.

---

1. These photons constitute the cosmic background radiation that can be observed today.

2

The Universe

WHILE IT IS true, when you look at your family tree, that you cannot say you are the direct consequence of your ancestors' purpose, it is equally true that you and your ancestor are connected, and that without him or her you wouldn't exist. And even if you imbue your ancestor with no powers of divinity, this means something. I am not advocating a return to ancestor worship, but it was a more rational practice than our modern mind allows. And we are not just related to our human ancestors. None of us can deny that we are the product of a remarkably complex process that preceded our arrival, and that this process has displayed a high degree of creativity. So the Judeo-Christian idea of a Creator was not irrational either. We are a creation of our universe, after all.

Certainly it is easy to mock the notion that there is a God hovering above us, willing and able to intervene if we ask the right questions, in the right way. But are we not still trying to ask the right questions, in the right way, of scientists rather than priests? Our universe is a dynamic entity and although it is creative, it possesses a profound integrity in the form of laws. There is much that we know about it and much that we don't. But whatever way we care to look at it, its creative history and its laws are our own. So, what *do* we know?

The universe seems to be 13.73 billion years old, and presently around 93 billion light years separate its farthest observable elements. Having started (at least in terms of our understanding of it) as a singularity — a hypothetical point at which the quantities used to measure gravity (such as the density of matter or curvature of space-time) become infinite — the universe expanded rapidly from an exceptionally hot, dense state, distributing itself into the space it created. The discrepancy between its age and size is due to the fact that space itself is expanding.

As of now, the universe is not very dense[1], consisting of only 4% of the sort of matter we are familiar with. Some 73% of the remainder is dark energy and 23% cold dark matter (neither of which we know much about). The jury is still out as to whether the expansion of the universe is being accelerated by dark energy beyond the ability of cold dark matter to constrain it, but the evidence is pointing to a rip, rather than a crunch or steady state halt.

With Einstein's famous equation in mind — $E=mc^2$ — where E is energy, m is mass and c is the speed of light (approximately 300,000 km per second), let's assume that our universe started from a moment of pure energy (the moment at which mass reached an infinite density). At that point energy became liberated, expanding rapidly as it went and cooling enough for what has been called quark-gluon plasma to form[2]. But temperatures were still so high that these

---

1. $2.11\text{x}10^{-29}$ kg/m^3, so a lot of space relative to matter. Density is interesting in that if the energy in the universe is neither net negative nor net positive, one would expect the relation between space and matter over time to be, let us say, Ω (the critical density). More dense than Ω and the universe is likely to fall in on itself. Less dense than Ω and the universe will dissipate into infinity. At the moment, all measurements suggest that the universe is expanding at an accelerating rate, so the total energy in the universe appears to be net positive. How can this be? We don't know.

2. Consisting of fermions, associated with matter, such as quarks and leptons; bosons associated with forces, such as gluons, photons and gravitons; and possibly the Higgs boson, which may give all the fermions their masses.

particles and their matching anti-particles[3] flew around at relativistic speeds[4], annihilating one another and reforming in a wonderfully wild and promiscuous dance.

That matter evolved in the universe may have been due simply to particles and their anti-particles (quarks and anti-quarks, electrons and positrons, protons and anti-protons) evolving slightly differently. As the temperature in the universe continued to drop, these particles and their anti-particles could no longer be created, so that it took only a small excess of one over the other (of quarks over anti-quarks, etc.) to lead to a mass annihilation as pairs cancelled each other out, leaving the remainder as matter. After the annihilations, the energy density of the universe became dominated by photons (the carriers of electromagnetic radiation)[5].

As the temperature continued to drop (to about a billion degrees Celsius) and when the density of the universe was about that of air, neutrons were able to combine with protons to form deuterium and helium nuclei in a process called nucleosynthesis. The uncombined protons were hydrogen nuclei. Continuing expansion allowed the temperature to fall further, and with the formation of atoms (principally hydrogen) the mass-energy density of matter came gravitationally to dominate that of photon radiation, which continued to move through space (the so-called background radiation that has helped scientists measure the age of our universe). Very gradually, and perhaps over as long as a billion years (the cosmological dark ages), small

---

3. In this early quantum world particles existed in pairs of positive and negative charge, each able to cancel the other out. This is not so odd. One would expect the emergence of matter to be tentative at first. What is new rarely arrives fully fledged, but rather as a whisper inside what currently exists. So matter had to make sense in terms of non-matter to start with.

4. Particle speeds comparable to the speed of light where physical phenomena depend on the relative motion of the observer and the observed object.

5. Along with the photon, which has zero mass and both wave and particle properties and travels at the speed of light, a characteristic of subatomic elements, were neutrinos, thrown off by certain types of radioactive decay. With close to zero mass and a speed just short of light, neutrinos from the sun pass through us (and all other matter they encounter) every day.

differences in what had started out as almost evenly distributed matter began to coalesce into clumps under the influence of gravity.

In what is, perhaps, a fundamental characteristic of the universe we are part of, perfect symmetry seems to be accompanied by a flaw — the grain in the oyster that gives rise to the pearl. Had matter and anti-matter particles been perfectly balanced, matter could not have evolved. Had the formation of the universe been perfectly symmetrical, matter would have been evenly distributed and there would have been no reason for it to start clumping because no element would have exerted greater attraction than any other, all being equally spaced[6].

Some clusters of hydrogen (75%) and helium (25%), produced within minutes of the Big Bang[7], were drawn together by gravity into dense molecular clouds. Inherently unstable, shock waves from colliding clouds (and much later from exploding stars that had changed into supernova) caused some areas of these clouds to become more dense. From about a billion years after the Big Bang, as clusters of matter collapsed in on themselves, gravitational energy was converted into heat and stars formed when the core of the compressed matter became sufficiently hot for nuclear fusion to occur, leading to a prolonged state of hydrostatic equilibrium (when the imploding force of gravity is offset by the thermal activity the compression generated).

The formation of stars and their eventual collapse is central to the dynamic of what I am calling the galactic system state. Almost everything about a star is determined by its initial mass. Consisting initially of the same elements that make up the gas clouds — hydrogen (75%) and helium (25%) — the fusion of hydrogen into helium that takes place when the core reaches a sufficiently high temperature leads to the

---

6. Measurements of the background radiation left over from the Big Bang, taken from the COBE satellite, have detected small temperature variations which suggests that matter was unevenly distributed at least as early as 100,000 years after the birth of our universe.

7. The name given to the fireball of radiation that expanded very rapidly at the birth of our universe from a state characterized by extremely high temperature and density.

fusion of heavier elements if the star is big enough (0.075 times the mass of the sun, which itself is large enough to fuse carbon). Stars are acting like great factories, throwing out elements they have created through fusion at high temperatures. Initially, they contained few heavy elements (such as iron), but as older stars have died and shed some of their material, new stars have formed with higher concentrations taken from their predecessors.

After a massive star has burned up its helium, the core contracts until the temperature and pressure are able to fuse carbon. As a star nears the end of its life, fusion can take place in layers, with each layer fusing a different element, the outermost fusing hydrogen, the next helium and so on until the most tightly bound element, iron, is formed at the core. In super-massive stars, the core can grow so large that when it collapses the shock wave causes the rest of the star to explode in a supernova, leaving behind a neutron star[8], often observed as a pulsar, or even a black hole if the explosion is massive enough[9]. Generally, dying stars blow off their outer layers and these are picked up by new star formations or by planets. Apart from hydrogen and helium, stars have manufactured everything that has gone into making the galactic system state. Apart from hydrogen and the small amount of helium we possess, they have also made all the other atoms that go to make up us.

It is not known exactly how planets are formed. The best guess at the moment is that when an interstellar cloud (containing original matter as well as those heavier elements created by stars that have died) starts to cluster (such clusters are called nebulae), further clusters can

---

8. A neutron star is composed of subatomic particles (mostly neutrons) and does not collapse because in the quantum world no two neutrons can occupy the same quantum state simultaneously. A typical neutron star has a mass about 1.5 times that of the sun, but a radius of only some 12 kilometers. Often these stars produce coherent beams of radio waves as well as visible emissions (pulses), believed to be caused by spinning particles accelerating near the magnetic poles which are out of alignment with the rotational axis of the star.

9. A black hole occurs when the density of material collapsing in on itself is so great that the gravity associated with it does not even allow light to escape. These formations have prompted some to speculate that they may be precursors to a new 'Big Bang' cycle.

form within them. Some of these become sufficiently concentrated to form protostars (stars in formation) and are surrounded by a rotating field of the remaining matter called a protoplanetary disk. When the mass of a star begins to release its energy, everything close to it is blown away and the remaining material starts to coalesce into bundles. The biggest bundles attract the most material until some bundles are large enough for gravity to pull them into spheres able to hold an atmosphere. A planetary world, like our own, is born.

All planets start in a fluid state and their denser materials sink to the center. Terrestrial planets (Mercury, Venus, Earth and Mars) are sealed within hard crusts, whereas in the gaseous planets (Jupiter, Saturn, Uranus and Neptune) the surface merges into the upper cloud layers. All the planets in our solar system have atmospheres (although most of Mercury's has been blown away by solar winds). The Earth's atmosphere, however, is different from that of the others because organic processes have introduced free molecular oxygen (more on that in a moment). If the heart of a planet is active, with flows of electrically conducting material inside it, as in Earth, the planet will possess a magnetic field (often far bigger than the planet itself) which deflects the solar wind[10]. Even planets that have become solid all the way through possess a weak residual magnetic field. To date, biological life has not been detected on any other planet besides our own.

At the moment, we do not know how biological life on Earth started. You may have begun to see a pattern here, which I will discuss in a later chapter, in that we find it hard to describe the movement from one type of material, one type of structure, to another. According to the New Oxford Dictionary, life is the condition that distinguishes animals and plants from inorganic matter, including the capacity for growth, reproduction, functional activity and continual change preceding death. The cumbersome nature of that description underlines the

---

10. The solar wind is a stream of plasma (charged particles) emitted from the upper atmosphere of the sun. Its effect can knock out power grids on Earth and be seen as the Northern Lights.

difficulty we have with the idea. We should, perhaps, be more wary than we are of the everyday concepts we take for granted.[11]

From my point of view, the transformations our universe has gone through must be seen as part of an evolutionary process, characterized by distinct system states, governed by their own rules, that have served as building blocks for new types of structure, new system states. Biological life is clearly different from the world of stars and planets that preceded it (in the evolutionary sense), just as the world of stars and planets was different from the simple atomic world, which the subatomic world of quarks and gluons that formed after the Big Bang made possible. As it was with the other types of structure, the emergence of biological life was tentative, until some invisible boundary of possibility was crossed, and it became rapacious.

What is clear is that biological life evolved as a result of interactions between chemicals. Carbon, the fourth most abundant element in the universe by mass after hydrogen, helium and oxygen is present in all known life forms, making up some 18.5% of the human body's mass. Within the temperature ranges found on earth it has acted as the backbone for a wide range of complex molecular structures that interact with one another in subtle ways, creating the diverse biochemistry that underpins the biological system state.

The Earth, as we know it today, is — unsurprisingly — compatible with the life forms we know today. But since its formation, 4.54 billion years ago, the Earth's environment has changed radically. Although its crust and oceans may have existed as early as 150 million years after its formation, the impacts that pock-marked the moon

---

[11]. Even Stephen Hawking felt compelled to devote almost 200 pages to *A Brief History of Time*, although his ulterior motive may have been to write a populist account that would cover his daughter's school fees! Published by Bantam in 1988, the book was immensely successful. Personally, I have my doubts about time, and think we would be better off if we thought of ourselves as existing in an unfolding present. Hawking's time deals with the equivalence of space and time in that events following the Big Bang can be analyzed as a causal sequence against measurable coordinates — hence the link between expanding space and time.

bombarded the Earth too, no doubt vaporizing some of its water in repeated cycles[12]. Simple organisms, capable of sustaining a degree of chemical integrity inside a membrane, may have needed exceptional conditions, such as deep sea sulfur vents, or extremes of heat and cold, in order to synthesize.

Whether these then split repeatedly, like bubbles, setting up metabolic pathways that crystallized into simple RNA (ribonucleic acid), a probable forerunner of DNA[13], is not known, but less than a billion years after the formation of the Earth's crust, fossil records show that simple-celled organisms (that have been named prokaryotes) had come into existence. Even today, the descendants of these organisms, archaea (of which plankton is a good example) and bacteria make up a large percentage of the world's biomass. There are typically 40 million bacterial cells in a gram of soil and a million in a milliliter of fresh water. Even the human body contains ten times as many bacterial cells as human ones.

Micro-organisms may have existed 3.5 billion years ago but multicellular organisms probably did not appear in the oceans until 2.5 billion years later. And judging by the fossil records, it was only as recently as 540 million years ago, after a veritable explosion of biological types, now known as the Cambrian explosion, that the ancestors of most modern animal types were formed. Although far from certain, this period of rapid evolution could have been triggered when an

12. It is not clear how the Earth came to have so much water, which covers about 70% of its surface. Water vapor is quite common in the universe and is another by-product of star formation. It is possible that the object that struck the Earth over 4 billion years ago and created our moon was a large icy body, like Jupiter's 6th moon, Europa. For the Earth to retain such a sizeable body of liquid water, it also had to be just the right distance from the sun — neither too hot, nor too cold.

13. Deoxyribonucleic acid (DNA) is a nucleic acid that contains the genetic instructions used in the development and functioning of all known living organisms, including some viruses. As it breaks down over a million years, there are no early examples. RNA is similar to DNA but generally has only one strand to DNA's two.

accumulation of oxygen in the atmosphere from photosynthesis[14], the free oxygen mentioned earlier, reached a critical level.

Some 500 million years ago, plants and fungi colonized the land, followed by early amniotes (mostly reptiles). Around 300 million years ago, amphibians appeared, followed by mammals (100 million years later) and birds (both descendants of reptiles) 100 million years after that. Over this period there have been at least five major extinctions. One of the greatest, 251 million years before our own time (since christened the Great Dying), eliminated about 96% of all marine species and about 70% of all those that lived on the land.

What was behind these extinctions is far from clear. Impact events, volcanism, disruptions to ocean currents due to tectonic shifts, the release of methane from the sea floor, and changes to ocean levels might all have altered the environment, particularly the availability of oxygen, to the detriment of previously established species, with gradual changes accelerated by more violent events. There is clear evidence of a pattern. Many of the more complex species seem to experience mounting stress before suddenly collapsing. This allows simpler organisms (such as dicrodium, a seed fern) to spread unchallenged until more specialized animals with complex ecosystems can once again re-establish themselves.

What is also clear is that the composition of species before and after such events changed. Biology, in other words, through the process of natural selection, was 'learning' from experience. Before the Permian Triassic extinction, for example, marine animals that lived attached to the ocean floor predominated. In the Mesozoic period that followed, a majority were free-living. It is hard to escape the conclusion that disruption has been a great evolutionary driver.

One consequence of the Great Dying was that it enabled the archosaurs and then dinosaurs to become the dominant land verte-

---

14. The process whereby some organisms use sunlight to synthesize foods from carbon dioxide and water, generating oxygen as a by-product.

brates, until they themselves became extinct some 65 million years ago[15], opening the way for mammals to assume the dominant role. A sobering observation is that about 99% of the species that have ever lived are now extinct, and that we are, today, living through a period of massive and rapid extinction caused, in the main, by the actions of man.

The genus Homo (man) is estimated to be some 2.5 million years old, having evolved from Australopithecus, a hominid that shared several traits with modern apes and humans and was widespread throughout Eastern and Northern Africa between 3 and 3.9 million years ago. Modern man, who has called himself Homo sapiens ("wise man") — a designation we can but hope is true — is only some 200,000 years old. All species of the genus Homo, save us, have died out. The last to do so may have been Homo neanderthalensis (24,000 years ago), although a recent find in Indonesia, named Homo floresiensis[16] could have died out only 13,000 years ago. The appearance of Homo, by the way, coincides with the first evidence of stone tools.

There is a suggestion that an explosion of a super volcano at Lake Toba on Sumatra, 70,000 to 75,000 years ago, emitted so much ash into the atmosphere that worldwide temperatures dropped by 5 degrees or more for several years, triggering an ice age which severely depleted

---

15. The most widely accepted reason for the extinction of the dinosaurs is that a 5-15 kilometer-wide meteorite hit the Earth in the vicinity of the Yucatan Peninsula. It is thought that initially its impact might have caused an unusual heatwave and then global cooling on account of the matter ejected into the sky as a result of it. However, the Earth's climate was changing in any event. At the peak of the dinosaur age (the Mesozoic era) there were no polar ice caps, significantly higher sea levels, little temperature variation from pole to pole and substantially more carbon dioxide in the atmosphere than today. Bear in mind, also, that over this time the continents were drifting apart from being connected, towards where they are today, and volcanic activity was decreasing. So dinosaurs may well have been struggling to cope with a fluctuating climate, even before the impact event.

16. Nicknamed the Hobbit on account of its small physique and brain, scientists are still fiercely divided as to whether its remains represent a new species or are merely that of a pygmy or larger human with a malformed brain and body.

the Homo genus (including Homo sapiens)[17]. DNA evidence suggests that modern man could be descended from a rather small pool of ancestors (from between 10,000 to as few as 1,000 breeding pairs), consistent with a significant disruption in human evolution, so our obsession with the weather could be justified. However, as the early dinosaurs once did[18], we have put setbacks behind us, and at 6,702,224,181[19] and counting, now dominate the planet.

In just ten pages we have traveled through almost 14 billion years of history. What should we conclude? Should it be, as some scientists have, that mankind is the result of so many improbabilities and occupies such a small part of the universe and its history, that our existence is irrelevant, save only to ourselves? Or should we imagine, as the Christian Church once did (and many Christians still do) that our uniqueness demonstrates, quite clearly, that we must be the direct consequence of God's purpose?

It is my contention that only if we look at ourselves in isolation, rather than as an outcome of an unfolding process, does the rather gloomy prognosis of those who say we are no more than an accidental blip on the rump of creation apply. If, as I have suggested earlier, consciousness represents the evolution of a new system state, in which sentient intent (the awareness of outcomes) rather than blind opportunistic evolution, becomes the driving force, we will be responsible for its direction.

In this, I find myself more in tune with the idea of God than I do with the idea of scientific abstraction. I'm not sure we should worry too much about the fact that we are a tiny part of a universe in which the matter we are derived from only represents some 4% of its whole. The

17. This has been suggested by Stanley Ambrose of the University of Illinois.

18. Dinosaurs are believed to have diverged from their archosaur ancestors (whose contemporary descendants include crocodiles and birds) some 20 million years after the Permian-Triassic extinction (the Great Dying).

19. A nonsense number, of course, in that we are unlikely to know the exact number of us at any given time, but 6.7 billion and counting seems to me to disguise the fact that each of us, individually, is included in that total. We are the 1.

rather amazing thing is that our minds are gradually embracing it all and there seems every possibility that consciousness is evolving elsewhere besides here on earth.

Consciousness does not exist in a vacuum but as an evolutionary outcome of the universe as a whole. So if the word 'God' is shorthand for the context within which the universe exists, then God's purpose is to be found within ourselves. When Einstein said that his work brought him closer to understanding the mind of God, he was probably thinking as a deist and expressing his wonder at the process of creation. Certainly we are part of an extraordinary universe and we would do well to try to understand what drives it, because what drives it, drives us. But increasingly, conscious intent places the creative onus on us.

3

Drivers

OURS IS THE AGE of the gene, and if men like Professor Richard Dawkins have their way, the gene will displace God and genetics will become the new religion, with Dawkins its High Priest.[1] Certainly science has upended much religious dogma, but there is often just a whisper of hubris in its claims.

This tendency to beatify the gene, with almost everything laid at its door (or on its altar),[2] is, I fear, seriously misplaced. As over 90% of all genetically-imbued life forms that have ever lived on Earth are now extinct, one might be inclined to question the gene's track record on its terms alone. More fundamentally, the universe has been around a lot longer than the gene and appeared to function quite well without it. Although important and fascinating, genetic evolution is principally a matter of biological mechanics, and does not directly answer the question, what drives the universe and so us?

---

1. In his book, *The Blind Watchmaker* (1986), Richard Dawkins argues, convincingly, that natural selection can explain the wonderful complexities we find in the biological world, and that an intelligent, all-seeing, *Creator* is not required. But it seems to me that in shooting his fox he is shooting himself.
2. W. D. Hamilton and Richard Dawkins have both argued that even altruism (which appears to go against an individual's interests) can be explained by genetic 'self-interest', on the grounds that the altruist is helping those with a genetic disposition of which he or she approves.

When Charles Darwin published *The Origin of the Species* in 1859, he made the remarkable claim that all life on earth had evolved from a single lineage and that a process that combined variation with natural selection had brought this about. He was widely ridiculed by the establishment, which at that time was closely associated with the Church of England. So Man was an ape, was he, people said, and not God's unique creation? Pha!

Six years later, an Augustinian monk, called Gregor Mendel, read a paper entitled Experiments on Plant Hybridization to the Natural History Society of Brünn, in Moravia, publishing it the following year. Mendel's exposition was based on his work with peas in the monastery garden and outlined what was to become the genetic basis of inheritance[3]. The importance of Mendel's work remained unappreciated for almost fifty years.

Darwin's mechanism of natural selection ran something like this: organisms produce a surplus of offspring, although their overall numbers tend to be stable on account of finite and stable food supplies, which implies a degree of competition. Sexual reproduction results in no two individuals being identical, and some variations will be better suited to an organism's environment than others. Over time, those individuals with the better variations will out-breed those without and pass on these variations to their offspring, so that over many generations actual species differentiation will occur, especially where organisms have spread into different environments.

Darwin, himself, did not have a particularly well developed idea about heredity and it was not until natural selection and genetic

---

3. By painstakingly observing the breeding pattern of some 28,000 pea plants, he concluded that variations in genes (not his word) accounted for variations in inherited characteristics. For each characteristic, an organism inherits two versions (now known as alleles) of the gene, one from each parent. At conception (now known as gamete production) only one of the alleles from each parent is combined in the offspring, allowing for variation. Mendel also deduced that characteristics are inherited independently from one another (so that color & size, for example, are a function of only their own genes) opening the way to still further variation.

inheritance were combined that evolutionary biology got fully into its stride. It has since been found that variation can come from mutations (alterations to a cell's DNA sequence due to error, or because of some external influence, such as radiation), the movement of groups between populations (such as took place when Europeans moved into South America) and the mixing that takes place on account of sexual reproduction. Genes can also be transferred horizontally between bacteria, speeding up the adaptation process (which is why these particular organisms can quickly become resistant to drugs), and between plants by hybridization.

Evolutionary biology is unquestionably important in understanding the biological system state. No argument there. But if, as I am suggesting, evolution is a process that preceded biology and will continue beyond it, we must dig deeper to find the drivers we are subject to.

Although an unanswerable question to some degree (which is why we keep coming back to a prime mover of one kind or another), an answer, of sorts, to the question *what drives the universe and so us*, is suggested by how we understand our universe to have begun. But we need to be careful here. As I am at pain in ***Notes*** to point out, what we see, and how we see what we see, is a function of our mental framework. Human mythology and more recently religion created a context within which we could place ourselves. Drawing on our experience and insight these stories allowed our consciousness to embrace 'everything' and account for all that bore down on our lives. In effect, they served to define 'reality' for us.

What the scientific method did was elevate the pursuit of measurable knowledge, a practice that goes back at least as far as the Ancient Greeks, into a framework as all-embracing as our age-old myths and more recent religions once were. It was not good enough merely to believe that something was the case. That it was had to be formulated in a way which could be tested by trying to prove that it was not. If the Earth was at the center of the universe, as Christian dogma maintained, one would expect to observe certain celestial patterns. The advance in optics that took place in the 16th century allowed the heavens to be observed more closely and to a man like Galileo Galilei (1564–1642) it became clear that a better idea was that the earth circled the sun. To date no credible evidence has been produced to suggest the contrary.

What gave the scientific method such momentum was not just one or two ideas that challenged the religious status quo (Nicolaus Copernicus (1473–1543), the Polish astronomer, had proposed a heliocentric order long before Galileo), but a thirst for improved ways of doing things that analytical thinking and experiment offered up across a whole range of human activity. More recently, advances in technology, observation, experimentation, theory building and mathematics have allowed physicists to work backwards from the expanding universe that can be observed today to its mathematical origin — a hypothetical singularity in which space-time collapses and mass achieves infinite density. The fact that the scientific framework collapses in this way (a strong indication that a model is incomplete is when it starts, under certain circumstances, to produce infinite values) should serve to caution us, not that what we know is wholly wrong, but that what we still have to learn is likely to be much.

Physicists continue to try to burrow beyond the singularity. The challenge is to come up with an explanation that meshes what seems to go on in the subatomic, quantum world with what Einstein's theory of general relativity describes went on after the Big Bang. It is theoretically possible that at very small scales there are more than just four dimensions (three of space and one of time) and that quantum fluctuations (triggering the creation of particle-antiparticle pairs) are part of a process in which our universe is simply one of many[4]. This would at least get us out of the bind of having to try to explain everything in

4. One version of string theory, which assumes that electrons and quarks inside atoms are not 0-dimensional objects but 1-dimensional strings, postulates that universes come into existence following collisions between membranes within an 11-dimensional space.

terms of our own universe[5]. And if we are indeed part of an infinite multiverse in which one was bound to embody an evolutionary dynamic that would result in consciousness, the least we can do is make the most of what has come our way.

Whatever the truth turns out to be, it is the evolutionary dynamic pertaining to our universe that we need to be most concerned with. The essentials of this dynamic include interactions which can create structures that are stable over time. In the quantum world matter consists of elementary particles (called fermions) that interact to form quarks and leptons, the former creating hadrons, baryons and nuclei that combine with leptons to form atoms. The way fermions attract or repel one another (each carries a charge and spin) is by exchanging force, in this case bosons which carry energy and momentum between fermions. The forces that appear to be at work at the quantum level have been called strong, weak, electromagnetic and gravity. Gluons (which operate over very short distances and are confined to the nucleus) carry the strong force; W & Z bosons (which are short-lived and have a relatively high mass limiting their range) carry the weak force; photons (which are massless and so have an infinite range and are the conveyor of light) carry the electromagnetic force; and gravitons (which are hypothetical particles needed to mediate the force of gravity in quantum field theory and would be without mass if they existed) carry the force of gravity.

The essential difference between fermions and the family of bosons (the force carriers) is that unlike bosons, no two fermions can occupy the same quantum state, giving them a certain rigidity that many associate with the formation of matter. The interaction between the force carriers and fermions has the effect of changing their character. Quarks become what has been called up and down, charm and strange, top and

---

5. Einstein introduced a constant into his theory of general relativity as without one a universe that was initially in a state of dynamic equilibrium would eventually collapse under the force of gravity. But when Hubble's work indicated that the universe was, in fact, expanding he abandoned this so-called cosmological constant, claiming it to be his biggest mistake. However, the belief is now growing that the equations which describe our universe do require a constant unique to it. But if we live in a multiverse, each universe will have its own constant, making ours no more remarkable than any other.

bottom, and leptons become electron neutrino and electron, muon neutrino and muon, tau neutrino and tau, enabling both to move beyond the quantum state, in which elementary particles exhibit wave-particle duality, and form atoms.

The reason I have started our search for drivers at a level most who are not physicists will be unfamiliar with (and I apologize to those who are physicists as they are likely to find my descriptions sketchy at best) is that I believe the evolutionary dynamic we are subject to is deep-seated and goes well beyond the biological. Also it seems to me evident that part of the evolutionary dynamic entails jumps from one type of interaction to another. Although the quantum fluctuations which started the formation of our universe almost 14 billion years ago, triggering the massive inflation of space and time we have come to call the Big Bang, lasted for only a moment in cosmological terms (temperatures had fallen sufficiently for atoms to form between 3 and 20 minutes after the Big Bang, but stars did not begin to form until some 400 million years later), it established the essential character of what we are part of.

So what should we take away from this? As we will consider in the next chapter, the establishment of boundary conditions seems to be central to the evolution of matter (and as I will argue later, to the evolution of meaning). It also seems clear to me that we are part of a process that has evolved through specific states, with each state governed by its own rules. Evolution is a progression in which structures build upon one another over time in a hierarchical manner. The idea of tension appears to be important, with the elements of structures being held together by energy-matter interactions: even space-time looks to be poised between competing forces and it is quite possible that entropy (the complete breakdown of all structure) will be the final outcome for our universe.

An important characteristic, I believe, is the interplay of forces operating at different levels within a structure. You see this quite clearly in the human sphere where something like the urge to wage war can overwhelm, for a time, more localized interactions such as friends and family. It is also hard to escape the conclusion that our universe is imbued with a propensity to create structure, although not static structure but structure that is dynamic and is, to an extent, impermanent, with a distinctly progressive thrust. Seen in this light, it is perhaps unremarkable that consciousness was a consequence of this creative evolutionary progression, and it is to be expected that it will vie with our pre-existing drivers.

It would be churlish, I think, to deny that the dynamic of our universe embodies its own epistemology (defines for us the nature of knowledge) but foolish to imagine we know even the half of it. There is something extraordinarily beautiful about the tentative emergence of matter, almost as if it was being conjured from thin air. But it is this very vulnerability — think of matter and anti-matter particles coming into existence only to annihilate one another in a wild dance until some small change, we do not know what exactly, allowed matter to predominate — which seems to lie at the heart of evolutionary creativity. As humans, we frequently crave stability and shun creative change, and yet we have often been at our most vulnerable when we have felt most secure and been at our most creative when under pressure.

While our desire for security is undeniable, we also possess great curiosity. That, too, seems to be reflected in the trial and error dynamic of our universe. Within each of its phases this dynamic has been to spur on whatever combinations were possible, although there were often long lulls between periods of activity. The so-called cosmological dark ages, in which nothing much changed in the universe following the great inflation, lasted for several hundred million years until stars began to form. None the less, trial and error did produce the precise number of chemical compounds we have, as well as the range of heavenly bodies we can observe because no other combinations could remain stable in the conditions that prevailed. And, of course, biological trial and error produced us.

One of the most marked characteristics of our universe has been its propensity to create boundaries. This is not so strange as there really are only three states of existence: nothingness, chaotic disorder (entropy) and something. Nothingness can only be conceived of in the context of the other two. The entropic state is, by definition, unbound which leaves us with something. 'Something' has to be an ordered interaction within a boundary and as such it embodies meaning. So the evolution of our universe has been the evolution of meaning, made up of countless interlocking hierarchical parts.

Throughout ***Notes*** I point out that humans repeatedly try to establish boundaries (by language, by ethnicity, by belief, by breeding, by conquest, by education, etc.), but that we don't recognize this as an outcome of the evolutionary process. If we did, we would realize that we are part of an evolved (and evolving) meaning set. And even if we exist within a multiverse consisting of universes we can never access and which embody different meaning sets or dynamics to our own (have different cosmological constants — see note 5 on page 25) at one level, at least, we remain part of that whole and so are expressing an aspect of it.

This brings me to the issue of God which I would rather confront sooner than later and head-on, and in so doing run the risk of offending believers and irritating non-believers alike. As the majority of those who read ***Notes*** must fall squarely or more or less into one of these two categories, all I can say is bear with me.

So let me say at the outset that if we are going to relate to the whole of which we are part, the idea of God seems an entirely appropriate construct. Why we should wish to relate to the whole is about belonging, about identity and about acknowledging our genesis. We are of the universe in every sense of the word. I also like the idea that each of us has an equal claim to that inheritance.

Religion, however, is a different matter. It is the way in which different groups of people attempt to address and celebrate the idea of God and, in particular, how they draw from the notion of wholeness a moral template for human behavior. That the religious boundary they throw around themselves, so as to give their lives meaning, has often led to conflict, hatred, bigotry and an unholy lust for power, can be explained in evolutionary terms and will be later. But religion need not be about a rather sordid exclusivity.

There is, of course, the difficult question (for anyone with a scientific mind, at least) as to whether God is an active agent in our universe with whom we can communicate directly or is merely, as Richard Dawkins so cleverly put it, a blind watchmaker. Rather to my surprise I am increasingly coming to the conclusion that the former view is right and that the latter view is wrong. Firstly, there is the matter of fact. We are of the universe and we are not blind (although we often behave as if we are) and are attempting to build our small part of it with intent.

Secondly, we are regularly communicating with the universe and it with us as we search for truth. From the great pyramid of Giza to the magnificent Gothic cathedral at Chartres, on to the Hubble space telescope of today, our efforts have often been heroic. Thirdly, and this is central to the issue of what drives the universe, I do not believe the evidence supports the notion that the universe we live in is fully deterministic. As I will argue in the last chapter of this section, there appears to be enough uncertainty about outcomes for their *nature* to be a consequence of creativity.

Put these three things together and it is not so crazy to say that man's task is to express God's will. If by God you mean the universe (or multiverse if there is one) and regard His will as the evolution of its creative potential, you are on ground that both science and religion could comfortably occupy. To do so, however, science must recognize that even a theory of everything is meaningless without context and religion needs to devote more time to defining the moral context of life and less time attempting to monopolize reality — a battle it has largely lost.

While the universe we are part of may not be fully deterministic, it is not without rules. Anything does not go. And although, as I will argue, I believe much of what we have done and still do is biologically driven, evolution — at least our small part of it — is increasingly for us to create. What we have to do is understand the rules and then learn how to reinterpret them in life-enhancing ways. Now, what a wonderful opportunity is that!

4

Boundary Conditions

I HAVE SAID THAT humans repeatedly try to establish boundaries, and throughout ***Notes*** I refer to the *boundary condition*, so let me explain what I mean by it. I picked the two words boundary and condition because what I am trying to draw attention to is the condition inside a structure that gives it its boundary. As has already been indicated, structure, like so many things familiar to us and which we take for granted, is a more complex concept than might be imagined. If you doubt me, try answering this simple question: why does structure exist at all?

We have seen that by working their calculations backwards from what can be observed today, physicists have arrived at the Big Bang, a moment in time just after the universe as we know it seems to have been infinitely dense. They have called this infinitely dense state the singularity. This process of discovery has been a little like trying to work out how a mature chicken evolved and getting as far back as the egg. At that point regressive calculations leave one stumped and asking the unanswerable question — what did come first? If it wasn't another chicken, perhaps it was God.

There are two aspects to this dilemma. One relates to discontinuity in evolution: the point at which a set of explanatory rules breaks down because a fundamentally new type of matter comes into existence with its own set of explanatory rules. This will be addressed in the next chapter on system states. The other aspect of the dilemma, which concerns us here, is why should there be anything at all? Or, to put it slightly differently, what is the difference between something and nothing? The statement by the French philosopher René Descartes (1596–1650) that *I think therefore I am* addresses the issue. Philosophers, just like physicists and theologians, have wrestled with the nature of existence for centuries. For my purpose, all I will say is that existence seems to require a boundary that distinguishes it from what does not exist.

We may never know exactly what preceded our universe (although I am optimistic that we will), but what we do know is that within what the physicist's singularity attempts to describe existed the full potential of everything that has evolved since. That, if you like, is the outer boundary of the adventure we are part of, whether or not it contains other universes besides our own. Whatever the nature of existence is, we are already part of it. The crucial question is what evolves from here? And this is why the establishment of boundary conditions is so central, because it is the mechanism by which meaning (in the form of structure) elaborates and evolves.

This has direct implications for us. Such a feeling as racism (much frowned upon today) is entirely natural and flows from the same spring as that which gave rise to species differentiation in the biological world and matter in the quantum one. What is evident is that many combinations will be attempted on account of more or less random mixing, but only some of these will possess structural integrity and work. However, those that do, such as planets, suns and moons, or the elements that make up the periodic table in chemistry, establish the nature of reality within that boundary condition.

Again, this has direct implications for us. As we know only too well, the development of human arrangements has followed a fairly haphazard path along which trial and particularly error have been the predominant process. Combinations that have been found to work have often exhibited a remarkable degree of tenacity. This is because they represent reality for those who are part of them. In the biological world, species vie with one another in a symbiotic dance of predator and prey. And while most species that have ever lived are now extinct, some structures, such as the shark, have exhibited great longevity.

Although human arrangements have been far more fluid than biological ones, some, such as the one history has come to call the Ancien Régime, characterized by a God-anointed king with temporal power, supported by an earthly church able to mediate between heaven and hell, and an hereditary class whose function was to discharge the monarch's writ, have proved extremely durable. What we will be looking at in ***Notes*** is how boundary conditions are established in the human sphere and why arrangements once in place have proved so hard to change. Just as species find it all but impossible to evolve backwards if the environment they occupy alters, so too have human arrangements.

The reason for this is that within a boundary condition characterized by competitive symbiosis, the dynamic is towards specialization (structures that can adapt will tend to do so in the direction of their unique advantage — that which enabled them to prevail at the time they did). In the human sphere this translates into the often erroneous assumption that, when confronted by problems, the best thing a social structure (or the individuals who make it up) can do is what it was doing before, only more so. That said, social structures do adapt faster than biological ones.

To take an example we are familiar with, the human body is defined by all the internal goings-on that make it function and appear the way it does. Indeed everything in the universe can be described in this way. The elaboration of structure from the time of the Big Bang has depended on such boundary conditions. All matter is made up of countless building blocks, each with its own integrity, and it is only the stability of a building block that enables a successor structure to evolve. Indeed, it is when stability has been achieved at one level that evolution seems to cast around for another.

The idea of these jumps in types of matter has already been alluded to. In the context of boundary conditions, what these mean is that we have to think in terms of hierarchical sets of matter (what I call system states and will discuss in the next chapter), each contained within a boundary. We do not know what drives evolution to function in this way, but the process must entail a set of structures bound together by a common set of rules achieving a degree of stability that enables a new class of structure to evolve out of them. It is quite possible that biological evolution is reaching a threshold and that it is within the brain, and through the social structures the brain is able to sustain, that the evolutionary process is now most active.

A central characteristic of boundary conditions is their permeability: the extent to which and the way in which they interact with all the other boundary conditions around them. And it is worth remembering that all boundary conditions (which is to say all types of matter) are temporary energy-matter combinations. They only last for as long as the energy that sustains them, and sustains the building blocks that make them up, is bent to that purpose. The energy that upholds suns, and even black holes, gets used up eventually. This merely goes to emphasize that we are part of a larger process unfolding within a boundary condition that defines the universe as a whole.

And it is not just the permeability of a structure's boundary condition that is important. Structures also discharge energy and while much of this probably dissipates across our expanding universe entropically, it is this release of energy, outside a structure's give and take with the other structures to which it is symbiotically related, that enables the evolutionary process to create new matter. In human terms, you can think of it in this way. Two painters expend much the same energy on a canvas, but only one possesses a creative gift. The creative work changes things — an evolutionary plus. The other work does not.

In evolutionary terms, the short life cycle of biological structures, together with their ability to recreate themselves, progressively with variations, has allowed a whole host of different boundary conditions to form, subject only to the laws that govern biology. But as has been said several times already, most of the variations that have ever lived are now extinct, suggesting that biology is stabilizing around a limited number of types. In the human sphere, however, there is a process underway that appears to be moving in the opposite direction. In biology, the members of a species whose characteristics are farthest away from those that have sustained it usually die out (unless they stumble upon an environment that suits them), while the boundary condition humans in affluent societies have thrown around themselves tends not to discriminate in this way.

Our actions have been enormously uneven, however, in that outside the affluent societies improvements in medicine and food production have resulted in a rapid increase in the numbers of people destined to live in grinding poverty. Traditional societies have often been utterly destabilized because only one part of the tension matrix that held their lives in balance has been changed[1]. This sometimes occurs in nature. If a species enters an environment previously closed to it, it can upset the status quo[2]. (The *tension matrix* is described in detail in chapter 6). As I will argue throughout ***Notes***, I believe humans are poised between the biological and what I call the cerebral system states. The boundary condition we are trying to establish for ourselves is still very poorly defined and unless we get on top of it, we are likely to end up in the worst of all worlds: one with a burgeoning population and only cold-hearted biology to bring it under control.

The underlying nature of boundary conditions raises some profound questions and like everything in philosophy (as well as in science and religion) does force one to make some assumptions about the character of existence and how it came into being. I have followed the lead of the physicists and started with the Big Bang, knowing full

---

1. In his novel, *Things Fall Apart* (the words come from William Butler Yeats's poem *The Second Coming*) the Nigerian writer Chinua Achebe (1930–) has one of his characters lament the destruction of his people's traditional ways by colonizers intent on 'civilizing' them — white men, he says *put a knife on things that held us together and we have fallen apart.*

2. The horse became extinct in North America around 11,000 years ago. When horses were reintroduced onto the continent by the Spanish in 1493 (today's wild mustangs are a descendant of these) it altered the flora on the plains and the way some Indian tribes hunted. The arrival of Europeans altered the continent far more, of course.

well that there is a class of questions physics cannot address.[3] These questions are important, both because we can ask them and because they will be central to the evolution of cerebral structure.

The important point is that boundary conditions exist by virtue of their context, and so — to some extent — are the creatures of that context. This is how we and the universe are one. To put this into human terms, our enemies occupy a place equal to our own. When the Indians of the North American plains hunted buffalo, they revered that which they killed, recognizing that they owed their lives to these sacred animals. Both were of one whole. But an *enemy*, what is he or it? Throughout ***Notes*** the answer I suggest is that our concept of an enemy is derived from our biology. It is a mutation of biology's interdependence, of the way biological species feed off one another, but turned — in our human world — upon ourselves.

In effect a boundary condition forms around a group of people, making them equivalent to a species, and groups, similarly bound, are driven to compete, replicating the dynamic tension evident in the biological system state. In other words, groups feed off one another, although not in a directly cannibalistic sense (even though lives are lost, often on a prodigious scale) but as a way of evolving new ways of organizing individuals. And this new way of organizing individuals is actually all about the evolution of cerebral structure. We are in a transition state between the biological and the cerebral. Our biological drivers are calling many of the shots because we simply have not yet grasped the ground rules of the cerebral system state.

Let us construct an imaginary situation. Political entity X is made up of two subgroups A and B, where the individual members of A make up 90% of the whole. When group A decides to demonize and then persecute its subgroup B, what is going on? In biological terms, political

---

3. No one has actually seen a Big Bang although we might get to see a little one if the Large Hadron Collider functions as planned. By firing subatomic particles into one another at close to the speed of light, scientists hope to recreate the conditions that existed just after the Big Bang and learn more about how the quantum world works.

entity X, assuming it is dominated by group A, is seeking to expel mutation B, whose members clearly have a different way of organizing themselves, at least to the extent of being distinct. Next, assume X goes to war with Y. Now what is going on?

Having expelled B, X has become A's creature, and seeks to augment its position and identity by defeating Y. But X and Y are similar structures, in that each is able to wage war. B could not wage war on A, only vie with A for control of X, an encounter it lost because (let's assume) its members had an identity separate from that of X: they saw themselves as being and were seen as being — to some degree — separate. Into the mix let's throw political entity W. Concerned that X might become too powerful if it defeats Y, W declares war on X.

Many millions of dead later, the combined efforts of Y and W overwhelm X. But does X disappear? No. What changes is the way it organizes itself. Cerebral structure — how human brains are linked in concert — evolves inside X, as well as — albeit to a much lesser extent — inside Y and W. And what of those few members of group B who were able to escape A's persecution? Their harrowing experience further sharpens their sense of separateness. Some rebuild their lives within Y, determined not to be excluded from the political process, which Y's inclusive method of organization makes possible. Others resolve to establish their own political entity Z.

Everything in the previous three paragraphs could be expressed in terms of biology. In biological terms, any concept of human morality would not only be irrelevant, but out of place. It is a great shame that the expression *survival of the fittest* was coined to describe Darwin's evolutionary theory, because many used the idea to justify conquest and the domination of one man over another, and evolution is not about that at all. Evolution is about the elaboration of structure. And as the existence of every energy-matter combination is finite, evolution cannot be about survival alone, but must be about a process, a journey, which in our case — or in the case of cerebral structure — translates, I believe, into a quest for ever increasing awareness.

What this means is that the boundary conditions that go to make up the cerebral system state must be thought of differently from those that have made up the biological system state. And this is quite reasonable in that system states, while compatible with those states they have evolved from, operate by their own unique sets of rules.

The anodyne alphabet example above of course describes, in raw outline, what happened to German Jews before, during and after the Second World War (and could be applied to any number of persecuted minorities over the ages). While it is dangerous to use examples from human history where emotions are still raw, the Jewish people offer an unusual example of a boundary condition, in that they have striven to maintain a separate identity even as they have lived within countries whose identity they did not fully share. The bouts of persecution that have followed them over the centuries, invariably when their host has been experiencing some difficulties, accords well with a biological structure's imperative to expel an 'alien' organism in order to protect its boundary condition.

What makes the Jewish people so unusual is their persistence. One can even argue that the story that defines their boundary condition (and we will discuss the role of *the story* in chapter 7) assumes a level of persecution as the price to be paid for that identity. But their strategy suggests something else as well. As a people they can claim a disproportionate number of talented individuals. Has a need to be useful to their hosts stimulated a striving for excellence? Perhaps. But as the fate of Henry VIII's ministers (not to mention his wives) demonstrates, talent is easily sacrificed when doing so pleases those the power structure of a boundary condition is designed to serve.

How the Jewish people's ferocious desire for their own identity and undoubted talents translates into a nation within a region whose own people's identity is very different, remains to be seen. To date, the state of Israel has run to script — remarkable and determinedly single minded. That the people this new nation has displaced have become the persecuted ones is a bitter irony. Boundary conditions matter because the character of their interrelationships leads to outcomes. As structural engineering goes, the creation of the state of Israel was pretty cack-handed. Until the Israeli people come to realize that they need an outstandingly successful Palestinian state as their partner in the region, the dynamic they are subject to will remain malignant. But do they know that such a choice is open to them or does the story that defines their boundary condition blind them to this possibility?

Choice entails intent which forces us to consider consequences, and this lies at the very heart of evolving cerebral structure. The idea that happiness might lie in our own hands and not in those of the gods is novel enough, but an awareness that our own happiness may not only depend upon the happiness of those around us, but may be a consequence of how we design the ways in which we interact, is positively revolutionary. Suddenly evolution ceases to be a random walk or crude game of survival in which today's winner takes all before losing everything to tomorrow's new contestant. It becomes the result of our conscious intent.

In the following chapters we will consider further the idea of *system states* and then look at the *tension matrix* which regulates interlinked boundary conditions. After that I will discuss *the story* which I believe makes sense of a matrix and serves as a kind of cerebral boundary condition with the two acting together constituting *cerebral structure* which we will then consider. In the last chapter of ***Part 1*** I will argue that the universe, of which we are part, is essentially a *creative enterprise*.

5

System States

AS I HAVE ALREADY suggested, the universe appears to have evolved through several distinct phases, with each phase as a coherent system, or set of arrangements, defined by a boundary condition embodying a unique set of rules that has determined its state. For ease of description I will give these system states names. Only slightly tongue-in-cheek, I am going to call the initial state of the universe (when mass was compressed to such an extent that energy overcame gravity) the Alpha state, and everything outside that state (which may be anything from nothing to a multiverse) the Omega state. The system state that emerged after the Big Bang — the Alpha state — I am going to call the *quantum*, the one after that, the *atomic*, followed by the *galactic*, and then the *biological.*

A useful way to imagine these system states is to think of a Russian doll. Starting with the smallest, the Alpha state, evolution has opened up into a series of increasingly elaborate states, each one taking on the likeness of the one before but adding something unique. Unlike the Russian doll, however, where each structure differs only in size, each of the system states through which our universe has evolved has been governed by a distinct set of rules, and this has allowed successive system states to build something new out of what has gone before.

The system states I am talking about are primary system states in that the prior state, out of which they evolved, does not need their methodology in order to exist. For example, the galactic state of planets, moons and suns would not be affected one jot if the biological state did not exist. That this can be so is because primary system states operate by different rules to those governing the states that evolve from them, even though their rules are compatible. For example, how solar systems evolved is different from how animal species evolved, but the latter could not have taken place without the former. The physicist, Murray Gell-Man wrote a lovely book, a few years back, describing how the quark, an element created in the quantum state, could become a jaguar, the sleekest of all the cats[1], although I am not sure he placed as much emphasis on system states as I.

An obvious question is why should primary system states evolve at all? The answer, suggested by evolution, is that when a type of matter (the range of energy-transfer protocols that characterize the structures within a system state) has exhausted its possible permutations, a degree of stability is established. What was previously the product of an environment (think of the early, rapidly expanding universe, in which the interplay between energy and space stimulated the quantum dance) becomes an environment itself. Evolution — energy's drive into structure — suddenly has a new platform on which to build, a new ingredient to use. It is as if someone has just mastered counting with 1s, and after some frustrated trial and error discovers that the use of a space, or a 0, would move things along in a whole new direction, with a new set of rules.

There was just so much structure that could be generated within the quantum state, but with the evolution of the atomic state, structural elaboration widened and deepened considerably. And remember, structure and substructure embody energy-transfer protocols and the

---

1. *The Quark and the Jaguar: Adventures in the Simple and Complex*, published by W. H. Freeman and Company, New York, 1994. Gell-Mann was awarded the 1969 Nobel Prize in physics for his work on elementary particles.

boundary conditions that govern them. Every single atom and its nucleus within the human body is converting energy — that same energy that existed within the Alpha state — into a human structure, in accordance with a nested array of evolved energy-transfer protocols, described by our DNA, each governed by boundary conditions, and this is possible only because evolution managed to jump from the galactic to the biological system state.

Systems theorists, in the human field particularly, place great emphasis on a system's complexity and adaptability. There has been an assumption, I think, that certainly adaptability, and possibly complexity too, are a necessary part of the evolutionary process. However, I think this is only partially true. Adaptability may more fairly be described as a subset of the no-change condition. A system adapts in order to preserve an energy-transfer balance between its boundary condition and its environment. In other words, it adapts so as not to change, and complexity may simply be a by-product of this process. While species differentiation was undoubtedly an outcome of adaptability, species themselves have tended to become more complex and more fixed. As the engineers behind the Space Shuttle know only too well, you can go on adding elements to meet new needs, but there comes a point when it is a radically new design that is required.

My point is that adaptability and complexity are as likely to lead into an evolutionary dead end (an evolutionary cul-de-sac) as to an evolutionary breakthrough. Evolution is not just about species divergence, galactic differentiation, chemical type, or elementary particle variation. It is about the creation of fundamentally new material and new rules. On this basis, evolution is as much about the progression through the primary system states (as I have defined them) as it is about what goes on inside them. The initial elaboration that goes on within each primary system state, a procedure that can fairly be described as adaptation with complexity as a frequent outcome, is most accurately described, overall, as a process whereby the new material establishes an equilibrium in relation to the old.

By now it will be apparent to you that I believe we should expand our understanding of the evolutionary process to include the universe as a whole. Also, I think we need to broaden what we mean by *life* to include all structured matter. This is not mere semantics, because what it does is allow us to place humanity in a revised context. Why is this important? At present we regard ourselves as being, essentially, biological entities. It is true that Christian theologians do not see it this way, and I have to say, that in broad-brush terms, they may be more right than the scientific establishment. This is not, however, a clarion call to elevate religious dogma over science, but a plea for science to be more aware of its own dogma, and a little less dismissive of religious insight.

Restricting ourselves to the notion that 'life' evolved on earth however many billions of years ago it was that biological organisms first appeared, tends to blinker us from the many billions of years more in which biology did not feature. Of course Christian dogma gets bogged down in this dreadfully, with God creating the universe in seven days and Adam and Eve being around almost from the start. In fact what we know about the Big Bang suggests our universe came into existence *as a process* in milliseconds (no leisurely seven days there), and its story is far more extraordinary than anything in Genesis. And although we have no evidence of a curious young couple chafing against the restrictions imposed upon them in God's pleasant garden, the idea of dynamic evolution — energy partially constrained by the functional prerequisites of structure (a less romantic way of describing our start than Adam and Eve's rebelliousness no doubt, but hardly less exciting) is absolutely paramount.

Having started in God's garden, a perfect world with Man and then Woman already in it, Christian theologians were confronted by the reality of man's behavior here on Earth, which seemed to fall far short of perfection. How to explain? Their best shot was to argue that Adam and Eve, in going against God's instruction not to eat from the Tree of Knowledge and thereby exposing themselves to carnal lust, bequeathed their sinfulness to all future generations. Evicted from the garden, mankind was thereafter condemned to temptation and to having to choose between good and evil.

In the circumstances, it was not a bad explanation, but I believe the evolution of system states offers a better one. Our Biblical problem arises, according to my analysis, because we are in a transition phase to a state beyond the biological. So it is not because we fell from grace, but because we have yet to fully work out the rules that pertain to the new state that is evolving through us — the exact reverse of the biblical progression.

The significance of evolutionary system states is that there is no logical reason why the process that has created them should have stopped. And if it hasn't stopped, one should expect a new state to emerge from the biological. The true magic of evolution — the jump from one system state to another — is understandably hard to describe because it is a genuinely creative process (and more on that aspect later). But our best chance of understanding the transition we are now in is by revisiting *the drivers*, and, in particular, by looking at how these drivers relate to the biological system state.

In answer to the question, what drives the universe, we came up with a general answer: the interaction between energy and matter. When energy freed itself from the constraint of gravity (a rather imprecise description, I admit), it appeared to embark upon a process of transformation in which it imbued structure with life. I can't think of any other way to put this. A nucleus seems to me to be as alive as you or I. Although the re-emergence of gravity in the quantum system state was almost infinitesimal, the structured matter that did evolve was bursting with activity, potential and — importantly for the concept of life — finality. Regardless of how many recombinations and system states this matter infuses, it will continue to exist only for so long as the energy sustaining it lasts.[2]

Within each system state, the initial drive to elaborate all the structures possible seems relentless and often chaotic. In the end, though, we are left with a precise relationship between quarks and gluons, a specific number of chemical compounds, an order to the heavenly bodies which have formed in space that can be understood and, in the biological world, organisms that have elaborated quite logically to fill every part of our biosphere.

---

2. Over time, it seems that energy will slowly leach away from all matter and dissipate entropically across our expanding universe.

Although the universal drivers are surely constant, one would expect them to take on the character of each system state. The drive to elaborate and create in the quantum state embodied relativistic principles absent from the atomic state (although by then, embedded within it). Similarly, the sheer scale of the galactic state, in which enormous structures were created, was unique to it. What has characterized the biological world has been the speed with which adaptive structures have formed, a consequence, in large part, of the genetic processes so eloquently described by the evolutionary biologists.

These biological drivers, as I call them, embody their own clear morality: biological survival first, species survival second and individual survival last. The survival of any individual member of a species is relevant only in respect of the other two. But the process, overall, works solely because every individual is imbued with a will to survive. When religion confronted human behavior, it was looking at it from an entirely different point of view — individual perfectibility (an idea, ironically, picked up by many of the 18th and 19th century thinkers most hostile to religion). As I have already said, my contention is that out of the biological system state a new type of matter is emerging, which I am calling *cerebral structure*, and although (as I will point out) there have been signs of it in many species, it is in our own that it has become most developed.

Our dilemma is that we have yet to evolve fully the rules that will work in the *cerebral system state*, which of necessity must be the outcome of trial and error, because what is being created is entirely new. As a result, we are being pulled along by our biological drivers as well as by those we are attempting to create, and the two frequently conflict. Religion has been well ahead of the game in trying to moderate human behavior, even if science is now well ahead in trying to understand it. If the two could but stomach it, it seems to me that the religious and scientific establishments have grounds for a truce here.

By way of illustrating how the way we look at things alters our approach to them, let me introduce you (or possibly reintroduce you, if you are already familiar with his work) to James Ephraim Lovelock (1919–). Lovelock captured the public imagination with his Gaia hypothesis, which essentially states that the Earth should be thought of as a single organism, which he named Gaia after the earth goddess in ancient Greek mythology.

Although my biological system state is not the same as Lovelock's single organism, there are distinct similarities in what we are both saying. Where we differ, however, is that for Lovelock, biological and non-biological matter on Earth should be viewed as being different parts of the same system, and that this system is self-balancing (in my terms, it will seek to maintain its boundary condition and so the integrity of everything within it). From my point of view, however, the Earth (minus its biological component) is part of the galactic system state, and the evolution of biological life resulted from a fundamental change in system state. To revert to the Russian doll analogy, I am saying that biological life is the next doll after that which includes the planets, stars and moons. Lovelock is saying that the Earth and its biological life are one doll.

From both our perspectives an equilibrium is being sought. Lovelock's relates to the Earth as a whole (including its biological life). Mine relates to biological life alone, given whatever environment it finds itself in, the Earth already being in planetary equilibrium. Under Lovelock's depiction, the biosphere (Earth, together with everything on it and in it) will go on adjusting so as to maintain its essential state. Mine suggests something quite different. Under my depiction, biological life will go on elaborating until it has exhausted all possibilities, at which point it will stabilize and remain stable, unless conditions on Earth change. However, neither of these scenarios fully captures what seems to be happening now, or indeed what has happened over the past.

The Gaia hypothesis does not conceptually separate biological matter from non-biological matter. Homeostasis (equilibrium) should be achieved when all parts of the system are in balance. Although the sun has a finite life, the energy it is releasing is being balanced by the energy it is producing (like a slow-burning coal) so, for the foreseeable future at least, a condition of homeostasis exists. Gaia's equilibrium is a much more angry one, in that the dynamic nature of the Earth — its tectonic shifts, volcanic eruptions, fluctuating climate and changing ocean currents — all call for adjustments that may be quite hostile to biological life. And this is before Gaia has to contend with a meteor or other visitation from outer space. No, unlike James Lovelock and the Greeks before him, I do not see Gaia as a wholly reliable friend![3]

The fact that there have been five catastrophic extinctions since biological life first appeared on Earth, and countless minor ones, should tell us — if nothing else — that biological life has had to fight every step of the way, a consequence of Gaia's tough love. It was not all doom, however. There were periods of biological stability. The dinosaur world did last for over 160 million years, after all.

Where Lovelock and I find common ground, I think, is that for both of us it would appear that the actions of Man are angering his Gaia and destabilizing my biological system state. In distinctly sacrificial language, he has said that by 2040 our present population of nearly 7 billion will have been severely culled by floods, drought and famine, brought on by climate change, a consequence of our addiction to carbon-based energy. In other words, our biological drivers are pushing us towards catastrophe, and Gaia towards a new equilibrium.

But this is where he and I part company, and where I may part company from the evolutionary biologists. Because in arguing that the universe is in the process of evolving a new system state, I am implying that the stresses and strains which the biological system state has been subjected to by its planetary environment helped stimulate, initially at least, this creative jump. Increasingly, though, humankind has been generating its own environment and almost certainly the problems we are about to experience are a direct consequence of the opportunities

---

3. The Gaia hypothesis was first proposed by James Lovelock in the 1960s and was welcomed by many environmentalists. Evolutionary biologists, such as Richard Dawkins, were skeptical that natural selection amongst individual organisms could produce an equilibrium for the planet as a whole, and climatologists, while accepting a link between organisms and oxygen levels, believe other factors affect the climate as well. Lovelock has since disappointed many in the environmental movement by arguing that nuclear power will be needed if we are to reduce our dependence on carbon-based energy.

cerebral structure has opened up, overlapping with our biological drivers. It is, therefore, the latter we need to weaken and the former we must strengthen.

In the following chapter I will outline what I call *the tension matrix*, essentially the framework within which each of must function. In the chapter after that I argue that the vision of the world we carry in our heads, and which I call *the story*, largely determines how we react to the tension matrix. I go on to define *cerebral structure* more precisely and then discuss creativity and its necessary ambiguity, because it is my contention that the universe we are part of is essentially *a creative enterprise*.

6

The Tension Matrix

THE TENSION MATRIX governs how a set of boundary conditions relate to one another. For example, all biological life on earth consists of multiple biological entities, each with its own boundary condition, which are all, to a greater or lesser extent, interdependent. They are the building blocks that have created the biological system state on earth. Energy flows through all of these structures and each seeks to maintain its integrity, frequently by absorbing the energy contained within other structures. These structures, in other words, exist in a state of dynamic tension with one another inside a matrix that describes how their boundary conditions interact.

Imagine, in your mind's eye, a woman in an African village (let's call her Shona) who must walk three miles each day to a well for water and three miles back. She must grind out her meager provisions to feed herself and her husband who tends their five cattle and small stand of corn, her four children (she has had a further three that died), as well as her father-in-law who is blind and infirm. The arid landscape and uncertain rains they have learned to live with. The customs of the village sustain them. This is the framework of their lives. Whatever aspirations and yearnings this woman has must be expressed within the parameters that make the lives of herself and her fellow villagers possible. This is *the tension matrix* within which she and her family live.

The need for food to sustain her dependents drives her through each day's tasks. Her desire for companionship ties her to the village and to her husband. Hers and his urge to mate produces children. The growth of her body from babe, to child, to young girl, to woman, to crone dictates the cycle of her life. The customs of the village serve to educate her in ways that encourage harmonious living and discourage discord. If you could draw a picture of all those things that influence her actions, you would see that she is fully stretched by many needs — personal, familial and collective — that determine the pattern of her life. Her life runs like a thread through a carpet of mutual obligations.

Each of the primary system states I have described can be characterized by a tension matrix that, in simple terms, establishes the framework of possibilities within which its dynamic works. Even the Alpha state is defined by the mass-energy interaction. The tension matrix that pertains to the biological state contains many of the same dimensions as those I described in the preceding page. Just like individual humans, organisms possess a degree of individual volition that increases as you move up the biological family tree. Just like individual humans, organisms utilize collective arrangements. Just like individual humans, organisms must interact with their environment in order to sustain themselves. Just like individual humans, organisms can replicate themselves. Just like individual humans, organisms have adapted to occupy specific parts of the biosphere. And just like individual humans, organisms have short life cycles, when compared to the structures that have evolved within the other system states.

The way of life described in the preceding page demonstrates another characteristic that typifies structures within system states — a tendency towards equilibrium. Even today there are groups of people whose way of life does not appear to have changed for thousands of years. We might regard Shona's fictional (but representative) way of life as tough, lacking in opportunity, unnecessarily restrictive, etc., and feel inclined to put forward all sorts of helpful suggestions as to how it might be improved. But if happiness is our goal, a settled way of life may be of far greater value than we appreciate.[1]

---

1. José 'Pepe' Alvarez, who was once an Augustinian friar in Spain but now works for the Peruvian Amazon Research Institute in the remote settlement of Iquitos, was recently interviewed by Paul Miles of the Financial Times

This raises a profound dilemma. Has the garden of Eden existed under our noses all along and is it we who have thrown ourselves out of it? And if so, and if happiness is our stated goal (as it seems to be), why on earth did we do so? Now let me revert to the story I started with. Imagine, if you will, that into Shona's village comes a new element, never before experienced: three young men, aloft a jeep, armed to the teeth and high on narcotics. They spray the village with gunfire, set several huts on fire, kill a number of the men who try to stop them, butcher some children for devilment, and rape as many of the women as they can lay their hands on.

Two and a half hours later they are back in their base, a hundred miles away, being congratulated by a man anxious to extend his power over the land the villagers have occupied for a thousand years. Unbeknown to these villagers, their land is believed to hold rich deposits of bauxite[2] which an alien people, many thousands of miles away, desperately need. Welcome to globalization — welcome to progress!

Now let us play a different version of this mind game. Instead of wild young men on a jeep, imagine that this once-isolated village is visited for the first time by professional slavers. Anxious to welcome these strangers, the villagers lay on a feast, notwithstanding their meager supplies. The slavers enjoy the hospitality and when the villagers are all lulled into a state of replete calm, round them up. Three months later, after a harrowing journey, and many deaths, those still alive are purchased by a Mrs. S. Baker at the Savannah slave market in Georgia, and taken to her plantation in Liberty County, bringing to 57 her total number of slaves.

The slave accommodation on Mrs. Baker's plantation is about average, and no worse than it was in the village. Shona's two oldest

---

(September 13th, 2008). Amongst many other interesting things, he said "people here are some of the happiest I have ever met even though they have nothing but a small hut, a wooden canoe and a paddle. . . . The key is enjoying simple things and every moment as it comes, and not worrying too much about the past or the future."

2. The chief commercial ore of aluminum.

children, a girl and a boy, survived the journey, as well as her husband. Her father-in-law and two youngest children died on the boat that carried them from Africa to North America. She has no idea that she came from Africa, nor does the idea of America mean much to her, save that one was 'before' and is becoming a distant memory and the other is 'after' and is real. Her husband and son work in the cotton fields all day, and, apart from having to endure the sour temper of Mrs. Baker's overseer, the work is no harder than it was in their village.

Shona's daughter has become companion to Mrs. Baker's and Shona herself has been given work in the kitchen. There is much that surprises her and even some things that please her, not least that water comes from a tap and does not need a six mile walk to be found. Every seventh day, which Shona learns is called Sunday, Mrs. Baker insists that her slaves gather in a meeting place, named church, where they sing and are spoken at in their new language. She enjoys the singing. They all do.[3]

In this second example, a new equilibrium has been established. The tension matrix is little different from before, save that what drives them is not the struggle to get food, but the need to satisfy their new mistress. When Abraham Lincoln leads the north to victory and slavery is abolished, their way of life is once again shattered. Shona and her family find that they have to sell themselves for money and that their family has to separate in order to survive. She discovers that they are hated and that they are free.

To understand how the tension matrix works, consider the scenario in which the three young men in their jeep arrive in Shona's village. It has an utterly destabilizing effect, because the boundary condition that applies to these young men is wholly different from that which defines the village. Not only are the young men immune to the customs of the village that ensure harmonious interaction between its

---

3. According to the 1860 US census, some 390,000 persons held around 3,950,000 unnamed slaves, an average of ten slaves per holder, although large plantations might have held over 200. There were over 6,000 slaves in Liberty County alone.

occupants, but they have access to new structure unavailable to the villagers: the jeep and their small arms.

And even the three young men are victims of a fractured tension matrix, because although they have their warlord and his community to return to, its boundary condition has been penetrated by that of the far-off interests anxious to get their hands on the bauxite. Without the financial and technological support the warlord receives from these interests, he would not be able to sustain his aggressive rule. He would, instead, have to act in cooperation with his community, whose members would be fully involved trying to sustain themselves.

But you do not need 'far-off interests' to destabilize a tension matrix. The *idea* of 'far-off interests' coupled with scale, will do just as well. First the scale. Whenever a group of individuals find one environment that is munificent (a location that can supply an abundance of their needs), they are likely to settle and increase in numbers. The idea that others could come and share their bounty (leaving less to go around) might prompt them to support a warrior class. On its own, this need not amount to much, but as soon as they are persuaded — in the interests of efficiency — to delegate food storage and distribution to another class of individual, the dynamics of their tension matrix have changed radically. They have shifted from an essentially collegiate set of arrangements to one that requires a ruling class.

But even this is a long way from the brutalized community the three young men who invade Shona's village belong to. If the boundary condition that defines the settled community remains intact and the elaboration of structure (the creation of a warrior class, and the creation of a ruling class) takes place gradually, traditions that protect individual interests (such as a process for dealing with conflicts and grievances) might easily evolve at the same time. A tension matrix will always tend towards equilibrium, because its purpose is to integrate individuals so that they can act in a way that sustains them. Anarchic systems will always be short-lived, because people do not like to starve.

The bestial systems we are familiar with evolve when individuals within a boundary condition are treated not just differentially — as in ruling class and warrior class — but differentially as human beings. In the second scenario depicted for Shona's village, she, and what remains of her family, are able to recreate a semblance of the community they once knew, but as slaves — a particular class of individual. However, apart from the wholly diabolical journey they were forced to take (and a natural calamity could have wreaked the same havoc on them in their village) Mrs. Baker's treatment of them is not particularly inhumane.

As Mrs. Baker's property, they are accorded a degree of protection, just as Mrs. Baker's horses are. Amongst most slave owners, cruelty to slaves is frowned upon as much as cruelty to animals is. Only when the Northern states, whose tension matrix is quite different, overwhelm the Southern states in the civil war, does the bitterness of whites on the losing side erupt in an orgy of nigger-baiting and nigger-murder. My point is not to defend slavery, but to condemn inhuman behavior and the kinds of tension matrix that allow it. The Nazi death camps and Soviet gulags were infinitely worse than Mrs. Baker's plantation, and the high-minded rhetoric of Northerners, with their insatiable demand for cheap labor to supply their burgeoning factories, was often less noble than it appeared.

The tension matrix that applied to Shona's village was consensual in the sense that almost everyone was in the same boat and the openness of their arrangements meant it was hard for any one person to steal a march on any other. Their harsh taskmaster was the environment. To this environment, they were invisible. But that has not stopped people over the ages imagining otherwise and believing that the right acts might influence events in their favor. This desire not to be the butt of merciless nature has given rise to priesthoods, and given priesthoods power that they have used to become a class apart, along with rulers and warriors.

Every tension matrix, by its nature, embodies coercive power — its purpose, after all, is to get individuals to act in concert for their overall benefit. But as soon as a tension matrix includes different classes of people, with some classes possessing more power than others, albeit for reasons initially believed valid (our warriors protect us from our enemies, our rulers make wise decisions on our behalf, our priesthood protects us from the environment's evil spirits), the potential for self-interested coercion is created. But worse than that: the tendency of the matrix to influence how we see the world becomes handmaiden to a particular power structure.

Over time, the tension matrix has come to incorporate numerous levels, from family, to neighborhood, to work environment, to region, to nation, to the multi-national structures that we are struggling to evolve. It incorporates informal rules and customs that differ between groups, and formal rules that are supposed to apply equally. It now embraces thousands of interlocking organizations, large and small, public and private. Often overlooked, because they are so ubiquitous, are all the physical structures that play a large part in our lives, from roads to airports to cities, to the remarkable technologies that we quickly take for granted.

We are now awash with information from a burgeoning media and can, if we want, observe news and politics twenty-four seven. Free-market capitalism has empowered millions and is reshaping the world in our own image. Regulators and regulated battle it out, with the latter often running behind the former as new schemes of arrangement are developed. We have created a dynamic jungle in which a wide range of abilities are rewarded and opportunities offered, but it is a jungle that has substituted remote media communities for actual communities, to the detriment of some. Worldwide, our tension matrix can now coordinate and sustain the activities of over 6.7 billion individual people. This is a staggering achievement — and we know remarkably little about it.

There are probably several areas we should concentrate on. The first is **intent**. The structures that go to make up the tension matrix have often evolved in response to crisis. This means that they are frequently hybrid in their objectives, as political interests use the opportunity to attach provisions that serve special interests. Although it is sensible not to try to solve problems that don't exist, more deliberate approaches to problem-solving, rather than waiting for a crisis to trigger action, would not go amiss.

The second area, closely related to the first, is **clarity**. We should design structures to do specific, measurable things. Coercive power, of the self-interested kind, thrives on ambiguity and clarity is its enemy. A third area is **neutrality**, or fairness. The structures we design should be acceptable to any individual coming into a situation for the first time. For example, if you were told that you could become part of a system in which you might, through no fault of your own, end up in dire straits, abandoned by the community you were joining, you would probably say no thanks.

Fourthly, greater recognition should probably be given to the **time cycle** associated with structures. Politicians and business leaders are often accused of acting on the basis of electoral or compensation cycles, when the problems they are supposed to be addressing are governed by quite different, often longer, cycles. All structures should be for a fixed term so that redesign, or even abandonment, can occur as circumstances suggest. A fifth area, often overlooked, is **collateral consequences**. Because we live in a complex, uncertain world, even carefully thought-out structures are likely to have unintended consequences. Processes need to be put in place that detect, acknowledge and deal with these. Individuals should not be left to suffer, simply because no part of the matrix can recognize their plight.

Finally, we must pay far greater heed to **boundary conditions** than we do. In Britain, today, for example, there is a large Muslim population, a consequence of the country's imperial past. Many young Muslims identify with their fellow Muslims in the Middle East, so that when Britain, as part of the Western alliance, interferes in that part of the world for strategic reasons, it finds itself with a fifth column inside its borders. At the very least, this should prompt Britain to reappraise where its strategic interests actually lie, and spur Britain's Muslim community into doing the same. A dialogue of the deaf is hardly helpful.

When the American Civil war was over in 1865, Mrs. Baker, in Liberty County, had to tell her slaves she could no longer afford them and they were free to go. Although granted the right to vote in 1870, white Southern Democrats, anxious to protect their power base, resorted to violence against any blacks who sought to exercise that right, often under cover of the Ku Klux Klan. In spite of bills to prevent the practice, segregation in the United States is still a fact of life. Blacks are imprisoned at over seven times the rate of whites, usually on drug-related offences.

The modern state is now so large and its tension matrix so complex that large numbers of people can quite easily fall foul of capricious systems without anyone but them knowing or caring. It took *One Day in the Life of Ivan Denisovich* (1962) and *The Gulag Archipelago* (1973–78) by the Russian writer Aleksandr Solzhenitsyn, to make the world understand the full horrors of the Soviet prison state. And if we imagine our democracies immune, we should probably think again. Notwithstanding its complexity, a tension matrix will only work for so long as most individuals within its boundary condition believe it will work. The collapse of communism demonstrated this.

In the main, the basis of this belief is a matter of fact: is the matrix delivering what people need? But needs are more than just food and shelter; they are about individual aspirations and perceptions of fairness, dynamic elements in themselves. And needs can also be about the avoidance of fear. This brings me to a central question: what makes a tension matrix work? How does it actually influence us in what we do? The answer is that we carry a vision of the world, of the matrix and how it works, in our head, and compare it to our moral compass or sense of self. It is this juxtaposition that injects tension into the matrix and gives it its potency. I call this interpretive mechanism *the story* inside which we live, and we will consider it next.

7

The Story

SO WHAT IS THIS THING I am calling *the story* inside which we live? In his prison hut, the imagination of Solzhenitsyn's Ivan Denisovich was constrained by its wooden walls, and yet expanded to fill every nook and cranny. No crumb went unnoticed, no change to his threadbare clothes was ignored, no expression on the face of a guard or fellow inmate was spared analysis. The expressive slowness of life and its closeness to death was all-consuming. This was the entire world for Ivan Denisovich, not only to be endured but to be savored. Just as Shona from the previous chapter had not questioned the three mile walk to get water or the three mile walk to carry it back, neither did Denisovich question the cold, the meager rations, or foibles of those around him. Instead, he was utterly absorbed in the richness of his existence. With his mind, he had turned his sentence on its head and dispatched his jailers to the mad house.[1]

---

1. In 1945, Solzhenitsyn was arrested, while fighting on the Prussian front, for writing to a friend unflattering comments about Stalin's conduct of the war. After being hauled back to Moscow and tortured in the Lubyanka prison, he was sentenced to eight years hard labor, to be followed by permanent internal exile. In 1950 he was moved to a camp for political prisoners in Kazakhstan and this formed the basis for his novel *One Day in the Life of Ivan Denisovich*.

If you left a man from Moscow in the jungle, would he be free? Perhaps less free than if you put him in the Gulag, Stalin's network of prisons for those who displeased him. Most of us are not dropped into a jungle nor into a Gulag Archipelago, but we are dropped into something just as overwhelming — an environment constructed by our predecessors, the tension matrix I described in the previous chapter. In the Brazilian rainforest, an Amazonian Indian would consider himself free. He would have grown up to understand it. The jungle and its ways would have become imprinted on his mind. Its story and his story would have merged. The jungle would come to offer him shelter, food and excitement. His life would be divided between the jungle and those other humans with whom he lived. Whatever customs they shared, the reality of the jungle would infuse their imaginations.

To be brought up in a modern city is no different. We have to learn how to read it, to recognize its dangers and spot its opportunities. Look inside the head of a teenager brought up on a rundown city estate and compare what you find with what is inside the head of one from that city's more prosperous neighborhoods. Their model of how the world works will be entirely different even though they live in the same metropolis and within the same tension matrix. For one, dealing in crack cocaine, belonging to a gang and stealing a few cars for kicks is the smart thing to do. For the other, getting educated, getting a well-paying job and partying like there is no tomorrow is the way to go.

It has come as a shock to many Britons to discover that there are young men of the Muslim faith, but British born and bred, quite prepared to walk onto buses and into trains, strapped with explosives, in order to blow themselves and as many others as they can, to kingdom come. The essential thing to be grasped about the tension matrix is that it is a construction, like a jungle or a city, full of pathways that individuals can take. Which ones will depend upon the story they carry in their heads. Each of us is born with a sense of self, with what I call a moral compass. I am not talking about a complex moral articulation here, although it might become that, but a feeling about our own identity and what it means.

In evolutionary terms, the biological volition to act independently, to some degree, that we have inherited from our forebears has mutated, within ourselves, into a conscious feeling that our identity is unique, that it should be protected, and that it should be acted upon. Think of teenagers you know (or just remember your own teen years) and recognize the struggle they have to be and to express themselves. Naturally the form this expression takes will be a function of an interaction between their genetic profile (their particular character) and the stimulus they receive from the tension matrix, mediated by the evolving story they carry in their heads.

Initially, this story is likely to have come from the humans they have grown up with, because it is through our fellow humans that we learn to understand the tension matrix we are born into. But over time our own experiences and whatever level of independent thought we can muster will craft our story into something uniquely ours. Our imaginary Shona might rationalize her position as a slave in Mrs. Baker's house entirely to her satisfaction, just as Ivan Denisovich rationalized his position in the prison. To both, freedom, in the sense of being released from the world they knew, might have been a daunting prospect, as alarming as being dropped into the Amazonian rainforest would be for a person who knew it not.

Our moral compass, essentially how we see ourselves in the story we carry, establishes a boundary condition that arbitrates between us and the tension matrix we inhabit and determines our actions. The Protestant prepared to be burned at the stake for his beliefs, like the Catholic prepared to do likewise, cannot exist outside his boundary condition, because what lies within it is his entire identity. The young man who becomes a soldier is no different. The very real risk of being killed is outweighed by the loss he would feel if he simply walked away. The legendary investor Warren Buffet has undoubtedly been helped in his chosen trade by a stubbornly independent frame of mind. Not for him to follow the crowd. Instead, he looks for the angle, the often overlooked and simple truth, rather than the conventional wisdom.[2]

---

2. In his authorized biography, *The Snowball: Warren Buffet and the Business of Life*, by Alice Schroeder, Buffet tells how he turned to a life of petty crime when he was forced to move to Washington following his father's election to Congress.

Luckily for Buffet, successful investing is considered OK in the United States, so the matrix — once he had located his niche — rewarded his behavior, rather richly as things turned out. The terrorist, by contrast, joins his or her identity to a cause such that the matrix he must operate within has been demonized by a competing matrix that he has chosen to attach himself to, in the same way as a soldier attaches himself to an army that demonizes an enemy. The terrorist is likely to have a short, narrow, albeit intense life, whilst the intelligent investor — so long as his capitalist world does not become a communist one — can look forward to a much longer, fuller one.

The matrix can, thus, mean different things to different people, depending on the story carried in their heads. In fact, no two people's story is likely to be identical, thanks to the biological notion of volition that has been translated into our conscious thinking process. That said, we all start out undergoing what sociologists call a process of socialization, essentially imprinting on our childhood brains a map of the world we have been born into, so that we can function in the man-made jungle where we find ourselves.

To understand the significance of the story fully, we need to have a good feel for the nature of the tension matrix. As I have described, it consists of hard structures (such as buildings, roads and machines) and soft structures, the latter being both informal (such as family loyalties) and formal (such as laws). The jungle analogy is quite apposite, in that the jungle dweller has the physical jungle as an environment in which he must live, with its cyclical and secular characteristics. Certain trees produce fruit at certain times each year and a river may redefine the jungle floor over centuries as it moves, to and fro, across its basin.

He loved his young life in Omaha, where he'd got things pretty much taped, and resented the dislocation. Luckily, he was never caught, and when his father threatened to take away his paper rounds unless he got back on track, he decided to rebuild his maverick identity along more conventional lines. He applied to Columbia University (after having been turned down by Harvard) to study investing, his unusual passion since childhood (he had worked out that if he kept rolling up the profits from his paper rounds they would grow like a snowball) under the legendary Benjamin Graham, co-author with David Dodd, of *The Intelligent Investor*.

Similarly, in the human jungle, buildings designed to provide some regular function have a finite life. The medieval town might have been state of the art in the 15th century, but come the 21st with its suburbs, automobiles and out-of-town shopping malls, it appears quaint to modern eyes — better looked at than lived in. The customs a jungle tribe evolve seek to ensure harmonious living on a small scale, and the transmission of information about the jungle that ensures its survival from one generation to the next. Its story repeats, again and again, with modest embellishments, no doubt, depending on the imagination and experience of the storytellers, in a state of static equilibrium.

In the largely human jungle (in which the stability of the sylvan environment has been replaced by structures of our own making), the tension matrices that we have evolved operate in a state of dynamic equilibrium, vulnerable to collapse during periods of chaos. It is when these structural failures occur that our biological drivers take over. Think of it this way. Our evolved biological responses have a far older pedigree than the story we inherited and built that gave meaning to our particular man-made matrix. If that matrix fails for any reason, our biological drivers quite naturally kick in. During periods of total war, for instance, a people's entire tension matrix is often largely destroyed. The behaviors we can observe in such circumstances originate from an entirely different moral framework (the biological one) to that associated with the story that previously defined the collapsed matrix.

When the millions of German prisoners taken at the end of the Second World War started to be released, many found that not only had their families been killed or scattered, but that the region they once called home was now part of a new country. And yet enough of the pre-war story existed in their heads, as well as in the heads of those around them, to make it possible for them to start rebuilding lives that at least bore some resemblance to the lives they had once known. What was different, of course, was the nature of the power structure — the rules, customs and practices that determined the exercise of collective action and which characterized the new tension matrix.

This illustrates an important aspect of the relationship between a story and a tension matrix: they do not fit exactly. And I believe this ties in precisely with how the universe works. If the universe were wholly deterministic, its functioning at any point of time would fully reflect its entire potential. Ignoring the fact that it can be cannibalized and will degrade, a car, for example, will only ever be a car. But that is not how our universe functions. It clearly embodies a creative dynamic (which I will discuss more at the end of ***Part 1***) made possible by a certain looseness between its boundary conditions, a pattern reflected across its evolutionary spectrum. In human terms, we call this freedom!

It is, of course, a rather limited freedom, but wholly real and central to the creative dynamic we are part of. Germany's Third Reich was a story cast like a net over a tension matrix that looked very similar to those of Britain or America. That it was morally malignant was overlooked because it did seem to address the aspirations of many Germans. A contemporary example is that of the credit crisis that is in full swing as I write.

Trade imbalances between developing and developed countries (particularly the United States) resulted in large surpluses being recycled from one to the other (because the developing countries could not absorb the money their exports were generating and the developed countries had more sophisticated money markets). This surfeit of credit eventually led to poor lending practices, over-consumption and inflated asset prices in the developed countries. Until debt reached unsustainable levels, politicians, regulators, bankers, businessmen and the general public all applauded. But when it was realized that a lot of the debt was never going to be paid back, the credit chain collapsed. Credit was withdrawn from the credit junkie and the global economy is now experiencing an acute case of *cold turkey*. Even the pushers and their suppliers are squealing.

My point is that a story, in justifying how a tension matrix is operated, allows for radically different outcomes. The Third Reich went to hell in a hand cart and the credit crunch that has gripped the world at the start of the twenty-first century looks as though it will cause a good deal of misery. It is not enough to look at a tension matrix and assume that its structure will do what it is supposed to do. The story that infuses it with life is also absolutely vital.

Two storylines infuse our evolved tension matrices with their dynamism. The first is a kind of layering of boundary conditions that we have come up with, which enables groups of people, with markedly different experiences and orientations, to function within the same matrix. The second element is the boundary condition, defined by the story of nationhood (an extrapolation of our instinctive attachment to family and community) that makes it possible for large collections of people to be pitted against one another as if they were a species of competing dinosaur.

What goes on in a typical restaurant, for example, is a good example of the first element of a story that infuses the matrix with life. Chefs, waiters and customers, all different in character and experience, interact each evening in a wonderful dance choreographed by an invisible story each participant has absorbed into his or her head by training and experience. While the matrix may define the set of relationships in a restaurant (finance, layout, contracts of employment, links with suppliers, opening hours, prices to be charged, etc.) it is the story each participant carries that governs its nature. Different restaurants embrace slightly different stories giving rise to a dynamic tension between them[3], which supplements the dynamic tension within each restaurant that individual differences engender.

The second element of a story that infuses the matrix with life is most clearly evident when a nation goes to war, although it is, in fact, operating in the background all of the time. I am not sure how best to categorize this second element and others will do it better than I am about to, but I call it *the here I stand moment.* What it does is open up (or make explicit — the pathway that already exists in all of us) a channel back into the deepest recesses of our feeling. It connects us to the universe we are part of and is a 'letting go'. In essence it entails passing the buck to our biological drivers.

Soldiers on opposite sides give themselves over to an instinct that derives from a species' biological imperative to survive (which, in turn,

---

3. I looked at this in my doctoral work (*Structure and Control within restaurants, 1989*).

is derived from a structure's volition to maintain itself — it could not exist otherwise). In human terms it is the subsuming of a person's identity within a 'greater' cause. It draws from the same well as that which prompts a man to risk his life in order to rescue another. At the bottom of that well we will find biology's tactic of sacrificing some members of a species so that the majority may live. Because we are conscious beings we have come to express these biological drivers in human terms: God is often invoked on opposite sides of the same conflict.

To the irreligious, such apparently illogical invocations demonstrate the fallacy of believing in God. But if, as I do, you regard God as a metaphor for the outer boundary of existence, it is not illogical at all. What both sides in a conflict are actually saying is that *we don't know how we got into this mess but it appears that the only way out is for one of us to win; God help us*! In other words, the evolutionary process is more important than any single individual. Within this framework, the loser in battle is as important as the victor, and the religious martyr is just as significant (and surely is more so) than his persecutors. Without these counterpoints the evolutionary dynamic would be stillborn, and is why establishments are loath to create martyrs.

What I am suggesting in ***Notes***, however, is that humans are in transition between the biological state, from which we have evolved, into this new state which I am calling the *cerebral state*. When we look back at the great conflicts that have enveloped humanity — the battle between Catholicism and Protestantism, or more recently that between totalitarianism and liberal democracy, for example — we do wonder why so much blood was spilled on account of what were essentially ideas, especially as they often seem arcane with the passing of time. The task that confronts us is how to engineer the evolution of ideas without having to revert to biology's predatory modus operandi. To this end, we will now look at the nature of *cerebral structure*.

8

Cerebral Structure

AS YOU WILL now know, it is my contention that the biological system state is serving as a platform for a new state, the cerebral system state, in which a new class of matter — *cerebral structure* — will evolve. This structure consists of boundary conditions containing tension matrices and the stories that explain them. One of the notable features of the boundary conditions that make up this cerebral system state is that they can adapt even faster than their biological precursors.

So what exactly is cerebral structure?

No doubt many who come across my suggestion for the first time, that cerebral structure is a distinct system state beyond the biological, will find it hard to embrace. And I wouldn't blame them. However, if you accept my contention that evolution should be thought of as encompassing the whole history of the universe, rather than just its biology, and that this history very clearly reveals distinct jumps from one type of matter to the next, then the suggestion — as outlandish as it may at first appear — is simply logical. That said, and as I have outlined already in respect of the other system states which I have identified, the emergence of one from another is exceptionally hard to describe.

This is because the material that will constitute the new state must start by being part of the state it evolves from: one moment it is not there as anything distinct, the next moment it is. As I have already mentioned, we have yet to pin down how biological matter evolved from the inert galactic matter that preceded it, so this problem is not new. But I believe the process is part of the creative mechanism which infuses the evolutionary dynamic of the universe and will be considered in the following chapter (the last in ***Part 1***). Here, I want to get a handle on what cerebral structure is, while acknowledging that describing the transition between system states is hard enough, without the added complication of being part of the procedure.

I have defined cerebral structure as being a tension matrix and its story. This is likely to be a crude definition, although I think it captures cerebral structure's essential elements. These are the ideas that are manifest in actual structures, from soft ones like language and the law to hard ones like a road network or city layout, as well as those explanatory ideas about how the world works that each of us carries in his head and relates to his unique sense of felt identity. Central to the distinction between biological structure and cerebral structure is that the latter evolves in response to conscious intent.

I am arguing that many of the problems we have experienced and are experiencing arise because we are stuck in a halfway house between the biological and cerebral system states, such that many of our actions (both at the individual level and the collective one) are biologically driven. In the past, this dichotomy has been characterized by such terms as *good* and *evil* and *original sin* and by the supposed conflict between a man's *soul* and his *body*. When it comes to improving the human lot, this has placed the emphasis on individual behavior when, according to my analysis, far greater emphasis needs to be placed on the systems we build.

In advocating that we must learn to leave our biological drivers behind, I am not suggesting that we abandon feeling. As I will say often, our feelings are the only things that tie our conscious minds to the universe we are part of. And neither am I intending to cast biology in a malignant light. It embodies much evolved wisdom and biology's components will be absorbed within the cerebral state, along with atoms from the atomic state and quarks from the quantum one. Cerebral structure can only ever be an expression of the universe as a whole. In trying to detect its emergence, the obvious things to look for are signs of consciousness. A clear marker of this is awareness.

The biological system state is awash with signs that require discernment. It is a world in which organisms are loosely connected by their ability to stimulate one another through visual, olfactory, audible and tactile signals. In the main, organisms give out and react to these signals in a hard-wired manner. But some processing goes on in brains (to the extent they exist) at both ends of the relationship. What this allows for is a degree of variation in how a signal is sent and how it is reacted to, depending upon an organism's mental capacity.

Doubtless too much wondering about when to send a signal or how to react to one when received was not generally life-enhancing and so it is hardly surprising that biological evolution did not give the development of mental capacity much mileage. That said, some species did manage to carve out a place for themselves by acting cooperatively and that will have required a greater capacity to interpret one another's signals. When combined with flexibility, which the ape's rather ungainly shape afforded, a need for mental acuity was established.

As one form of communication amongst the members of a group is chatter (a cacophony of sounds that carry meaning — just listen to a tribe of chimpanzees going about its business), a pathway to the evolution of language was created. Now language is believed by most to be the evolutionary breakthrough that moved man away most dramatically from his animal ancestors. If you think of grammar as its matrix, meaning — the relationship between sounds and feelings — is the boundary condition of language.

After sounds came words and then writing, but the crucial breakthrough, I think, occurred when our ancestors' brains started to differentiate between subject, verb and object. He or she could do something to him, her or it. Although this embryonic cerebral structure was only establishing a tentative boundary condition, reflection — as a deliberate process allowing for intent — was pushing feeling into a new context beyond that of the purely biological.

As soon as you start thinking in terms of subject, verb, object you are drawn to the notion of cause and effect. This is likely to suggest to you that everything before now was caused by something and that everything after now will be a consequence of what is done today. Almost all human histories that I am aware of have some prime mover, something that starts the ball rolling[1]. And of course when you get to that point it is only a small step to recognizing that if the prime mover got things to where they are now, that same prime mover has the future in its hand, so why not communicate with him, her or it so as to ensure a future to one's liking?[2] The basis for some overarching story is established.

Well you can see where this is going. In no time (in just a few thousand years) we moved from myths to religious priesthoods, to our contemporary scientific establishment, from *Mbombo*, the white giant of Africa's Bukuba people who vomited out the sun, moon and stars, to our own Big Bang.

But we need to back up a little, because something is missing. There exist small groups of people today (in the Amazon region, for example) who possess language but whose customs and style of life reflect what we would call a stone age existence. Their tension matrix consists of the biological environment which surrounds them overlaid by their interpersonal relations. Their story is about their experience of each other and that environment. Their emergent cerebral structure is characterized by a conscious awareness of and affection for their harmonious existence. Their dynamic is to maintain a status quo that fully satisfies them. Clearly for such communities there is no pressure to evolve. So the experience of those communities that did evolve must have been different.

---

1. Possibly unique amongst people, the Piraha of the Amazon rainforest have no creation myth or concept of time, history or mathematics. They seem to live in a perpetual present based entirely on their immediate experience and, by all accounts, are very happy as a result.

2. Buddha held that conjecture about the origin of life was a waste of time and that individuals were much better occupied trying to improve their self-awareness.

If we go back to the time when people began to settle along the Nile, it is not hard to imagine that this fertile region would have attracted newcomers. Those already there would have been keen to protect what they had and slowly a military cast would have evolved and some leader would have been chosen to manage things. Farmers would have worked a little harder and a little more productively so as to support their protectors. And then there would have been imponderables to deal with, such as would the Nile flood, replenishing the land they relied on? A scientific establishment (called by us a priesthood) would have been appointed to look into this. Over time a gathering of tribal farmers, who happened to alight on some of the world's most productive land, would have elaborated into the complex society we know as Ancient Egypt.

It is important to recognize what has happened here. There is very little differentiation amongst the individuals in an Amazonian tribe. There is the male-female distinction, naturally. There are the progressions of age. There might be some tribal headship function associated with collective decision-making and adjudication, but by and large the experience of each sex will be the same for all members of that sex. Every individual will be able to experience the full richness of life as it is known to the tribe. Now consider the position of an individual in a complex society, like that of Ancient Egypt.

The most obvious difference is one of scale. The individual is associated with an identity that is beyond his immediate experience. Another difference is that it is not just the male-female roles that cannot be exchanged, there are a whole host of others from Pharaoh to priest, from soldier to goldsmith, from master-builder to miner. The individual can no longer experience every aspect of life as it is known. He has become part of an entity that has a purpose greater than he and what is more, those in charge of that entity can direct aspects of his very existence. To overcome this dislocation, an elaborate story evolves to justify the structure and the individual is exposed to a regular diet of public ritual to reinforce it.

Something else has also happened. The dynamic is one of increased productivity. In the Amazon tribe the pressure is to gather enough food and no more, and even the steady climate mitigates the need to store food for a time when it might not be available. Not so in Ancient Egypt. The Pharaoh's granaries are regularly filled, his armies are equipped and provisioned and his building works are limited only by his imagination and the skill of his people. What is more, this surplus and the organizing ability that has made it possible enables the Pharaoh to project his power and to engage other structures in battle.

Remarkably, this basic model has existed for over 5,000 years. During this time political entities have assumed the mantle of biological species, engaging in a competition with one another that has spurred ever increasing productivity. This has enabled the human population to grow from a few million to almost 7 billion. It has to be said, however, that this was not an intended outcome (worries about overpopulation surfaced throughout the period), but the direct consequence of our biological drivers taking advantage of organizational and other innovations that our minds were able to devise. In effect, our unfolding cerebral structure has served to destabilize the biological system state.

One of the innovations that has made this model so effective is that of hierarchy: a large number of individuals, with different abilities, can be tied together within a functional boundary condition and be directed by a single intelligence. In the First and Second World Wars, millions of men, encompassing a wide range of skills, were embedded within structures whose sole purpose was the annihilation of similar structures on the opposing side. Unbelievably no one thought it particularly odd that single individuals directed these military engines. The analogy that comes to mind is that of Tyrannosaurus Rex, a mighty killing machine with an unremarkable brain.

Luckily, within these massive hierarchies (which, if they did not become nations became empires) a range of lesser hierarchies also evolved. These were often headed by individuals with particular abilities and had the effect of levering up those abilities to the benefit of the structure as a whole. Only comparatively recently, however, has the range of these skill-based hierarchies truly multiplied and this has largely been due to the fact that an increasing number of individuals have been incorporated into the decision-making process. The innovation that enabled this was free-market capitalism.

Although consumerism has empowered a great many people, it only addresses one aspect of our lives. The problem we encountered, as cerebral structure started to form, was how to make individuals complete again (that is to say undiminished, equal parts of the entities they constituted) while at the same time keeping the wide and growing range of differentiated functions that have made these entities so productive. On the face of things it looked as though we had moved backwards from the tribe that is in harmony with itself and its environment.

The morality of such a tribe is underpinned by the fact that there are limited disparities in power between individuals, communication is immediate and transparent (it is hard to engineer a conspiracy undetected in a small group), there is no competitive pressure to over-consume and in extremis any individual is free to walk away. In addition, the experience of each person is largely the same, giving rise to a boundary condition infused with shared empathy.

The great monotheistic religions sought to counter the complex and often inhuman cerebral structures that were evolving by wrapping them within an overarching moral story. Their mission was to make the individual, who had been sliced and diced like a collateralized debt obligation, whole again, at least in the eyes of God. You might have been a prince or a pauper, it was said, but your true worth would be recognized (just as it would have been in a harmonious tribe).

While the best exponents of the various faiths surely curbed some of the biologically driven excesses that were rampant, religion itself got caught up in the cerebral structure of the day, becoming a boundary condition intent on defending itself before anything else, and therefore as biologically driven as the rest. That said, and notwithstanding Marx's jibe about it being the opiate of the masses, religion and religious practice undoubtedly gave large numbers of people the great comfort of knowing that they were not living their lives alone.

However, it took innovations such as constitutional law, democracy, taxation and its corollary, government expenditure that leveled the economic playing field, to put substance behind the idea that all those within a cerebral structure actually mattered. Without the great improvements in communication that brought the plight of individuals to light this could hardly have occurred. Unfortunately, mass communication also served to stir up our biological drivers, pitting group against group, nation against nation, and this resulted in suffering and loss of life on an industrial scale.

The way the drivers within the biological system state work is that any advantage is pushed to its limit. Generally that limit will be determined by the biosphere itself and a new equilibrium will be established. The dinosaurs may have come to dominate the earth, flourishing for some 160 million years, but having secured their place they stopped evolving — there was simply no pressure on them to continue doing so. But when calamity struck, the biological system state went into overdrive. Evolution refilled the spaces calamity had created with new structures and T-Rex was not one of them.

The evolution of cerebral structure here on earth is in its infancy, and may yet be stillborn if we cannot evolve systems that allow us to guide our trajectory with intent, instead of relying on our biological drivers to fill the gaps. The dynamic that has driven cerebral evolution so far has been twofold: competition between cerebral structures, often built around the story of nationhood, and individual competition within cerebral structures to redress the disparities in power that we have engineered.

As individuals we rub along with one another on a one-to-one basis, thanks to a protocol of manners we learn growing up (some more thoroughly than others). But as soon as we become part of a functional boundary condition (we join the army, a company, the prison service, or are part of a distinct social class) we largely suspend our personal morality and act in accordance with the mores of the organization or group we are part of. A company, for example, will take on people in good times and shed them in bad, a survival strategy straight out of the biological system state. And it is right that a company should behave in this way, but also right that there exist other structures to take care of those individuals adversely affected.

We have been slow to react to systemic injustice, and were often grudging when we did, largely, I suspect, because we failed to understand it, disguising our ignorance with self-interested prejudice. A given social order functions like a species unable to think outside its own context. In an attempt to maintain their human dignity, even those disadvantaged by it often reinforce the boundary condition that circumstance has drawn around them by exhibiting some pride in their prescribed status.[3] Luckily we live in a universe that is not just dynamic but creative (the topic of the next and last chapter here in ***Part 1***) and so need not remain committed to structures that are so obviously repugnant. But only by coming up with a new moral framework that embraces all individuals and which we can apply to the structures we are building, will we be able to free our evolving cerebral structure from our biological drivers.

---

[3] As was the case with women, self-awareness can help a disadvantaged group to redefine the context that governs its member's lives. India's *Untouchables*, for example, are becoming a growing force in that country's politics. Although the caste system has been outlawed under India's constitution, prejudice is still widespread against Dalits (or outcasts) as they are called, a hereditary class of individuals who's work was traditionally limited to the most menial of jobs.

9

A Creative Enterprise

THE LEAST CONTENTIOUS argument in ***Notes*** is surely that the universe is a creative enterprise. From the Big Bang to the present, structure has been created in an impressive amount and variety of types. But this is deceptive. A plant can produce large volumes of cars and over time these cars might include different models. But one would never say that an automobile factory was creative. Creativity implies more than the mechanical expression of a script. A great conductor, with a great orchestra, seeks to draw something extra, even from a great piece, than the notes written down in the score.

To create anything you need to have at least two of something, or one thing that can simultaneously assume two conditions (the situation in the quantum state). The reason for this is simple enough. Creation is the product of an interaction in which the outcome cannot be wholly predicted. If you only have one thing and that thing is a primary thing which cannot be reduced further, you are stuck. However, we know that the universe was not stuck. It has generated new structure at a prodigious rate.

But you might say, hang on one moment, supposing a primary thing is subject to a temperature variation that causes it to become something else, couldn't that get evolution going? And of course it could (and probably did), but a temperature variation suggests that there is something outside this primary thing. Well perhaps, you might concede, but what if the primary thing generates its own energy, because we know that mass and energy are interchangeable from Einstein's equation, and in expanding brings about a temperature gradient within the space its expansion is creating.

OK, I would have to admit, you have got me, but only up to a point. The fact that this primary thing expands implies that its nature is to fluctuate, otherwise what causes it to expand in the first place? And if its nature is to fluctuate it must exist within a boundary condition infused with dynamic tension. This leads to that hypothetical singularity in which, for an instant, everything collapses into the primary thing. But this primary thing occupies an inherently unstable state that can only be resolved by expansion. Such a chicken and egg riddle is resolved by assuming a state prior to that which gives rise to the primary thing, thereby enabling it to interact with itself and restart the process of structural elaboration.

This is not mere semantics, because it tells us two important things about what we are part of. Firstly it implies jumps, or as I am calling them changes in system state, in which energy-matter combinations mutate through hierarchical sets of relationships, each with their own particular rules. Biologists are still unsure how organic matter mutated out of chemical matter, but the process is hardly a one-off. The universe had evolved through several distinct states before the advent of biology. Secondly, while the process may be deterministic in one sense (looking back we can work out the steps it has taken), there appear to be a substantial number of outcomes consistent with the rules we know to exist. The proliferation of biological structures alone is testament to that.

But, and this is a big 'but', there may be an underlying trajectory in the evolution of the universe (or multiverse, if that is what we are part of), towards — and almost certainly beyond — conscious life as we know it, that can only be attained through trial and error. In other words, while the evolutionary journey may be open-ended to a degree, there may still only be a succession of possible evolutionary states. Predicting when and how our universe will end cannot tell us what states remain to be assembled between now and then. But as part of this creative enterprise and possessing, as we now do, a sense of conscious intent, they are surely for us to discover and help build.

Down the ages, thinkers have been aware of the creative duality of the universe (the notion of dynamic opposites, of good and evil, of desire versus wisdom) and have espoused the idea of perfectibility through trial so as to attain an improved state of being (such as the Christian, Judaic and Islamic belief in heaven, the Buddhist belief in nirvana and even the Communist belief in a proletarian utopia). Unfortunately, there has been an assumption, particularly within the great monotheistic traditions, that suffering was necessary before the promised land could be attained. This gave rise to the Marxist criticism that religion gulled the masses into putting up with their subservient lives because they were promised heaven later (a trick the communist priesthood itself would one day play).

It was not until Protestantism refocused people's attention on improving the here and now, instead of preparing themselves for a hypothetical tomorrow, that the creative tension we are subject to could be expressed in the direction of reforming those structures that affected the quality of day-to-day life. The Ancient Greek tradition in this regard, developed further by the Romans, fell by the wayside during the Middle Ages, a time when the prevailing story regarded social hierarchy, servility to superiors, and the inferiority of women as morally defensible and Catholic dogma to be a complete expression of philosophical knowledge.

The problem for the Roman Church, a problem currently shared by much of the Muslim world, was that its boundary condition became all-embracing and so worked against creative change. Unlike Buddhism, which attempts to influence how an individual lives, Roman Catholicism sought and radical Islam now seeks to dominate how individuals live. With its call for personal responsibility, Protestantism returned Christianity to the individual level and created enough space for the evolution of secular structures that culminated, amongst other things, in the American polity.

The challenge we face today is how to create a moral order that remains dynamic and does not become a dead hand. This will only happen if we can embrace a story and a matrix that can not only accommodate a plurality of views, but can also draw out of their interaction an improved story and an improved matrix to go with it, without descending into the bloody conflicts that have characterized our past.

As a first step, we have to recognize that the boundary conditions, essential to our functioning collectively at all, are both permeable and temporary. Their temporary nature is about as hard for us to relate to as is the fact of our individual mortality: we all know we are going to die, in an intellectual sense, but act as if we will not. Boundary conditions are just as hard to let go of, and when they are undermined — as happened progressively over the 18th, 19th and 20th centuries in respect of the traditional order — our collective arrangements tend to fall apart. Whenever our cerebral structures fail in this way our biological drivers take over.

As was argued in the previous chapter, feelings must remain central to human evolution (and so to the evolution of cerebral structure), because it is these which tie us to the universe we are part of. Any attempt to intellectualize them will lead us into those dark places we visited in the early part of the 20th century. To counter the risk of this, the primacy of the individual must be asserted in every structure that we build. What this means in practice, to give just one general example, is that we should challenge the idea that a faceless bureaucracy is efficacious to the smooth running of society.

The German economist and sociologist Max Weber (1864–1920) was undoubtedly right to point out the benefits of rule-based administration over systems that were capricious and prone to back-door influence. But what such rule-based systems tend to do is freeze out individual feeling entirely, placing men, women and children into administrative boxcars whose destination can all too easily be the *gulag* or *gas chamber*. And while the solution is to make structures directly accountable to those they serve, the fact that prejudice can overwhelm principle makes the law, as the guardian of principle, of crucial importance. But the law is only as good as the people who use it.

After the American Civil War (1861–65), many in the South, whose way of life had been destroyed, were bitter. They might have lost their slaves, but no one could force a white man to love a nigger. That was their view. On Thursday December 1st 1955 a diminutive forty-two-year-old, called Rosa Parks (she might have been our fictional Shona's descendant), boarded the Cleveland Avenue bus in Montgomery, Alabama, after a long day's work. As was customary, she sat in the section assigned to "coloreds". But the bus filled up and the driver moved the sign behind Parks, so that the whites standing could take a seat at the front of the bus. For no reason, other than she was tired of being pushed around, Rosa Parks refused to budge and was duly arrested.

The incident sparked an outcry amongst the blacks, who boycotted the bus system. A series of legal challenges were mounted and in November 1956 the United States Supreme Court ruled that segregation on buses was unconstitutional and so against the law. Churches were burned, shots were fired into buses, and Rosa Parks and her husband were forced to move from the area. Stories do not change just because one side wins a battle, or even a war, but they begin to change. The permeability of boundary conditions, one way or another, is a given. In 71 BC, Spartacus may have lost, but he and those slaves who had followed him in rebellion reminded the Roman world that their mighty structure was built on tenuous footings. The mass crucifixions that followed the revolt contained the seed of a another story which would eclipse that of Rome.

The great upheavals of the 18th, 19th and 20th centuries were about people wanting a greater say over their lives, in the absence of any structure that would allow them to have it. The traditional structures were largely blind to this need, even though many individuals could see that change was necessary. The disadvantaged were forced to work in unthinking concert, often with pitiable results.

In what has become a classic of its kind, Thomas Kuhn, in his book *The Structure of Scientific Revolutions*,[1] describes what he calls paradigm shifts, when one scientific idea about how the world works gives way to

1. Thomas S Kuhn, *The Structure of Scientific Revolutions*, University of Chicago Press, 1962.

another. An example would be the evolution of physics from a Newtonian understanding of the universe, which was essentially mechanical and described with great accuracy the motion of the planets tied to one another by gravity, to Einstein's relativistic world in which mass and energy were interchangeable and space-time was curved, with light deflected by gravity. When men and women who had spent a lifetime mastering the Newtonian story were suddenly presented with Einstein's new one, in which the time interval between two events on a moving body appears greater to a stationary observer, their very identity was being challenged.

Arguments there certainly were, and heated ones at that, but there were no pitched battles and I do not believe anyone was murdered in the name of one or other of these stories. When poor Galileo Galilei challenged the earth-centered dogma of the Roman Catholic Church, he was not so lucky. Threatened with torture, the aging polymath recanted his heliocentric views and was condemned to house arrest. Our biological drivers tell us to create boundary conditions and then to defend them. And this makes sense. A great deal of energy goes into creating and maintaining a tension matrix (a structure that has both form and function) and the story that underpins it. Luckily for scientists, the whole scientific process — just like the process of creative destruction embedded within market capitalism — is predicated upon creative change.

So we are making progress in building systems that accommodate change without having to hit each other over the head in order to decide which person's or group's way is better. The democratic process, for all its faults, was a clear evolutionary advance in this regard. However, our continuing recourse to warfare and its bloody aftermath indicates that we still have some way to go. Quite simply, we have largely stumbled to where we are by a process of trial and error driven, I suspect, by one part intent to two parts biological instinct, and that may be flattering to intent.

Take the saturation bombing of Dresden in the Second World War, in which the allies killed women and children by the houseload. It must have felt like sweet vengeance to all those who had suffered so much at the hands of the Third Reich. But over time we have come to ponder this, as we have countless other atrocities committed in wars past, and now wonder if getting ourselves into such situations is really the best humanity can do. Europe, at last, appears to have seen the light and is embarking upon a new set of structural arrangements.

And it is not just from our mind, in the sense of it being some intellectual abstraction, that our desire for change comes, but it is felt, just as our need for vengeance is felt. And this is the crucial point. That which drives us to commit acts that are seen as evil draws from the same well as that which leads us into acts of the greatest compassion.

In *His Dark Materials*, Philip Pullman's wonderful trilogy, the writer has invented a world in which *The Authority* seeks to separate children from their *daemons* (their human souls) before they can become sinful beings. Although Pullman's target is the Church (*The Authority*), his criticism is really a criticism of all institutions, which can — at their worst — become citadels of form over substance in which the position of office bearers is considered more important than their purpose. What little we know about Jesus of Nazareth suggests he would often have been driven into a blind fury by the bodies that have perpetuated his name.

Corporate structures, in free markets, have to be permeable to customer requirements, to shareholder interests, and even to employee needs. Indeed, they are designed to be. Our political systems (in the democratic world, at least) are also subject to public sanction, but the underlying structures that the politicians sit astride, and nominally manage on our behalf, are entrenched, unwieldy, and are hardly ever permitted to fail on account of poor performance. In Sweden, great efforts have been made to ensure that bureaucracy is accountable to the individuals it serves. Other nations do not have to have the same high level of collective provision the Swedes have opted for, but their citizens have every right to insist on the same level of accountability.

The extent of structural ignorance in most societies is astounding. People accept the status quo because it is the status quo. And why not? Change is often hard work and can be unsettling. But even though the dynamic of the universe seems to reach for equilibrium, these moments are always temporary. And so we might as well design systems that allow for change, in response to individual needs, rather than run on with outdated structures that demoralize us and eventually collapse, throwing all associated with them into disarray.

We are part of a creative enterprise, as I have said. Where it is going, none of us can possibly know. But what we can know is whether it accords with our own moral compass. And this need not be a highfalutin, complicated sort of thing that only smart people talk about on the radio after midnight. It is what we, as human beings, feel. Rosa Parks felt it, and decided to act. Luckily for her, she did not have to be crucified to make her point. Progress? Certainly.

And this raises, perhaps, the most fundamental point: what do we mean by progress? If I am saying that cerebral structure will evolve progressively as a result of our intent, does that not presuppose that we have to know where we are headed? Not if intent entails expressing a human value as opposed to a concrete objective. The idea of heaven was not a bad one at all. It did give us something to dream about during many centuries in which there was as much darkness as light. But if we think of ourselves as living in a perpetual present, it is heaven here on earth that matters.

Reflecting on the progress we have made, three things are evident. The first is that we have increasingly created our own environment. The second is that change has always come from the aspirations of individuals acting in concert, sometimes cooperatively and sometimes competitively but always in opposition to the status quo. And thirdly it is clear that the stories and tension matrices we live within have directed our collective actions — for good as well as ill.

While the need to survive will always place great emphasis on maintaining our boundary conditions — without them, we are sunk — so our need for order will remain a high priority. Our survival and the evolution of cerebral structure depend on their being a plurality of boundary conditions (a diversity of approaches) because we simply cannot be sure what will work. Creativity is just that. It is about coming up with something that did not exist before, and so could not have been anticipated, like a new form of musical expression.

The creative act is not a painless act — far from it. It entails struggle and effort and false starts, with no guarantee we will attain the dimly-imagined goals we strive for. But if our mission is to enhance life at every turn, honest attempts that do not work out will be every bit as important as those that do. A tension matrix that motivates people in this way and a story that nurtures our best aspects, rather than our worst, is surely what we should aim for. Process is everything. The harshness of Leonardo da Vinci's (1452–1519) world has long been forgotten, but his Mona Lisa smile lives on.

Part 2

HERE, IN ***PART 2***, I step back from theory and in a somewhat rough and ready, selective and not always chronological fashion, outline a portion of our human history. My purpose is to place what we already know alongside the processes I have just outlined so as to illustrate my argument. The ground I cover is well known to historians and quite well known to the rest of us, so it will be clear enough, I think, if I have stretched my facts too far. Inevitably, I suppose, the Roman Empire features large, even though it could only have come into existence because there was already a thriving Mediterranean culture. At one level, empires are parasitic: their particular skill is applied to what is already there. So apart from a nod to Ancient Greece and another to the land of the Pharaohs, the story of much that has influenced us is untold here.

My Eurocentric account traces the collapse of Rome's secular authority and the slow birth of Western Europe in which a hierarchy of secular obligations (called feudalism) tied a predominantly tribal region together under the spiritual authority of a Roman Church, the remaining depository of Roman literacy and administration. As this order matured, it was challenged by a new set of ideas that came to be called Protestantism. Very slowly, nations emerged run by men and women whose emphasis was on individual ability and on new ways of doing things. This required a revised definition of merit which challenged traditional obligations.

The French Revolution stands as a ghastly foretaste of what irresponsible ideas loosed onto a hollow structure can do. By contrast, the American Revolution demonstrates what can be achieved by energetic minds free to build anew without the structural encumbrances of an earlier age. We also examine the struggle for power between France and those tribes along its northern border who would eventually merge to become Germany and challenge the peace of the world.

Naturally my history touches on the unlikely story of the English, a people who combined the democratic instincts of their Anglo-Saxon and Viking forebears with the feudal order of their eleventh century Norman conquerors. From a lackluster start, and protected by their island status, they slowly asserted themselves, coming to dominate Scotland in the north and Ireland to the west. By the end of the seventeenth century they had executed their king (144 years before the French did) and redefined politics.

Bursting with ideas and industry, and rechristened Britain, soon to be Great, their country led the industrial age in the eighteenth century and used its new power to build an empire that had spanned the globe by the end of the nineteenth. A hotchpotch imperium with over 400 million souls, it comfortably exceeded that of the Romans who had once regarded the occupants of their distant province, Britannia, as little more than primitives.

But it was not to last. The twentieth century saw slaughter on a prodigious scale and political collapse almost everywhere save in the English-speaking world. Once again, new ideas came to the fore, turning whole nations, inhabited by millions, into killing machines under the control of single individuals. The United States, weaned from the breastmilk of the British empire, came to dominate half of the world, while the Union of Soviet Socialist Republics, together with communist China, came to dominate the remainder. It was also a century of great technological and commercial progress.

As the twenty-first century gets into its stride, the USSR has collapsed, communist China has embraced capitalism and looks set to dominate Asia, the Europeans are struggling to build a union and

Americans to control an empire that is slipping from their grasp, while the rest of the world muddles along as best it can. What I hope this short history reveals is the extent to which humans have simply not been in control of their destinies. Trial and error, mixed with outright opportunism, have driven the process along, often at huge individual cost. Traditional societies have been emasculated by something called progress, and unintended consequences have been the rule and not the exception.

And yet. . . . this largely biological process, as I believe it to be, augmented by great ingenuity, has brought the human population up to a record 6.7 billion and counting. From a biological standpoint, success! But I think it would be true to say that we feel out of control. And that is what ***Notes*** is all about, because we are the stirrings of a cerebral structure that is straining to break free from the biological system state. By describing the processes I believe we are subject to, my aim is to make it easier for us to do just that. If we fail, the system will certainly self-correct. Biology is a numbers game after all. But its morality is not ours and the consequences for us would likely be grim.

10

Historical Perspective

OUR HISTORICAL JOURNEY starts 200,000 years ago in the African savanna when Homo sapiens developed out of Homo erectus, spreading into Eurasia around 40,000 years ago and into the Americas some 20,000 years after that. But I will open with a brief look at the end of the 15th century when Europeans began their migration to the Americas. The tension matrices of those who first made it to the Americas had not evolved as much as those who came later in sailing ships like gods from another world. If we are ever visited by extra-terrestrials, we can but hope they will be more responsible than we have been whenever we have found ourselves with an edge.

Biology demands that any advantage a species has it should use to exploit its environment until an equilibrium is found. The first settlers to the Americas appear to have found one in their sparsely populated land. By contrast, for Europeans, as successors to those communities that an ice age and a drying Sahara had forced to cluster around the Mediterranean, their environment had increasingly become each other. Any advantage one community discovered stimulated its competitors into evolving an advantage of their own. This dynamic so separated these two streams of people that when they came into contact again the cerebral structure of Europeans completely destabilized that of the then indigenous Americans.

* * * *

The European migration to the Americas, which I suppose started in 1492 when Columbus sailed the ocean blue, led, in a comparatively short period of time, to the subjugation of its people. Hernán Cortés and his Spanish conquistadors landed on what is now the Mexican Gulf coast in 1519. By 1521 they had largely gained control over the Aztec Empire, a loose confederation of principalities, using a mixture of political guile (they allied themselves to the Aztec ruler's most reluctant tributary), superior technology and smallpox, to which the Europeans had some immunity and the native population had none.[1] When Francisco Pizarro reached the north-west of South America in 1532, with just 180 men,1 cannon and 27 horses, it took him barely a year to crush the Inca Empire and claim it for himself, for his Spanish king and for Christendom.

In 1494, after the discovery of the Americas, the two great maritime powers of the day, Spain and Portugal, signed the Treaty of Tordesillas, dividing up the new territory (still almost completely unexplored) between them. Over the next 100 years, most of South America came under their control. In the north of the continent it was different. Although New Spain (now Mexico) was to become the Spanish Empire's most important overseas possession, her settlements in Florida and California were largely unsuccessful. After Jacques Cartier explored the St Lawrence River in 1535, French interest in the new continent grew rapidly. At its height, until displaced by the British, New France ran inland from Hudson Bay in the north, all the way to the mouth of the Mississippi in the south.

Slow to start, it was not until 1607 that the English established their first successful settlement at Jamestown, on a small river near Chesapeake Bay. Over the ensuing 176 years, until the then 13 colonies, which had unfolded down the east coast like stepping stones, secured their independence from King George after an eight year struggle, an increasing flow of adventurers and religious non-conformists, together with some 50,000 shipped convicts, displaced the native

1. By some estimates, as much as 80% of the indigenous population was affected.

population and set about building what would become the most powerful nation of the late 20th century. To the north, Canada was finally granted complete independence in 1982 although it has — so far — elected to remain loyal to the British crown.

The previous three paragraphs have sketched out some 500 years of history as it relates to one continent (the Americas) and how the people whose continent it once was were displaced by a superior cerebral structure, albeit one with several faces. But where did this cerebral structure come from? What made the cerebral structure of Cortés and his thugs 'superior'? And why did cerebral structure not evolve faster along the banks of the mighty Mississippi, one of the longest river in the world at 2,320 miles, and surely the waterway with the most fertile valley?

* * * *

If, as the evidence suggests, Homo sapiens did develop in the African savanna some 200,000 years ago, as a hunter-gatherer, spreading into Eurasia 160,000 years later, and only reaching the Americas 10,000 years ago, we probably have an answer to the last question. The most recent ice age only ended 11,000 years ago, and would have pushed south those people who had tried to move north. The groups that found their way into the Americas were likely to have been small (the land bridge to that continent was not generous) leaving many of the rest to seek refuge around the Mediterranean. As the ice sheet retreated, the monsoon that had kept the Sahara moist for a while also moved south, so that by about 3400 BC the area was once again dry as toast.

Circumstances having forced Homo sapiens to work out how to live in concentrated, permanent communities, it does not take a great leap of imagination to envisage a population cluster growing around the fertile mouth of the Nile. The remains of simple settlements dating as far back as 5500 BC have been found all along the productive Nile valley, but it was not until around 3000 BC that evidence of elaborate social structure can be found. For close to 3,000 years, until Egypt became a province of the Roman empire in

30 BC, her society functioned in a highly organized, stratified way, with administrative offices, a legal system, a system of writing and — of course — pharaohs. And all this was held together by powerful religious-scientific beliefs: Ancient Egypt's story.

In c1274 BC, Rameses II, the Egyptian Pharaoh, fought an epic battle with Mawatalli II, ruler of the Hittite Empire at Kadesh (where Syria now is) on Ancient Egypt's northern border. Although the encounter was inconclusive, his struggle with the Hittites impressed upon Rameses the need for Egypt to keep its military technology and tactics competitive with those of its neighbors. The resulting written peace agreement is believed to be the first international treaty of its kind. Why was a recorded agreement deemed superior to an unrecorded one?

Farther north, on the island of Crete, evidence has been found of a Bronze Age civilization living around 2600 BC. Depending more on trade than on agriculture and warfare, the Minoans (as they have been called) had time for art. Their city streets were drained and paved with stone slabs, and some buildings extended to three floors. It is thought that a major volcanic eruption on the island of Santorini (about 100 km away) sometime between 1630 and 1550 BC set the Minoans back. In any event, the Mycenean Greek culture familiar from Homer (c800 BC) started to dominate the area after 1600 BC until its progenitors appear to have been overrun by tribes from the north in 1100 BC.

By the 8th century BC, however, the Greeks had rediscovered writing (adopting the Phoenician alphabet) and by the 6th century the city states of Athens, Sparta and Corinth were flourishing. So successful were the Ancient Greeks in developing a collegiate form of government and in applying rational thought to the day-to-day problems of life that their population increased rapidly and colonies were established around the Black Sea, and as far afield as what is now the South of France, Eastern Spain, Southern Italy and Tunisia. This odyssey continued until the outposts of Ancient Greece were gradually absorbed within the Roman Empire (from around 146 BC).

And what of Rome itself? From an obscure trading post on the banks of the Tiber in the 8th century BC, it progressed through tribal monarchy to a Republic in 476 BC and then into an imperium (although many did not regard this as progress) when Julius Caesar was appointed perpetual dictator in 44 BC. It reached its height in AD 116, dominating the entire Mediterranean region from Syria in the east, to Britannia in the west, spanning some 2.5 million square miles. But by AD 293 the empire was proving impossible to hold together, and emperor Diocletian split it into two, East and West. The Western Empire eventually collapsed when the German chief Odoacer forced emperor Romulus Augustus to abdicate in 476. By then, Rome had already suffered the indignity of being sacked by East Germanic Vandals in 455.

The Eastern Empire managed to hold the line, reaching its peak in 1000. But with Islam a rising threat, it too went into a decline which even the crusades could not reverse, finally coming to an end when Mehmed II captured Constantinople in 1453.

Although their achievement speaks for itself, there were a number of things that worked in the Romans' favor. First was Italy's peculiar shape. Protected by the Alps to the north, it jutted out into the waterway it was to dominate. Once the hinterland beyond the city had been subdued, it made an ideal base from which to build an empire encircling the great sea. Secondly, the Romans were not stepping into a vacuum. Both the Phoenicians and the Ancient Greeks had built up flourishing trading networks around the Mediterranean. Thirdly, Homo sapiens had made great strides since at least 500 BC in the fields of government, agriculture, trade and technology. What the Romans did, with masterly efficiency, was bend all of these to their political ambitions. Every facet of an individual's life found expression within the Roman system.

There was security; there was food; there was law; there was education, although it tended to favor the children of the nobility and the successful; there was an opportunity to participate — to some degree — in government; there was an abundance of consumer goods; there were excellent public facilities such as roads, baths, temples, forums and water; there were public shows and spectacles for all to enjoy and share; there was genuine opportunity for advancement and there was, above all else, the idea of Rome itself, the pinnacle of civilization. Roman leaders were pragmatic and focused They ate, drank and often slept politics (literally), and were wholly unsentimental about the use of power. Finally, of course, making up perhaps as much as 30% of the population, about the same percentage as would make up America's southern states in 1800, there were slaves, that raw material which underpinned, and in many ways powered, the Roman commonwealth.

When Rome was at its peak, the mighty Mississippi was not yet *Ol' Man River*,[2] separating free states from slave states, because human beings had not spilled into the New World in sufficient numbers. But it was rolling along, none the less, unaware of the part it would play one day in a new story that would help to define a new empire, whose roots would stretch back not just to Ancient Rome and Ancient Greece, but into the Nile valley of Ancient Egypt and on into the heart of Africa itself.

* * * *

A people's cerebral structure is their tension matrix (the way they organize themselves), made up out of interlocking boundary conditions, and their story, which gives this matrix life and meaning. Two thousand years ago a fundamental shift began to take place, quite as profound as that which gave rise to the transformation of traditional society into what we call our modern world. In both instances *the story* began to change. Although Romans had many gods, their state was a secular blend of meritocracy and aristocracy. If there was one overriding object of worship it was Roman greatness, made manifest by magnificent public works and an economic system that showered the Roman people with goods and services and sensations of every kind. When abundance became as commonplace as the power that underpinned it, did some people begin to wonder if that was all there was? I suspect they did.

---

2. Written by Jerome Kern and Oscar Hammerstein in 1927 to conjure up the forces that carry our life along, it was made famous by the African American singer, Paul Robeson whose rich bass voice matched the river's power.

Ah gits weary,
An' sick of tryin'.
Ah'm tired of livin',
An skeered of dyin'.
But Ol' Man River,
He jes' keeps rolling along.

* * * *

That wonderful plea to his god by the young Augustine of Hippo (354–40) — *grant me chastity and continence, only not yet* — gets to the very heart of it. Of Berber descent, Aurelius Augustinus, to use his Latin name, was born in the provincial Roman city of Thagast (the modern Souk Ahras) in what is now Algeria. Although his mother was a Christian, he opted for the Manichaean religion when he went to study rhetoric in Carthage. According to his own account he was thoroughly seduced by the pleasures of the flesh and his concubine for thirteen years bore him a son. After a period of much anguish — he had agreed to leave his concubine for an arranged marriage but could not go through with it — he converted to Christianity and took a vow of celibacy.

St. Augustine, as we now know him, is revered by Catholics, Protestants and Orthodox Christians, a remarkable achievement in itself. What drove all his thinking and his extensive writing was the apparent conflict between what it was right to do and what one might want to do. The Manichaean religion he had started with originated in Persia based upon the teachings of the Babylonian prophet Mani (c210–275) and was one of the most widely followed in its day. Manichaeism holds that there is no omnipotent power, but rather two opposing powers and that a man's soul reflects what is good in him and his body reflects what is bad. As a Christian convert, Augustine asserted the omnipotence of good and for the rest of his life struggled valiantly to explain evil.

> What I am arguing in *Notes* is sympathetic to each of these views but different from both. As biological entities, we are naturally subject to our evolved biological drivers. To say that these result in immoral or moral acts is meaningless because biological morality is solely concerned with the evolution and existence of the biological system state.
>
> Due to the fact that humans have evolved to compete organizationally (acting as if a particular tension matrix and its story were a species), these same biological drivers have come into play within the context of human activity itself. That we have been able to compete in this way is due to consciousness (without which we could not have organized as we have), but consciousness has given us an awareness of outcomes that is absent in biology.

St. Augustine's battle with what he regarded as the urge to commit sexual sin was a battle between what his mind had decided he wanted to do and what his biological body wanted him to do. He knew from first-hand experience how easy it was to get drawn into a life of 'decadence' and rationalized it by drawing on Judaism's Old Testament story. He maintained that Adam, in disobeying God and eating from Eve's apple, had introduced sin (later called original sin) into the world. He and subsequent theologians, then got tied into knots over the issue of free will. If man could not resist being sinful, how could he be saved? Only through God's grace, he asserted, and anyway God had already selected the elect (those who would be saved), because in His infinite omnipotence He knew who would freely choose the righteous path.

> Augustine's problem (and ours) is that our conscious mind inhabits a different system state to our biological mind, and the little voice we hear that cautions us against a course of action we feel driven to is our ability to imagine a future outcome. And what makes it even trickier is that the potency of the future outcome we imagine is also derived from feeling. Cerebral structure is not some intellectual abstraction but an ability to recast the feelings we have within the context of an imagined world of our own invention. As individuals, we don't have a free hand. Cerebral structure is not some private fantasy but a composite world of our collective making in which we have to interpret the feelings of others as well as our own.

* * * *

That two of the world's great monotheistic religions, Christianity and Islam, should have appeared within a few hundred years of one another suggests that individuals were hungry for something more than Roman order in their lives and the wealth it had brought them. Christianity became the Empire's official religion in AD 380 and Muhammad had been preaching Islam in Mecca and Medina for many years before he died in 632. Remarkably (in that you would hardly think it now), both religions were offshoots of Judaism, one of the world's oldest monotheistic belief systems. When the Western Roman Empire collapsed, the only coherent structure left was the Roman Catholic

Church, which did eventually spread into all of northern Europe, easily exceeding the boundaries of the old Western Empire.

The fact that there was religion in the early part of the 1st millennium is not extraordinary. For all of recorded human history, we find that Homo sapiens has needed some way of dealing with the unknown. Where do we come from? Where do we go when we die? What is the point of existence? To what do we belong? Do we matter? How can we control those fateful things that affect our lives? One way or another, we have sought answers to these questions through what we call religion. But what was extraordinary was its particular flavor, which I believe resulted from a deep reaction to Roman rule.

Although only a footnote in Roman history, the slave revolts of 73–71 BC were an ominous portent and the name of Spartacus, who led them, lives on to this day. A growing number of people, I suspect, and not just slaves, were hungry for something that elevated them above the status of well fed and well entertained pawns on the Roman Empire's chessboard. And that something had to be a story that was bigger than the idea of Rome itself. The instruction that one should *Give to Caesar what is Caesar's, and to God what is God's*, was wonderfully seditious. It allowed people to identify with an existence that was not Roman. If you were to see a parallel in fundamentalism today you would be right.

Of these two great religious movements, Christianity was the most radical and Islam the most prescriptive. But what both Islam and Christianity offered was a parallel world in which the ordinary man and woman had a place, determined not by economic or social status but by behavior. Suddenly there was an alternative to the often brutal and materialistic disposition of the Roman political system. By the 4th century AD, Western Europe had had its fill of the Romans.

The unconquered Germanic tribes to the north were on the move. Perhaps buoyed up by a better climate, their numbers had increased and they were looking for new lands to colonize. Their sap was rising, just as the energy of the Romans had started to wane. Although hostile to Christianity at first, they came round to it, and when the Romans could no longer afford to maintain their western frontier and pulled back, Church organization with its monasteries and bishops was the only unifying structure that remained.

Between the 5th and 8th centuries, Roman institutions crumbled and Europe became decentralized and predominantly rural, with Germanic tribal leaders establishing their own hegemonies. To the south, Muslim Arabs spread out from Arabia into North Africa and Spain. It was not until the coronation of Charlemagne, as head of what would become known as the Holy Roman Empire, in 800, that a degree of secular order returned at least to the central part of Europe. However, with his death, the area returned to a fluid state, a situation compounded by Viking raids in the north, and Saracen raids to the south.

Throughout the 11th, 12th and 13th centuries, the region became increasingly urbanized, with Paris holding a population of some 200,000 by the end of the period. Europe's unique Gothic architecture started to develop. Kings in England, France and Spain began to consolidate their power. The Papacy asserted its authority over the entire region, however, even sending a crusade to the northern Baltic and Finic regions to bring their people into the family of Christendom. Crusades to the Holy Land were less successful, but the last great Moorish strongholds in Iberia fell to Christian Spain in the 13th century, although it was not until 1492, the year Columbus sailed to the Americas, that Granada was taken and Islamic rule was finally driven from the peninsula. With travel growing safer, trade increased and the treasure trove of Arab learning found in Cordoba, which included many of the Ancient Greek texts, gradually found its way into Europe's institutions.[3]

---

[3] At the height of the Cordoba Caliphate, in 929, the city had a population approaching 500,000. In addition to some 700 mosques and 60,000 palaces, Cordoba had 70 libraries, the largest of which held around 600,000 books. The largest Christian library at the time had only around 400 manuscripts and even by the 14th century the University of Paris library only held 2,000 books. Cordoba was originally founded by the Roman, Claudius Marcellus, and was host to both Seneca the Elder and Younger. Today it has a population of around 321,000.

The 14th and 15th centuries were a time of turbulence in Europe. A minor ice age brought the great famine of 1315–1317, and if that wasn't enough, the Black Death followed in waves on its heels, reducing an already weakened population by as much as a third over the following thirty years. This had two unexpected consequences, however. A shortage of labor drove up wages, and the power of the Church, which had appeared powerless in face of the plague, was weakened in people's minds. French and English dynasties fought each other for the best part of 100 years, resulting in a strengthening of the English and French nations. High Church politics descended into farce, with an Avignon Papacy based in France alongside the traditional Papacy in Rome. To bolster Church funds, the sale of indulgences was accelerated, and a sense that the Roman Church had become a corrupt organization caused people to look more to their local churches for spiritual guidance.

When Martin Luther, an Augustinian monk and professor at the university of Wittenberg, nailed his ninety-five points of debate to the door of the castle church in 1517, he was doing no more than raising questions many had been asking. Had the Roman Church become an institution too concerned with its own welfare and lost sight of Christian truth as expressed in the Bible? For the next 200 years the Protestant Reformation, as it became known, dominated politics across Europe as religious excitement mixed with national enthusiasm and personal agendas. Luther was protected by Frederick, Elector of Saxony, and Lutheranism was eventually adopted by all the German princes, eventually spreading north into Scandinavia.

Luther's co-rebels (and often fierce rivals) John Calvin in Geneva and Ulrich Zwingli in Zurich (a radical offshoot of whose followers are the Amish in America) were protected by their city councils. In England, Henry VIII had completed his break with Rome by 1536 for reasons that blended his desire for a male heir (the Pope had refused to annul his marriage of 24 years to the Spanish Catholic, Katherine of Aragon, which had produced only one surviving daughter) with his lust for Anne Boleyn (who, unlike her sister, refused to sleep with him unless they were married) and his urge to expropriate Church lands for the benefit of the Royal treasury. This decidedly non-ideological approach to the matter led to the Anglican Church, a sort of halfway house between the rituals of Catholicism and more somber ways of the Calvinists. But it was Calvinism that inspired the Puritans and their heirs who were responsible for England's brief flirtation with republicanism under Oliver Cromwell (between 1649 and 1658), and who populated England's early colonies in the Americas.

The Roman Catholic Church did not concede ground willingly. Mercenary armies were used to fight the renegades across the German principalities as well as in what is now Holland, and which, back then, had all been part of that hopeful construction, the Holy Roman Empire. Spanish power, augmented by gold from the Americas, was the main instrument of Catholic ideology, forcing even Catholic France to side with the rebels, so as not to be encircled by Spanish territory. Gustavus Adolphus, the great Swedish king, had to wade into the fray in 1630 with 4,000 soldiers, to push back Catholic incursions. So brutal were these wars, waged for 30 years between 1618 and 1648, that the German states may have lost as much as 30% of their people.

> When a people's story starts to bifurcate, the tension matrix they are part of has to be directed in one way or the other. As protostates, anxious to assert their independence, the German principalities possessed tension matrices that were more accessible to the reformers than was the matrix of dominant Spain or even France. The matrix model of the period was based on warfare, and so warfare was what the people of Europe engaged in to resolve their differences.

Remarkably, much of the cerebral ferment that erupted at this time can be traced to the great merchant republics of the 14th, 15th and 16th centuries, particularly Venice and Florence. Ruled by hard-headed business dynasties, more interested in new ideas than traditional ways, they attracted great artists such as Giotto, who moved away from the flat symbolism of religious art to the more naturalistic style of the Ancient Greeks and Romans, great architects like Brunelleschi and Alberti who made good use of perspective that was being rediscovered at the time, great political thinkers such as Niccolo Machiavelli, great polymaths like Leonardo da Vinci and Michelangelo, and, latterly, the great scientist Galileo Galilei.

The learning of the ancient world found eager minds, hungry to break with the conventional orthodoxy. As Socrates, Plato and Aristotle had been, some 1800 years before, men like the Dutchman Desiderius Erasmus (1469–1536) were anxious to apply reason rather than dogma to the problems of the world (earning for themselves the epithet *Humanists*), and printers such us Johannes Gutenberg (c1400–1468) in Germany and William Caxton (c1415–1492) in England found new ways to disseminate this knowledge to an audience well beyond the narrow confines of ecclesiasticy.

In Elizabethan England, William Shakespeare (1564–1616) would give the common man and woman a spry and entertaining insight into the human condition, as it affected both ruler and ruled alike. And some sixty years later, following England's bankrupt experiment with Puritan republicanism, one of its most ardent supporters, John Milton (1608–1674), would agonize over mankind's Christian failure in his epic poem, *Paradise Lost.*

> Why was the pursuit of knowledge — prevalent in Persia, Ancient Greece and Rome — abandoned in favor of Christian and Islamic orthodoxy? Could it have been because religious dogma confers certainty, whereas enquiry does the opposite? Had Europeans simply grown tired of Catholic certainty by the end of the Middle Ages and become more confident in their secular structures? Does this suggest that the creative endeavor can only flourish under certain conditions, such as when the benefits of ***progress*** are visible?

* * * *

To say that the Industrial Revolution, which began in England around 1750, grew out of this intellectual ferment would be no exaggeration. England had tried republicanism and concluded that a monarch accountable to a parliament made up of not just landed interests but also the new up-and-coming business and professional classes would be a better bet. Agriculture had become steadily more productive over the previous century, so with a settled polity, a financial system that had grown in sophistication, along with Britain's maritime trade, and an expanding population eager to find new work, the conditions were right for entrepreneurs, using coal, iron and steam, to build a world in which the machine would become slave to the needs of men.

The 18th century was full to bursting with ideas, and I suppose it was inevitable that some would grow in unexpected ways and reap a bitter harvest. Born in Geneva in 1712, Jean-Jacques Rousseau moved to France where he was to become one of the most influential political philosophers of his age. Central to his thinking was the belief that social structure had corrupted man in that its arrangements pitted one against the other while still leaving them interdependent, and so subject to the vices of pride and cruelty. His solution was a new social order, whose rules would be mandated by all, but enforced by a government subject only to the law and not to the will of the people.

His ideas were well sown, and their harvest was indeed great, but it proved to be as bitter as hell. The Revolution in 1789 that exploded the debauched and corrupt social order which had evolved in France, certainly from the time of the self-styled Sun King, Louis XIV, whose exercise in absolutism was a parody of everything government should have been about, owed much to his intellectual genius. But all it succeeded in doing was to disband a regal dictatorship and put in its place a collective terror, unconstrained by even those few humanizing customs which are inherent in tradition. Rousseau's belief that private property was one of those aspects of society that corrupted men influenced Marx, and his idea that there could be such a thing as the will of the people expressed by a government, accountable to no one but itself, justified the twin disasters of Communism and Fascism that blighted the twentieth century, and stole so many of its children.

The truth is that ideas had been drifting around Europe from at least the 15th century, like the restless Germanic tribes that had circled the Western Roman Empire over those last centuries of its decline. But this time the citadel to be overrun was the Catholic Church and its secular counterpart of kings and princes, which had re-established a degree of order into the chaotic vacuum left by the departing Romans. No one knew exactly what was at the heart of these ideas, save only that to a growing number it seemed reason should be placed before tradition and dogma. No longer, they thought, was it good enough to say that this was the way things had always been done. For many, however, this was justification enough, and the argument that what mattered was how things *should* be done smacked of hubris. For 500 years, imperfect reason has battled it out with blind tradition, and the struggle is not over.

> In biology, evolution moves in the direction of specialization, but this makes it increasingly hard for a species to alter course. Unknowingly, social structures seem to be subject to this dynamic.

* * * *

When England's last great Tudor monarch, Elizabeth I, died without an heir in 1603, James VI of Scotland became James I of England. Although brought up in the Protestant faith, he showed an inclination of tolerance towards Catholics, and the Protestant Reformation in both countries seemed far from secure. Many Scots had moved decisively into the reformed camp under the fiery leadership of the Calvinist clergyman, John Knox (c1510–1572), but not all. In England, even after the Puritan parliamentarians, led by Cromwell, had executed his son, Charles I, in 1649, their hold over the public imagination was not total. Following Cromwell's death, the English could think of no better solution than to reinstate his victim's son as Charles II, a return to monarchy paralleled in France 155 years later, by the brief return of the Bourbons[4] after the eventual failure of that country's Revolution and its Napoleonic adventure.

By 1688 the English parliamentarians had had enough of the Stuart dynasty, as James's was called, and Charles II's son, James II was deposed in a bloodless coup (save in Ireland and Scotland where the change was resisted by Jacobites, as supporters of the old dynasty became known) in favor of the Dutch and avowedly Protestant King William and his

4. "They have learned nothing and forgotten nothing" observed Talleyrand, that wonderfully cynical statesman who escaped the guillotine to serve first the Revolutionary Directorate, then Napoleon, and finally the reinstated monarchy.

Protestant wife, Mary (who was also James II's daughter), after they agreed to a Declaration of Rights, enshrining the powers of parliament.

Encouraged by Scottish businessmen who wanted access to English markets, and Scottish Protestants willing to sacrifice nationhood for their cause, Scotland and England were formally joined in 1707 by the Act of Union, creating Great Britain.[5] Parts of the Scottish nobility rebelled in 1715 and again in 1745, with the tacit support of France, of which James I's mother, Mary Queen of Scots, had been queen consort. Neither of these Jacobite uprisings was successful, although for a heady moment, in the rebellion of '45, Edinburgh was retaken.[6] Having unwisely advanced into England, and having received no help from the crumbling French crown, the Jacobites were finally routed at the battle of Culloden, near Inverness, in 1746.

> When stories that impact all areas of life collide, people seem to see no alternative to conflict in order to establish an outright winner. At the time, compromise appears to be an insult to their identity. They cannot conceive of themselves outside the boundary condition they have established. Naturally the power brokers on both sides play to this biological imperative.

* * * *

One of those to return to England from Holland, after what became known as the Glorious Revolution had placed William and Mary on the English throne and the Declaration of Rights onto the

---

5. A large number of Scots had also invested in a scheme to colonize the Isthmus of Panama hoping that they might gain a lock on trade between Europe and the Far East. This Darien scheme, as it became known, was opposed by the English and failed miserably, bankrupting many. In negotiating the Act of Union, generous bribes were offered by the English enabling some Scots to recover a portion of their losses.

6. Briefly imprisoned by the Jacobites was John Witherspoon, a Protestant clergyman, who went on to become the 6th President of Princeton University and a signatory of America's declaration of Independence. The Jacobites believed in the idea of nationhood and traditional allegiances; men like Witherspoon not only believed in the reformation of religious practice, but in the sovereignty of the individual citizen and in the complete reformation of government.

statute books, was John Locke (1632–1704). Locke believed that man was defined by consciousness and that each of us starts out in life with a blank slate, although with a natural curiosity and ability to generate ideas by both deduction and intuition. He saw no justification in the notion that monarchy had any divine right to rule, and that the relationship between the individual and his government was more akin to a social contract. Revolution, under some circumstances, might be unavoidable. Like the Frenchman, Charles Secondat, Baron Montesquieu (1689–1755), he argued that government would only protect individual liberty if a strict separation of power between the executive, legislature and judiciary were maintained. He saw property as being the natural consequence of labor, and consequently believed that government had no right to sequester it arbitrarily. His influence on the Founding Fathers of America — Hamilton, Madison and Jefferson in particular — was considerable.

Another to influence Madison was the great Scottish philosopher, David Hume (1711–1776). More cautious than Locke about the wisdom of changing customary government, he was none the less concerned about how best to balance the need for individual liberty with the need for strong government, arguing that neither should be sacrificed. Like the celebrated Scottish moral philosopher and political economist Adam Smith (1723–1790), he understood that trade and industry would generate wealth, and that a wealthy people would become a more civilized people. Smith's great genius was to articulate how individual self-interest could be channeled by a well regulated free market, into collective well-being. To both men, the Marxist idea that only government, idealistically driven, could construct an earthly utopia, would have been an abhorrence.

The stories that we build are inevitably the product of our experience as well as of our intellect. Men like Locke, Hume and Smith were of the professional, middle class (part of Marx's awful money-conscious bourgeoisie). And while they certainly wanted the matrix to be run by the likes of themselves, rather than by the hereditary class of old, they espoused a moral ideal (that men and women could live better lives) and a belief that the matrix should be redesigned to liberate individual potential. For them, process was infinitely more important than any utopian goal.

Something the French Revolution did do was throw into sharp relief the ideas that had shaped the American Constitution, adopted in 1787, only a year or so before Robespierre's bloodbath began. How could two movements that had drunk so freely from the same intellectual well result in such different outcomes?

If you regard, as I do, the Napoleonic wars and Franco-Prussian wars in the 19th century, and the First World War, the rise of Fascism and Communism and the Second World War in the 20th as being part of the unfinished business that Martin Luther's challege to Catholic orthodoxy symbolically began in 1517, part of the answer must be that Europe had an enormous amount of embedded structure to adapt to the new story which America did not. But I am getting ahead of myself. The amazing highs and terrible lows of the 20th century, so artfully set up in the 19th, will be threaded into the carpet I am trying to weave in a moment. But before doing so I want to turn back to imperial expansion.

* * * *

The word 'imperial' has negative connotations today, particularly after America, as the new kid on the block, displayed a sniffy disapproval of Britain's empire at the end of the Second World War — and promptly proceeded to expand her own. The truth is, that as far back as we have human records, groups that have found themselves with an advantage have used it to dominate other groups. The Roman and Ancient Greek advantage we have touched on. But empires existed before them and after them. That of the Mongols, for instance, based upon their skilled use of the horse in warfare, encompassed all of China, including Korea, extending, at its height in 1279, to the borders of Poland and Hungary in the west. By 1683, the Ottoman Empire, successor to the Arab Caliphate and, like it, held together by Islam and princely alliances, encircled the eastern Mediterranean, from Budapest in the north all the way round to Algiers in the south-west, embracing most of the Middle East along the way.

Their maritime skills gave Spain and Portugal an early lead across the Atlantic, and, for a while, the Americas became their playground, to be raped and pillaged and reformed in their own image. And as we have shown, the English and French soon followed in the north. But the Americas were not the only landmass that excited European interest. By 1674, the Dutch had established their presence on the West coast of Africa, as well as due south at the Cape, the route they took first to India and then on to the Far East, to gather up tea and spices for the markets in northern Europe. The Portuguese were doing the same, and by 1800 the British were fully engaged in this lucrative trade, which included shipping slaves from West Africa to plantations in the West Indies and South America.

By then, Britain's industrial might was starting to grow and manufactured goods could be shipped out and sugar, tobacco, spices and tea shipped home. Over the following century there was no part of the globe that escaped European interest, and by 1900 the continent of Africa belonged not to itself but to Britain, France, Spain, Portugal, Italy and the new country of Germany (more on this later). Britain's industrial and maritime strength had secured her the lion's share, including Southern Africa, most of East Africa, all of India, Burma, Malaya, Australia, New Zealand and Canada. America, meanwhile, had pushed her frontier all the way to the Pacific, having purchased the French-controlled territory of Louisiana from a cash-strapped Napoleon in 1803 for $23.2 million, followed by the purchase of Alaska from an equally cash-strapped Tsar Alexander II for $7.2 million in 1867. Russia, itself, now stretched from the Baltic in the west to the Pacific in the east.

In the Far East, the 19th century was catastrophic for China, one of the world's oldest civilizations. The ruling Qing dynasty had been in power since 1644, and the country had remained largely isolated from developments in Europe. And why not? What could a nation that had invented paper, the compass, gunpowder and printing, and which had achieved most of the characteristics of a nation state by the 14th century, learn from a people with a lesser pedigree? But, as European merchants pressed into their world, the Qings and their people realized, too late, that there was much they needed to learn.

British traders, anxious to exploit China's large population, were told she had no need for manufactured products, and if they wanted to purchase the silk, tea and ceramics, which were in great demand back in Europe's capitals, they would have to pay in silver. Governments in London and Paris balked at this, and the British, imaginatively, introduced opium instead. Twice (in 1838 & 1856), the Qing rulers tried to put a stop to this trade and twice they were humiliated by the greatly superior British navy and army. Discontent spread throughout the country and two rebellions erupted in 1856 and 1862 which resulted in many (almost certainly in the millions) being killed.

After suppressing these rebellions, the Qings set about modernizing their army and navy. But their neighbors and rivals, the Japanese, having studied Western techniques, had already done so, and inflicted a crushing defeat on China in the Sino-Japanese war (1894–95) as well as on the Russians (1904–1905), whose system of government was also on the point of collapse.

The idea of 'empire' shone brightly in the minds not just of Europe's leaders but in the minds of her people as well. It spelt opportunity. Americans were finding it on their own, under-populated continent. The inhabitants of the cluttered old world had to seek it by going farther afield, and their advanced trading and military technologies enabled them to do just that.

> In biology, a change that upsets the balance (such as a disease, or an alteration in climate) can open an opportunity for one species to steal a march on another. In the human sphere, an improved matrix (due to advances in technology and methods of organization) can confer the same destabilizing advantage on one group of people at the expense of another.

* * * *

What was it about the 19th century that brought unparalleled wealth to the world, and yet saw traditional structures, across the globe, unable to cope and frequently destroyed? Let us look for clues in the reign of Louis XIV (1638–1715), often thought of as France's greatest king but to my mind the true author of the French Revolution.

It is hard not to associate Louis XIV with the opulent splendors of Versailles, and in many ways that extravagant palace is a fitting monument. His reign was really the last magnificent gasp of the Ancien Régime. He was not the monarch who put his country on the road to modernity. Certainly the nobles and clergy needed to be forced into a more structured relationship with the country's government. They could be an unruly lot, inclined to pursue their own agendas. But to remove their power and yet encourage their sumptuous ways was the worst possible response. In an age when the nature of government was being thought about with some clarity and originality, it was a decidedly retrograde step to draw all power into his own hands, and the height of folly to make a virtue of it.

Louis ascended the throne aged four and his first minister, Cardinal Mazarin, governed the country until his death in 1661. Mazarin owed his position to Cardinal Richelieu, who had served young Louis' grandmother, Marie de Médicis, a descendant of the Florentine business dynasty, and father, Louis XIII. Richelieu had had two overriding objectives: to strengthen the French state, and to resist the power of Ferdinand II of Spain, who was also the Hapsburg emperor of the fractious Holy Roman Empire, that patchwork of principalities that sat at the heart of Europe, along France's northern border. Indeed, it was he who persuaded Gustavus Adolphus to enter the fray against Ferdinand in support of the Protestants. To finance this struggle, he raised taxes, but largely exempted the nobility and clergy, which caused riots that he brutally suppressed.

Mazarin continued Richelieu's anti-Hapsburg policy and was twice driven out of France by parliamentarians and nobles for continuing with Richelieu's push towards centralized, authoritarian government. Both men favored executive efficiency over collegiate responsibility, a myopia which would ultimately lead to the downfall of the French state. Louis XIV, it has to be said, loved every aspect of his increasing omnipotence. Just look at the portrait of him painted in 1701 by Rigaud, every inch the bird of paradise, displaying a shapely pair of legs inside tights, but otherwise cloaked in ermine, gold, velvet, satin, silk and lace with an expression of arrogance, beneath his fine wig, that only a Frenchman could have mastered.

As can often be the outcome in the short term, the French monarchy's move towards centralization and executive efficiency did augment state power. At home, the strength of the clergy and nobles was much reduced, but this hollowing out of the body politic concentrated not only power, but also responsibility in the hands of very few, moving France away from any semblance of parliamentary government. The country's anti-Hapsburg policy was also largely effective in the near term. France's borders were more secure at the end of Louis' reign than they had been at the start, but the path to this had been backward-looking and disguised problems that would come to haunt France over the next 250 years.

Louis XIV's exceptionally able finance minister between 1665 and 1683 was Jean-Baptiste Colbert, Marquis de Seignelay, (1619–1683). Colbert improved France's internal market, cracked down on corruption and sought to strengthen the country's corporations and guilds. He succeeded in improving France's trade balance at the expense of its trading partners (mercantilism) and would have brought the country's accounts into balance had it not been for his king's ruinously expensive wars. His achievements, however, served to accelerate France's evolution towards a centralized corporate state, a type of structure that still characterizes the nation today.

* * * *

One of these problems was the French state's inability to manage, and so to benefit from, social diversity. In the 16th century, France was home to a large population of French Protestants (followers of John Calvin), perhaps as many as two million at their peak, out of a population of eighteen million. Tension between them and the Catholic majority reached breaking point with the St. Bartholomew's Day massacre in 1572, when a large group had assembled in Paris to celebrate the marriage of the king's sister to the Protestant Henry of Navarre (the future Henry IV). On someone's orders (it is not clear whose) the city gates were locked and the slaughter began, spreading across France. When it was over, some 2,000 had been killed in Paris and up to 10,000 in the rest of the country. Pope Gregory XIII ordered a Te Deum to be sung in celebration. Over the following years, many hundreds of thousands of Huguenots, as they came to be called, fled France, taking their talent and work ethic with them.

When Louis XIV's grandfather, Henry IV, was assassinated, the old king's policy of religious tolerance was abandoned, and the *Sun King* saw no reason to reverse Cardinal Mazarin's policy of quiet hostility towards the remaining Huguenots. While Louis was prepared to sup with the Protestant devil in order to thwart Spain's ambitions to the north of France, at home he could imagine no benefit in religious diversity. Instead, he looked to the past, seeing heredity and the Catholic Church as the source of all legitimacy.

Having married the daughter of Philip IV of Spain, the French King's foreign affairs took an unexpected turn when the childless Charles II of Spain named Louis' grandson heir to the Spanish throne on his death. The prospect of France gaining control of Spain's entire empire, was too much for the other European powers, and the Holy Roman Emperor, Leopold I of Hapsburg, decided to push his own claim to the Spanish inheritance, with the support of England.

Although the war that raged between 1701 and 1714 took some 400,000 lives, the pivotal battle was Blenheim in 1704. The forces of England, the Dutch Republic, Denmark and Austria, under the brilliant leadership of the Duke of Marlborough and Prince Eugene of Savoy, crushed the French and Bavarian forces, demonstrating to Louis and his admirers that there were limits to the *Sun King's* power. At the war's eventual end, France had to accept that King Philip V of Spain (Louis' grandson) would be excluded from the French succession.

France also had to relinquish several territories outside her borders, including the Spanish Netherlands, and give England a 30 year monopoly on the lucrative Spanish-American slave trade. So much for the moral high ground! Shortly before his death, Louis actively supported the Jacobites in Britain (those who opposed the bloodless coup that had put the Protestant William III on the English throne), sending troops to Ireland in support of the 1715 uprising, but in this, too, he was unsuccessful. The emerging story was that sovereignty lay with individuals rather than with bishops and kings and Louis fought against it to the last.

> Although reformers like Rousseau and Locke could see that sovereignty ultimately rested on that rather nebulous concept 'the people' and that the Church had become a self-serving bureaucracy, the story of nationhood seemed entirely appropriate to them. They were thus blind to the conflicted nature of European politics which the idea of nationhood greatly exaggerated and the Roman Church had, in fact, sought to curb.

* * * *

It is certainly harsh to lay the Franco-Prussian war of 1870–71 at Louis's feet — it took place 155 years after his death — but what this campaign reaped, the *Sun King* surely helped sow. It demonstrates, I think, the extent to which a people's cerebral structure (their tension matrix and its story) directs their actions. First, however, let us try to get a handle on that strange thing, the Holy Roman Empire, which Voltaire (1694–1778) described as neither holy, nor Roman, nor an empire.

After the Romans had pulled their troops out of the Western Empire around AD 450, the tension matrix that remained was an array of Germanic tribes and the Roman Catholic Church, a scattered network of monasteries, bishops and their churches. Shorn of Roman support, the Church authorities set about winning over tribal leaders. What the Church had to offer was a more sophisticated religion than the Germanic tribes were accustomed to, and a system of administration, that included writing, which was far superior to their own. As rough and tough as the tribal leaders were, some could see the advantage in having such a body on their side.

By 768, jostling between the various tribal leaders had resulted in one of the Franks securing dominance. He started the royal lines of France, Germany and the Holy Roman Empire as Charles I, and is better known to us as Charlemagne. At the time of his death in 814, he had forced the Saxons in the east to accept Christianity, defeated the Lombards in Italy, held the line against the Saracens (Muslims) at the Pyrenees and had been crowned *Imperator Augustus* by Pope Leo III in 800.

Over the following centuries the empire split, with what is now France establishing a separate identity. The remainder evolved a complex process for selecting its leader. This was partly based on lineage, partly on support from its various princes, who made up a sort of electoral college, and partly on papal blessing. When in 1519 Charles V of Spain inherited the Hapsburg lands in Austria, he became a natural candidate for the position, and with the help of the wealthy banking dynasty, the Fuggers, managed to persuade enough electors to support him rather than his rival, Francis I of France. He was crowned Holy Roman Emperor by Pope Clement VII in Bologna in 1530, the last to receive a papal coronation.

The Reformation, started by Martin Luther in 1517, would eventually give many of the German dukes and princes the opportunity to improve religious practice (as they saw it) and to assert their independence from Rome and Charles V. It would also set the stage for the religious wars of 1618–1648 (the Thirty Years War) and the empire's eventual collapse when it was formally dissolved in 1806 during the Napoleonic wars.[7] The enigmatic nature of this odd political construction — this Holy Roman Empire — almost exemplifies the clash between the two stories (individual consciousness versus national or collective consciousness) that has stalked the minds of Europeans (and still does), often unsettling their arrangements.

> Germany today is a federal state and as such, is more reflective of its origins than the monolithic entity it became under the Third Reich. It is at least arguable that one reason the Reich was able to establish itself is because Germany, having only become a nation state in 1871, possessed only a limited experience of nationhood and its structures, making the *idea* of nationhood even more intoxicating.

7. At its height the Holy Roman Empire embraced most of present-day Germany, most of Austria, all of Liechtenstein, Switzerland, Belgium, the Netherlands, Luxembourg and the Czech Republic, most of Slovenia, parts of eastern France, as well as all of northern Italy.

* * * *

It is, perhaps, hard for us to understand the mental gridlock that gripped Europe as the 18th century drew to a close. The ideas which had dominated European politics for a thousand years — the ideas of monarchy, of its divine right to rule, of lineage and heredity, all wrapped up in the very substance that underpinned the Roman Catholic Church (as well as the Orthodox Church, for that matter, heir to Christianity in the Eastern Roman Empire) — were losing their grip on people's imagination at an accelerating speed.

Protestantism, first and foremost, was about taking individual responsibility for one's life. It was about not accepting that kings had any divine right to rule or priests any divine right to stand between oneself and one's God, taking a 'cut' in the process. English Puritans had already committed regicide in 1649 when they executed their king, Charles I, and Protestant states had sprung up across northern Europe at the same time as ideas about the nature of society and government were coming under sustained review. Not in an orderly fashion, of course, because officially there was no alternative, but rather in fits and starts, with the Roman Catholic Church fighting a rearguard action at every turn, against what it regarded as terrible backsliding. The Church was aided and abetted by those dynastic families whose legitimacy was so irretrievably entwined with its own.

As Louis XIV approached death, he lost three male descendants in the space of three years, and was succeeded by Louis XV, his five-year-old great-grandson. Although the regent, Philippe Duc d'Orléans, endeavored to involve the nobility in government, he found them so lacking in practice that he reverted to the ways of his uncle, Louis XIV. Abroad he concluded an alliance with the Netherlands and Britain to prevent Philip V of Spain from claiming the French crown, should young Louis, who was none too healthy, die. When the young king attained his majority in 1723, aged thirteen, he relied on ministers to rule on his behalf. By all accounts, the king was more intelligent than his great-grandfather had been, and was well aware of the problems besetting France and the monarchy, but by nature he was reserved and shy and unwilling to push through serious reforms.

In the war of the Austrian Succession (1740–48),[8] in which France allied with Prussia against its traditional Hapsburg adversary (which was supported by the Dutch and British), France did well. However, in the eventual peace treaty, Louis handed back most of what Austria lost, preferring France's stable borders as they were. This statesmanlike gesture won him only contempt from the popular press in Paris, whose readers were beginning to exhibit feelings of nationalism and a lust for popular power. When Prussia, under the mercurial Frederick II, later invaded Saxony (1756), it easily overwhelmed the Saxon and Austrian armies, making Louis' gesture seem even more foolish. It also brought home to France that Prussia was now its rival in the north, not Hapsburg Austria. While Prussia was absorbing Saxony, Britain declared war on France and when that was over, seven years later in 1763, France had lost most of her North American territory. At the time of Louis XV's death in 1774, the prestige of France and of the monarchy was at an all-time low.

In just sixty years France had descended from the glorious pedestal erected by Louis XIV to this slough of despond, and worse was to come. The underlying problem was not this or that king, but a rigid, centralized matrix, defined by a story of declining relevance, unable to adapt to the shifting boundary conditions, both inside and outside the country. Across Europe, urbanization and the growth of mass media were starting to empower the citizen and stimulate feelings of popular nationalism. People almost everywhere felt that the tensions inherent in those structures that regulated their lives were reaching breaking point. Change was in the air. Something had to give. But which aspect of government, and how, and what would take its place?

* * * *

Fatherless at 11, married at 15, and king at 20, one can feel only sorrow for Louis XVI who became king on his grandfather's death.

---

8. The war was started under the pretext that Maria Theresa of Austria was ineligible to succeed to the Hapsburg throne and involved nearly all the ruling houses of Europe. Prussia, an emerging power that was developing a professional army, rather then rely on mercenaries as was more customary, had designs on its neighbor — a clear foretaste of actions to come.

French society was a powder keg waiting for any excuse to explode. The up-and-coming bourgeoisie of Paris had contempt for the nobility, who had utter contempt for them. Almost everyone viewed the monarchy as feeble and many considered its religious foundations outdated. The working poor felt abandoned and the Roman Catholic Church feared the worst. And all, of course, had a point!

People expect the tension matrix they are part of to support their lives. If it does not they lose faith in it and in the story that justifies it. Since the reign of Louis XIV, France had been fighting expensive wars and was almost bankrupt. Her infrastructure had been neglected in favor of external engagements. By reducing the number of effective eyes through which the problems of the country could be understood, the steps Richelieu, Mazarin and Louis XIV took to centralize government ended up weakening it. The Little Ice Age had seen temperatures in Europe reach their low points in 1650 and 1770 (and would again in1850), causing crop failures and widespread starvation and the cruel effects of the 1770 downswing still lingered. In an attempt to replenish state finances, taxes were raised, but many on whom this fresh burden fell were ill-equipped to pay them.

Not only were the rising middle classes alive to new ideas that would involve them in government, but numerous members of the old hereditary order were becoming disenchanted with the system as it was. The story that had sustained the nation appeared threadbare. Evolution seemed beyond the tired sinews of the state and to an increasing number only revolution offered an exit from the tangled thicket of conflicted interests that was paralyzing the country.

In 1793 the thirty-eight year old king was executed in front of a cheering crowd, after the brilliant young lawyer, Maximilien Robespierre, elected first deputy for Paris to the National Convention formed by the revolutionaries after the September riots in which Paris mobs killed and mutilated priests, nobles and just about anyone they could lay their hands on, regardless of age or sex, said in an impassioned speech that *Louis must die, so that the country may live.* Nine months later, Louis' 37-year-old wife, after a show trial in which she was accused of many nefarious things, including molesting her son, enjoyed the same fate. On the 24th of July 1794, Robespierre himself, once a disciple of Jean-Jacques Rousseau, was guillotined without trial as the revolutionary bloodlust consumed even its own.

The Royal cause had not been helped by a proclamation issued by the Duke of Brunswick, who had advanced on Paris in 1792 at the head of a Prussian army, that if the king of France was hurt in any way, the people of Paris would suffer for it. This, in part, fueled the September Massacres. In the event, a citizens' army managed to repel the duke, but the revolution was on a knife's edge. With British help, the town of Toulon had risen up against the Republican government, and was only brought into line when a young artillery commander from Corsica recaptured the city. Again, in 1795, young Napoleon Bonaparte came to the aid of the revolution when royalists and counter-revolutionaries organized an armed protest against the National Convention. His quick success earned him the gratitude of Barras, head of the Directory formed to run the country, as well as that of Barras's former mistress, Josephine. The Little Corporal's glittering career had begun.

> Revolution is like a forest fire, seemingly destroying everything. The structure that takes its place, however, is often a version of what existed before because the existing tension matrix, stripped of any traditional comforts (seen by the usurpers as sops to preserve the old order), is all the revolutionaries have to work with. What is gone forever, though, is the old story, as are most of those who once occupied positions of power. Although the justification for the matrix changes, empowering new individuals, its nature may mutate into a crueler version of what it once was.
>
> This is because relationships become highly volatile (the old basis upon which allegiances were formed having gone while the new basis remains to be fully formed) leaving terror (perhaps our deepest biological driver) as one of the few coordinating mechanisms to carry weight.

* * * *

By 1811, Napoleon, now Emperor, controlled most of Spain, much of what had been the Holy Roman Empire and a large part of Poland. But not everything was going his way. In 1805, 27 ships of the British navy, under the command of Admiral Nelson, had defeated a Spanish-French fleet of 33, capturing or destroying 22 and losing none. So when the Emperor marched on Moscow in 1812, he embarked on a fateful course which another European leader would follow some 130 years later when he, too, was thwarted in the West. The Russian tactic was to retreat, destroying any food as they went. In Moscow, Napoleon found a deserted city and no Tsar to negotiate with. The onset of the brutal Russian winter forced him to retreat. Having started with around 650,000 troops, the remnants of his Grande Armée eventually struggled home with only 40,000 men. Russian casualties were probably some 400,000 and civilian casualties several hundred thousand more. War was on the threshold of the industrial age.

Napoleon never fully recovered from this crushing failure. With support waning in Paris, he abdicated and Louis XVI's corpulent brother was restored to power as Louis XVIII.[9] Bonaparte's escape from the island of Elba and his return to power for 100 days after successfully, and alone, confronting the army sent by the king to capture him, is well known, as is his eventual defeat at Waterloo. More than any man, he captured the spirit of the age. Reckless perhaps, profligate with human life certainly, brilliant without a doubt, he played out the part history had prepared for him and proved to the European mind that people did not need kings in order to achieve greatness. To more sober minds, however, the French experiment signaled that the machinery of government, across Europe, was rotten to the core.

* * * *

In spite of being defeated, France was restored to its original borders at the Congress of Vienna, and the Bourbon monarchy reinstated, largely because no one could think of an alternative. Two Bourbon

---

9. Louis XVI and Marie Antoinette's ten-year-old son died in prison in 1795 under revolutionary guard and so never reigned. But under the rules of hereditary succession, which the poor little chap had no hand in devising, he was deemed to have been Louis XVII.

kings ruled until 1830 when a far less bloody revolution than the first deposed Charles X and placed Louis-Philippe (from the house of Orléans, and much loved by the liberals) on the throne as a constitutional monarch. He struggled on until 1848 when yet another revolution deposed him. After the constitution of the Second Republic was finalized, Louis-Napoleon (a son of Napoleon Bonaparte's brother, with excellent brand recognition) won the presidency by some 3 million votes to his rival's 2.4. Determined to reform the country, but finding himself confronted by a parliament dominated by monarchists, he staged a coup and in 1853, to the disgust of many republicans (including Victor Hugo), the second French Empire was established with him as Emperor Napoleon III.

> The return of monarchy as a system, followed by the election of a leader (who happened to be a Napoleon), followed by dictatorship illustrates how hard it is for a new system to be introduced. The tension matrix which regulates those within a national boundary is far more complex, with its many interrelationships, than people realize and changing it is far harder than they expect. This is one reason why evolution, rather than revolution, invariably turns out to be more effective.

As a young man, Louis-Napoleon had been involved with the resistance, fighting Austria's domination of Northern Italy. This sympathy for Italian Nationalism caused him to stand back when Prussia crushed Austria in 1866. But by 1870, tensions between Prussia and France boiled over into war.

Prussia was supported by the North German Confederation and the South German states of Baden, Württemberg and Bavaria. The French, drained by their earlier adventures, were completely outclassed on the battlefield. Emperor Napoleon III was captured by Count Otto von Bismarck's Prussian forces in September 1870, and the Second Napoleonic Empire collapsed. The Prussians went on to take Paris, and in the peace treaty of 1871 the French were forced to cede much of Alsace-Lorraine, once part of the old Holy Roman Empire, and home to a substantial German-speaking population. In January of that year, the German states formally agreed to unite under the Prussian King, and the German nation came into being. Almost all the steps which would lead to the First World War, in just forty-three years, were now in place.

* * * *

We have come a long way from the *Sun King* and his divine monarchy. Could he have acted differently and if he had, would it have made any difference? In an ideal world, he would have stayed within his borders and concentrated on domestic reform. The nobility would have been subject to tax, but also granted power as part of a legislative assembly. The bourgeoisie also needed to be given a legislative chamber. The arrangement could have been similar to the English Houses of Lords and Commons, although to be fair to the French king, the English were having their difficulties with this arrangement. However, a rough template did, at least, exist. Finally, French Protestants could have been accorded equal rights. This would have reduced the power of the Catholic Church and led to a better-balanced society.

But while Louis might, possibly, have had the power to do these things, they were invisible to him. He suffered from the blindness of his age. The nobility were as often bored competitors as energetic partners. The common man was invisible. The increasingly assertive middle class were merely a distraction. Territory was still defined by the bloodlines of centuries that ran through it. And the Roman Catholic Church remained power broker of last resort, determined to secure what it saw as its rightful place, at any price.

> The way we see the world is probably nine tenths received wisdom and one tenth our own reasoned interpretation. In Europe the new ideas, which would lead to a new story and were first nurtured in the merchant city states of the Middle Ages, gained most traction in the north, away from the Catholic strongholds (particularly Spain). But it was in the New World that the new story fused most completely into a new and fully-functioning tension matrix.

When the Second Continental Congress adopted the words Thomas Jefferson wrote for the thirteen colonies' Declaration of

Independence in 1776, that *We hold these truths to be self-evident, that all men are created equal, that they are endowed by their Creator with certain unalienable Rights, that among these are Life, Liberty and the pursuit of Happiness*, only 61 years after the Sun King's death, he was looking at the same world but in an entirely new light. Even the self-righteous revolutionaries, who drenched the French capital in blood seventeen years later, were fatally tainted by the past.

* * * *

I picked on Louis XIV, not because he was a greater villain than any other, but because he was emblematic of a story that was losing its appeal. Indeed, as a sovereign who ruled by divine right his reign was a glittering example of its kind. For many, feudalism was not the near-slavery we think of it as being today, but a system of loyalty with its roots embedded in the tribal system. A king represented one's identity in a personal, human way, that the idea of a country did not, and this was just as true of the aristocrats who ruled their domains and owed loyalty to their king. The Roman Catholic Church functioned as a sort of moral bureaucracy and power broker of last resort, mixing high politics with an often genuine concern for the poor.

The Protestant Reformation was really a revolt by the middle class against a system that had evolved before such a class became significant. Indeed the Church used to afford the best opportunity for young men of ability from humble backgrounds. But commerce and urbanization were changing this. It was as if the tension matrix was evolving in ways that the story could no longer explain. Imperial expansion served as a safety valve, but it also served as a distraction from much needed reforms at home. And this was America's great good fortune. She could build anew.

Europe's dynasties may often have been splendid and their courts the height of civilization, but their raison d'être was rooted in territory, bloodlines and conquest. They were simply not designed to think about internal matters (other than to the extent of ensuring their supremacy), a weakness shared — I believe — by the United States

Presidency today. As their partner, the Roman Catholic Church could not have detached itself from this story even if it had wanted to. It depended on the tribal families as much as the tribal families came to depend upon it.

Europe's tragedy, I think, lay in the fact that the idea of nationalism displaced the idea of a divinely-ordained monarchy while absorbing the idea of tribal rivalry, reinterpreting both in a form of feudalism as potent as any that had gone before. You were no longer expected to die for your liege or king, but for your nation. Fascism and Communism would become extreme expressions of the state's new religion. They would become stories, like the story of democracy, that justified the modern world's new tension matrices.

To repeat, cerebral structure is the method of interaction between individuals through man-made structure, hard and soft, both formal and informal, embedded within a boundary condition that can best be thought of as a story (defining its parameters and context), which gives rise to collective action. And remember, this description can apply to an entity, as well as to any larger entity inside which it functions, such as a political party and the democracy it is supposed to energize. Naturally, the stories (and the boundary conditions) that define these nested (hierarchical) cerebral structures must be broadly compatible.

If you read Jefferson's words they are both inspiring and hard to fault. So how do you explain that the Americans treated the indigenous population of their continent no better than the Portuguese or Spanish did? How do you explain America's eviction of Spain from Cuba in the Spanish-American war of 1898 (described in a letter from the ambassador in London to Colonel Theodore Roosevelt, the future president, as a splendid little war) and America's subsequent treatment of Cuba? How do you explain that when America gained the Philippines from Spain (along with Puerto Rico and Guam), following that country's easy capitulation, she immediately (and rather brutally) suppressed the First Philippine Republic, established by Emilio Aguinaldo, after a long fight against the Spanish occupation? Does this make one think of Vietnam, or even Iraq?

These questions do not have easy answers, but part of the answer lies in a structure's biological imperative to maintain its own integrity. What lies outside it lies outside its understanding. In human terms this translates into what looks like hypocrisy and double standards, but is really a complete blindness.

These apparent contradictions between America's self- proclaimed story and her actions against those outside her borders suggest that she sees herself as a beacon of liberty at home but as a nation abroad. Like the Romans before her, her leaders believe she has discovered a better way and see no inconsistency in forcing that way on any who resist her power. Individual liberty may be America's creed, but the idea of nationhood still defines her tension matrix.

* * * *

Although intended to be given to America by the French on July 4th 1876, to mark the centenary of the Second Continental Congress's Declaration of Independence (and to poke a finger at the British, no doubt), the Statue of Liberty didn't actually arrive until ten years later due to funding problems and logistical difficulties. But no matter. It has remained an enduring symbol ever since. Inside the pedestal, engraved on a copper plate, are the words of the poet Emma Lazarus:

Give me your tired, your poor, your huddled masses yearning to be free

and throughout the 19th century, Europe, in particular did just that. From 8,385 in 1820, immigration increased to 1,713,000 between 1841 and 1850, of whom more than 781,000 were Irish fleeing from the wealthiest empire the world had then known because the potato crop so many were forced to rely on failed, and they had nothing to eat. War and turmoil in Europe caused 435,000 Germans, 267,000 British and 77,000 French to join the exodus in search of a better life. By 1881–85 around 1 million Germans had settled in the Midwest and over the following decades Swedes, Norwegians and Italians all poured into the promised land.

The power of a story that resonates within that vault wherein our deepest aspirations lie should never be underestimated.

* * * *

The 19th century was remarkable. At the start of it, a young Sam Clemens was learning his trade as a pilot on the mighty Mississippi. Steamboats plied that changeable lady by the score upstream and down, between St Louis and New Orleans, carrying the well dressed and poorly dressed, the adventurer, the opportunist, husbands and wives and their children, all alive with prospects yet to be met, together with supplies of every hue to feed the hopes of Lady Liberty's huddled masses as they spilled into their new land. By its end, the Civil War and the railroad had done for the trade and *mark twain*, a measure of depth on the river, had become a household name.

The century was a grand one for writers. There were Leo Tolstoy, Anton Chekov, Charles Dickens, Jane Austen, Walter Scott, Edgar Allan Poe, Victor Hugo, Emile Zola, Hans Christian Anderson; one could easily go on to fill the page. Science, too, was changing not only people's perceptions of life but how they lived. There was Darwin, of course, and Thomas Edison with his laboratory full of potential light bulbs. Born in the previous century, Samuel Morse, an ardent Calvinist who could see no moral objection to slavery, turned from painting to inventing and came up with his code and a telegraph to propel it down the wires. By 1845 telegraph lines radiated out from New York to Philadelphia, Boston, Buffalo and Mississippi. Twenty-three years later, Edison's Universal Stock Ticker was in action and would deliver the news to troubled investors in 1929 that their fortunes were as easily lost as won.

It was a century in which giant corporations of the future were formed. Alexander Graham Bell left Edinburgh in 1870 for Canada, but the following year started working part time at the Boston University School of Oratory. Caught up in the scientific excitement of the time, he concentrated increasingly on his talking machine and was awarded a patent in 1876. Bell and his partners offered to sell the patent to Western Union for $100,000, but its directors balked at the price. The following year the Bell Telephone Company was formed, and by 1886 over 150,000 people in the United States owned telephones.

In 1802, Eleuthère Irénée du Pont, a French chemist, with capital and gunpowder machinery imported from home, started his company on the Brandywine Creek near Wilmington, Delaware. By the time the American Civil War was finally over in 1865, and some 620,000 soldiers had been killed, DuPont (the family's now anglicized name) had supplied the Union Army with half its powder. His heirs would go on to build the company and become investors in General Motors. Supplying people's lust for war was always good business. In Sweden, Alfred Nobel, a brilliant chemist and engineer, patented dynamite in 1867 and the more powerful gelignite in 1876. His company, Bofors, became a major arms manufacturer and a premature obituary, describing him as *The Merchant of Death*, is believed to have influenced his decision to establish the Nobel Prize. In Germany, the Krupp family built its first steel foundry in 1811 and was soon making cannons for the Russian, Turkish and Prussian armies.

Wherever you looked, men with talent, drive and expertise were changing the ways of the world. After graduating from the Franklin County Mining School in Missouri, George Hearst spent a few years on odd jobs, interspersed with a good deal of poker, bourbon and tobacco. But when he heard gold had been discovered in California he took his chance and in 1850 headed west. After a miserable first winter he switched to the new technique of quartz mining (extracting gold from layers of quartz) developed by a Prussian engineer, Jacob Brache. Within fifteen years his company had interests in many of the most productive mines. In settlement of a gambling debt, he acquired *The San Francisco Examiner*, which his only son, William Randolph, would build up into a publishing empire of popular journalism with 28 newspapers across the country, inspiring Orson Welles's classic film, *Citizen Kane (1941)*.

* * * *

Yes, wherever you looked, the structure of society was being changed. The silk industry in Lyon was in crisis by mid-century, on account of a silkworm pandemic (in fact, several). French traders started to import raw silk from Japan, whose worms were resistant to the European disease, and to set up offices in Yokohama. Stimulated by this contact (and not repelled by it, as the Qing rulers in China were), the Japanese invited the French engineer, Léonce Verny, to help them modernize their arsenal and even participated in the 1867 World Fair in Paris. The French-built *K tetsu* became the first ironclad warship in the Imperial Japanese Navy; Henri Pelegrin helped construct Japan's first gas-lighting system for the streets of Yokohama; and the French legal system, which had been partially modernized under Louis XIV (a process completed by Napoleon I) was so much admired that the French legal expert, Gustave Boissonade was invited to Japan in 1873, where he spent the next 22 years helping the Japanese modernize their own.

Her enthusiasm for western technology enabled Japan to overwhelm China's Imperial forces (1894–95) and to defeat the Russian navy in 1905, further weakening two ailing political structures that would both turn, in only a matter of years, to a new kind of story within which to organize themselves — Communism. This success, however, would eventually rebound on Japan herself, and with a vengeance. Determined to keep the United States away from her expanding empire, she launched a daring attack on the US Pacific Fleet at Pearl Harbor in 1941. Three years and eight months later, the industrial powerhouse she had so unwisely stung would drop two atomic bombs, one on Hiroshima and the other on Nagasaki, killing around 200,000 people, forcing her to accept utter defeat.

But that was still in the future. In the 19th century, friendly contact between France and Japan was the pattern, and the influence was not all one way. Japanese art, with its lack of perspective, subtle arrangements and strong colors greatly influenced the Impressionist movement as a whole, and Degas and Monet in particular. And Pierre Loti's successful 1887 novel, Madame Chrysanthème, based on his encounter with a young Japanese woman, so captured imaginations in the West that it would become an inspiration for Puccini's opera, *Madame Butterfly (1904)*, and even the musical *Miss Saigon (1998).*

> One of the contradictions implicit in globalization is that it is differences that stimulate the exchange but barren homogenization that is its logical outcome.

* * * *

The Imperial dream was alive and well in the 19th century, blending man's natural lust for power with his often genuine wish to pursue an ideal — a powerful brew. On February 8th 1870, his fifty-first birthday, a gentle John Ruskin, who was an ardent believer in Christian socialism (that is socialism without big government), stepped up to the podium to give his inaugural lecture, as Slade Professor of Fine Art, to a packed audience at Oxford University. Entitled *Imperial Duty*, these are some of the sentiments he expressed:

> There is a destiny now possible to us — the highest set before a nation to be accepted or refused. We are still undegenerate in race; a race mingled of the best northern blood. We are not yet dissolute in temper, but still have the firmness to govern, and the grace to obey. We have been taught a religion of pure mercy, which we must either now betray, or learn to defend by fulfilling. And we are rich in an inheritance of honour, bequeathed to us through a thousand years of noble history, which it should be our daily thirst to increase with splendid avarice. . .
>
> And this is what she must either do, or perish: she must found colonies as fast and as far as she is able, formed of her most energetic and worthiest men; seizing every piece of fruitful waste ground she can set her foot on, and there teaching these colonists that their chief virtue is to be fidelity to their country, and that their first aim is to be to advance the power of England by land and sea. . .
>
> But that they may be able to do this, she must make her own majesty stainless; . . . The England who is to be mistress of half the earth, cannot remain herself a heap of cinders, trampled by contending and miserable crowds; she must yet again become the England she once was, and in all beautiful ways,. . . . polluted by no unholy clouds.

In the audience was a young man of sixteen, called Cecil John Rhodes, the fifth son of an English country minister, who prided himself on never having preached a sermon longer than ten minutes. By the time of his death in 1902 Cecil Rhodes had been Prime Minister of the Cape Colony in South Africa for six years (1890–96), founded Rhodesia (the now tragic country of Zimbabwe, where in 2008 annual inflation was running at over 2 million % and average life expectancy had fallen to 39 years), started De Beers, the diamond mining company, and amassed one of the largest fortunes of that time.

Under his will, money was set aside to fund scholarships so that qualified individuals from around the world could study for a year or two at Oxford. Among the many who have benefited are the country and western singer, Kris Kristofferson, America's 42nd President, William Jefferson Clinton, and his Secretary of Labor, Robert Reich. It is hard to say whether Ruskin approved, but Mark Twain, another contemporary, had few doubts: "I admire him, I frankly confess it; and when his time comes I shall buy a piece of the rope for a keepsake." A wonderful insult but Rhodes was merely a reflection of his age.

* * * *

The 19th century was a period in which new structure was being formed on a scale that was bigger and at a speed that was faster than ever before, and so it was inevitable that powerful individuals would become associated with it, as these things do not just materialize out of thin air. When Andrew Carnegie sold Carnegie Steel to J.P. Morgan in 1901, he was one of the richest men in the world with a fortune, in 2007 dollars, of around $298.3 billion. That this was a man born in Scotland, the son of a hand-loom weaver, a mighty poor trade at best, tells us a lot about the age. The 19th century was full to bursting with things that *could be done* and importantly — particularly in America — with few things in place that would act to stop them being done. What was needed were men and women with drive, intelligence and application to see the connections, forge the links and then create expanding structures able to produce more than they absorbed.

> We shouldn't lose sight of the fact that these individuals, as great as many were, could not have achieved what they did had the tension matrix they were part of not been amenable to their talents.

Inevitably, as these new corporate structures relied on countless ordinary individuals to make them work, there was often great tension between the need to keep enterprise costs down and each individual's desire to pay his and his family's way. Naturally, a lone voice raised in protest against the often impersonal managers of a corporation was a feeble-sounding thing, so men organized.

Between 1873 and 1896, the world was plunged into a severe depression. The reparations Germany forced France to pay after the Franco-Prussian war, together with the collapse of the Vienna Stock Exchange the war helped trigger, served to destabilize Europe. But there had been rampant over-building in railroads, as well, on both sides of the Atlantic. This led markets to collapse and credit with them. Added to that, the greenback, which had been issued to finance the Civil War, was shunned in favor of gold and silver, freezing international trade, as no one wanted to part with silver or to take on paper, of any kind.

In 1892 Carnegie Steel attempted to cut the wages of its skilled workers, but the National Amalgamated Association of Iron and Steel Workers of the United States refused to accept this ultimatum and took on the company. Union workers were locked out of Carnegie's Homestead plant in Pennsylvania and bus loads of non-union immigrants were shipped in, under the protection of 300 agents from the Pinkerton detective agency in New York City. The confrontation lasted for 143 days. Men were killed on both sides and the Pinkertons were forced to withdraw. Eventually, 5,000 townspeople were confronted by 4,000 state militia. The strikers' cause was not helped when an anarchist, Alexander Berkman, contrived to shoot and stab the plant manager, Henry Clay Frick. He failed to land a fatal blow and was sentenced to 22 years in jail.

The union eventually capitulated and the Amalgamated Association never regained its strength. From a high of 24,000 in 1891, its membership had shrunk to just 6,300 by 1909, as mill after mill refused to sign a contract and the union proved too weak to force the issue. Employing organizations grew in scale and importance throughout the 19th century. Although, in theory — and sometimes in practice — if an individual did not like what one company had to offer, he could move to another, some companies grew so rapidly that they came to dominate their communities. This was not always bad for workers.

> From a design perspective, the tension in a tension matrix should capture the aspirations of individuals and channel them in such a way as to put pressure on the overall structure to evolve in a direction that will (hopefully) meet them, but without causing the structure to fail.

* * * *

Henry Ford prided himself on paying high wages (about double the going rate in 1914), reckoning — quite rightly — that if he could attract the best workers, the efficiencies of his new mass production system, in which steel came in one end of the plant and a Model T popped out the other, would still be highly profitable. And in England, the Lever brothers built up their soap-making business around not only a factory but a model town for their employees called Port Sunlight, after their immensely popular *Sunlight Soap*, which they were producing at a rate of 450 tons a week by 1888. The Protestant ethic that Lever, Ford, Carnegie and many of the century's great industrialists shared made them want to improve humankind's lot. Tough they certainly were, but they took their mission seriously.

And this sense of moral purpose was not confined to business. As a young man, William Wilberforce, the son of a wealthy merchant, often sat in the gallery of the House of Commons listening to debates with his friend William Pitt, who became Prime Minister in 1783. In that year, Wilberforce traveled to Paris with Pitt's future brother-in-law where he met Benjamin Franklin, General Lafayette, Marie Antoinette and Louis XVI — what a conjunction of fates!

> Franklin was father to a nation, Lafayette achieved the status of a military pop star, while Louis and Marie Antoinette would be humiliated by their country's Revolutionary press, before being decapitated in front of their excited fellow citizens under the blade of Joseph-Ignace Guillotine's scientific killing machine — on the orders of the self-appointed National Convention. [In the absence of any accepted process, new structures often have to reach for legitimacy in the most bizarre fashion.]

Over the years that followed, Wilberforce came into contact with a group of Quakers (a branch of the Reformed Church, which included many notable business leaders) anxious to put a stop to the trade in slaves.[10] His own deep Christian views caused him to make their goal his life's work, and in 1833 the Slavery Abolition Act was eventually passed, just three days after his death. Although Wilberforce was exceptional, he was not unusual in wanting to improve the lot of those outside his own social sphere, a reaction Karl Marx (1818–1883) did not allow for when he outlined the mechanical way in which capital would inevitably exploit labor to the point of destroying itself, at which point 'the people' would take over the means of production, through their government, and set themselves free.

> All deterministic models suffer from the fatal flaw that they do not allow for the creative potential that is so clearly evident in the universe. A tension matrix that inhibits such creativity is similarly flawed.

When Britain, allied with France and the Ottoman Empire, sought to blunt Imperial Russia's interest in the Middle East, Florence Nightingale, another committed Christian from a wealthy family, went to the disease-infested Crimean battlefield in 1854, and using common sense, exemplary organization and attention to hygiene, transformed the practice of nursing. Another reformer, Anthony Ashley Cooper, the 7th Earl of Shaftesbury, concerned himself with improving working life in factories, pushing through the Coal Mines Act of 1842 and the Factory Acts of 1847 and 1853 which regulated hours and conditions.

---

10. Between the 16th & 19th centuries it is estimated that some 12 million Africans were forcibly transported to the Americas. As many as 20% probably died en route and at least 40% of the remainder died in direct consequence of the work they were driven to do. This despicable trade degraded all those directly involved, with instances of brutal depravity all too common. Cities like Liverpool prospered from it and sugar from the plantations was a commodity much prized by the expanding middle class. As immoral structures go, that of slavery is right up there with what was meted out to the Jews in the Second World War. And lest we forget, Africa sold its own.

Many, like the great liberal thinker John Stuart Mill (1806–1873), took heart from the French experiment, even if appalled by its excesses, and attempted to articulate how the new order might be constructed. Mill, following the economist David Ricardo (1772–1823), was a firm believer in the benefits of free trade. At home, however, he sought to distinguish between income from land (which he called unearned) and income from professional work and other labors (which he called earned), advocating that the former be taxed along with inheritance. Unlike Marx, he saw production as a technical matter and only the distribution of wealth as being a reflection of the social order, which he, and many others from the professions, wanted to change.

It was as if the middle class was redefining the story, together with the tension matrix it supported, to suit its own perception of how life should be. And great liberal though he was, Mill could not detach himself completely from conservatism — *no government can expect to be permanent unless it guarantees progress as well as order*. What he really meant was that no government could expect to be permanent unless it guaranteed order as well as progress. In many ways, his view reflected the innate conservatism of the English. Whilst Karl Marx became totally wrapped up in what he believed to be the scientific determinism of his ideas, Mill (like most of the great British reformers) was more interested in what would work in practice.

The first Liberal Government under the high Anglican, William Gladstone, was resoundingly elected in 1868 and continued to push through reforms. And by the end of the century it was not just Charles Dickens who was heightening awareness about life in industrial Britain. Social reformers like Sidney and Beatrice Webb, who helped found the Fabian Society (a sort of left-leaning think tank) as well as the London School of Economics, were doing so using the tools of scientific research. But working men were not content to leave reform to aristocrats and members of the middle class, however enlightened. As more people became entitled to vote, the Union Movement gradually entered politics putting up 28 members under its own Labour Party banner in 1895. Although this new entity won only 44,325 votes, it was the start of a process that would eventually lead to it eclipsing the Liberals and gaining full power.

The 19th century is remarkable on almost every measure that touches on structural change. Improvements in health, hygiene and food production allowed populations to increase rapidly. People moved in large numbers into cities and across borders, often to America. Globalization was a fact, although individuals still thought in terms of nations and wars were fought in almost every part of the globe. New companies were formed, new products sold and new political parties invented, bringing freedoms to men and women they had never known. Countries everywhere were attempting to reform their creaking political systems. Even the sprawling Ottoman Empire tried to modernize and Russia did finally abolish serfdom in 1861. The ideas that bound individuals to their societies were fast fracturing under an avalanche of opportunities. What a setting for ambitious men!

* * * *

As the calendar turned over into the 20th century, the British foreign secretary, Lord Lansdowne, and Hayashi Tadasu, Japan's minister in London, met in Lansdowne House, just off Berkeley Square. One hundred and twenty years earlier, in the same house, the foreign secretary's great-grandfather, William Shelburne (the 1st Lord Lansdowne) had met with his friend, Benjamin Franklin, to work out how best to end America's struggle for independence.

On this occasion the agreement struck acknowledged Japan's interests in Korea and Britain agreed to remain neutral if these were pursued. Japan, for its part, agreed to remain neutral while Britain protected its own interest in India and the Far East. Both parties agreed to come to the other's aid if attacked by more than one power. For the British, the treaty represented a warning shot against Russian expansion towards India, through Afghanistan, or into China through Manchuria. For Japan, it represented a green light for its imperial expansion on the mainland. Between 1904 and 1905, Japan annihilated both the Russian Far East Fleet and their Second Pacific Squadron, taking over Russia's possessions in Manchuria.

The onset of war between Russia and Japan set alarm bells ringing in London, as France was technically allied to Russia at the time, and the last thing either France or Britain wanted was to be drawn into war on account of what was going on in the Far East. So in April 1904, Lansdowne signed another agreement, this time with the French, which put aside all the overseas differences that had plagued the two countries since they had embarked on their respective colonial expansions three hundred years earlier. However, this agreement angered the new Germany, whose own colonial ambitions had been constrained — she had been late to the feast — causing her to think more in terms of continental expansion. After all, the remnants of the old Holy Roman Empire, outside Germany's current borders, still contained substantial populations of German-speaking people.

> Our histories are embedded within our structures and influence our perceptions, and so actions, more than we might think. When European immigrants passed through Ellis Island into the new America, they left their histories (and often their names) behind.

Britain had just fought an expensive war against Dutch and Huguenot settlers who had established an independent republic north of the Cape Colony, in southern Africa. When gold was discovered thirty miles south of its capital, Pretoria, the popular press in London, egged on by Cecil Rhodes, then prime minister of the Cape Colony, demanded that this renegade republic be brought under the control of the British Empire. The war that followed was expensive, dirty and not Britain's finest hour. The Afrikaners or Boers, as the Dutch-Huguenot settlers were called, resorted to the guerilla tactics used by American colonists in their war of independence against the British.

The British response was to adopt a scorched earth policy in an attempt to deny the guerilla fighters any local support. Women and children were herded up into poorly run concentration camps where they suffered from starvation and disease. Outside, their farms were destroyed and the ground salted. In all it is estimated that some 20–28,000 Boer civilians (mostly women and children) died in the camps. There is no accurate record of how many black Africans died in the camps, although some 107,000 were also interned, segregated from the whites, of course. The British military command, under Lord Kitchener, regarded these deaths as "an abysmally low priority" when set against the military objectives, which were, after a succession of embarrassing setbacks, ultimately achieved. Faced with overwhelming odds, the Boers were forced to accept defeat and their republic became part of the British Empire, and part of what is now South Africa.

Lansdowne had been Secretary of State for War during the run-up to this war, and must have been only too well aware of the military over-stretch that was beginning to become apparent in Britain's far-flung empire. And doubtless he was as appalled as most people back in London were by the reports coming out of the camps. When these were confirmed by an independent commission established by the government to investigate, under pressure from its Liberal opposition, the camps were removed from military control and placed under a civilian authority, appointed by the government. But by then the war had only three months to run, and the damage was done.

When he moved to the Foreign office in 1900, shortly after the start of the Boer War (which ended in May 1902), Lansdowne must have seen his main task as being to defuse as many of the Empire's hot spots as he could. The agreement with Japan (in January 1902) and then the *Entente Cordiale* with France, signed in April 1904, doubtless seemed like steps in the right direction.

The agreement with France probably pleased him particularly, as his mother was half French. Her father was the illegitimate son of the former French Foreign Minister, Talleyrand, and had been one of Napoleon's generals. After the restoration of the Bourbon monarchy in France, this rather dashing man had fled to Britain (finding his enemies in war more hospitable than his enemies in peace) and married a Scots heiress, Lansdowne's grandmother.

By way of illustrating the impossibility of predicting the future, Lansdowne's grandson would one day marry an American whose ancestors included French immigrants to the New World. A computer system made by the company one of these helped found stood ready, for many years, to launch missiles at the Soviet Union during the cold war that was to develop later in the century. The world Lansdowne was trying to control was moving far faster and changing more completely than he, or any of his colleagues, could possibly have imagined.

* * * *

At the start of the new century, Britain, France and Germany were rearming rapidly. Japan was already well advanced in this and Russia would soon experience the consequences. At the heart of Europe, the German people were bursting at the seams. There was an air of impending crisis. The mindset amongst leaders in most of the major powers was focused outwards, rather than on internal development. This was to prove fatal at a time when populations (especially working populations) wanted more control over their lives. One form this took was a rise in nationalism.

When Gavrilo Princip, a young Serb nationalist, took a potshot at the heir to the Austro-Hungarian throne — a remnant of the Hapsburg and Holy Roman Empires — and killed him, Germany rattled its saber, demanding that Serbia be brought into line, which caused the Tsar to rattle his saber on behalf of the Serbs, Russia's ethnic cousins. Eager to expunge the humiliation she had experienced in the Franco-Prussian war, France, Russia's ally, started saber-rattling too, which brought Britain into the circus, as France's new ally. Within weeks, a war that would claim some 20 million lives had begun.

This war, which macabrely would become known as *The Great War*, started — for Britain, at any rate — at the end of August 1914, some ten years and four months after the *Entente Cordiale* had been signed. Just two months into the war, on October 30th, Lansdowne's son was killed, along with 700 of his fellow officers and some 54,000 of their men, in what was ultimately a successful attempt to stem a lightning first strike by the Germans through Belgium, intended to take possession of the Channel ports.

Two years later, when the war had ossified into a trenchant stalemate and the death toll had escalated into the millions, Lansdowne circulated a paper to his cabinet colleagues arguing for a negotiated ceasefire on the basis of each country's pre-war boundaries. This received a hostile response. Lansdowne then redrafted his proposal in the form of a letter to be published and invited the editor of *The Times* newspaper to Lansdowne House to consider it. The editor was appalled and declined. Eventually, Lansdowne's letter was published on November 29th 1917 in *The Daily Telegraph*. In part, it read as follows:

> We are not going to lose this war, but its prolongation will spell ruin for the civilized world, and an infinite addition to the load of human suffering which already weighs upon it. . . . We do not desire the annihilation of Germany as a great power. . . . We do not seek to impose upon her people any form of government other than that of their own choice. . . . We have no desire to deny Germany her place among the great commercial communities of the world. . . .

The communication was generally treated with scorn. The writer H.G. Wells cynically observed that it was the letter of a peer who feared revolution more than national dishonor. And this about a public servant who had not only been Foreign Secretary and Minister of War, but also Governor General of Canada and Viceroy of India: not exactly a profile of the idle, self-interested aristocrat, so derided by the new revolutionaries. Even many of Lansdowne's colleagues put it down to their friend being an old man (he was 72) whose judgment had been clouded by the death of a much loved son. Woe betide any man who goes against the prevailing story!

In spite of a spring offensive in 1918 that brought the Germans to within 75 miles of Paris, they were unable to push home their advantage. Suffering over 270,000 casualties, they were soon pushed back to where they had come from, although this was still 900 miles from Berlin and outside German soil. But with the American entry into the war the previous year, their enemy's resources were increasing while their own were being depleted. One by one, the Central Powers, as Germany and her allies were called (which, by then, included the Ottoman Empire) sued for peace. In November, an armistice was signed in the railcar Adolf Hitler would insist on using to accept France's surrender in 1940, and the spoils of war were divided up.

Lansdowne had been both right and wrong. Civilization did not come to an end, although the type of civilization he knew did. We now know from German documents that it is unlikely the German high command would have accepted a ceasefire on the basis of a return to the status quo. Up until the spring of 1918 they thought they could win, and just might have, had their logistical support been better. To expect the allies simply to stop, having made so great an investment in men and materials, was naïve. In all this, Lansdowne was wrong.

But in another sense, he was dreadfully right. If cerebral structure is going to evolve without recourse to the extreme violence that has characterized human history to date, we are going to have to rise beyond our biological drivers and design structures that meet individual aspirations, even when it is not clear to individuals themselves what these are. We are not talking here about some utopian fixed point, but about a continuing process, and the fact that Lansdowne was prepared to stand up and be counted was the thing. In a lifetime of determined public service, that single, rather hopeless act was, perhaps, his greatest contribution.

* * * *

When the First World War finally came to an end in 1919, the tensions that had been bubbling up beneath the surface had expressed themselves with a vengeance and the world was a different place. The Tsar and Russian aristocracy had been swept away in the revolution of 1917 and the Soviet Union, together with Poland, emerged from the debris of the Russian Empire. Although allied troops had not set foot on German soil, the German surrender led to unrest, the abdication of the Kaiser, the formation of the Weimar Republic and a regime of reparations that crippled the German economy. The Austro-Hungarian and Ottoman Empires came to an end and much of the latter's territory in the Middle East was parceled out amongst the victors as 'protectorates', in the face of growing Arab nationalism.

The remnants of the old Holy Roman Empire that had not mutated into Germany but into the Austro-Hungarian Empire became independent states. The rump of the Ottoman Empire was reconstituted as the Republic of Turkey and Christian Armenia earned a genocidal footnote in the history books. In Africa, as elsewhere, the spoils were distributed over the heads of the people. German East Africa, three times the size of present day Germany, was divided up between Belgium, Britain and Portugal.

The United States did not enter the war until 1917, some three years after its beginning. With only an insignificant army at the start, Congress had drafted four million men to fight by the close, and her high-minded President, Woodrow Wilson, had pushed for the creation of a League of Nations, to prevent such a catastrophe from occurring again. This earned him Nobel's Peace price in 1919. Japan also entered the war (but in 1914), following her agreement with Britain, and ended up obtaining control over some of Germany's interests in the region, furthering her ambitions on the Chinese mainland, as well as securing *Great Power* status and a permanent seat on the council of Wilson's new League.

Britain's imperium also rose to the challenge, with India alone deploying 1.3 million soldiers, partly in the hope that this show of solidarity would earn Britain's gratitude and advance her own nationalist ambitions. Soldiers from Canada, Australia and New Zealand all played vital parts too, in a catastrophe which needed to be justified by calling it the *Great War*. Of the European nations, only the Netherlands, Switzerland, Spain, Portugal and Scandinavia managed to keep themselves clear of the bloodbath.

Victors they may have been, but Britain and especially France were shattered by their exertions. Towards the close, the French army had sustained so many casualties — some 1.4 million killed — that it almost mutinied. A large part of Britain's overseas investments had been liquidated to pay for the conflict. At home, around 16,000 conscientious objectors, who had been imprisoned on a regime of bread and water during the war, had to face notices saying *No conscientious objectors need apply* when they were eventually released and needed to find work.

Britain had mobilized close to 6 million men of whom 750,000 were killed and 1,700,000 were wounded. Wives lost husbands, children lost fathers, and families had to pick up broken men as best they could. And as if that was not enough, a virulent flu pandemic declared war on the human race, killing, by some estimates, 40 million more around the world. What a far cry 1919 must have seemed from those happy summer days, five years before, when young men, from all over Britain, flocked to the recruiting tables, worried that the adventure they sought would be over by Christmas.

* * * *

It is hard to come up with a word to describe the world in the 1920s. A ghastly war was over. Nobody quite knew why it had happened or what it had been about. The official version, that it was all Germany's fault, probably convinced no one, but to anyone who wasn't a German it must at least have seemed like a sticking-plaster-of-an-idea they could use to bind together the tears that were shredding the social fabric they once knew. The old story, the one that had bound people to the political entities they were part of, was disintegrating in front of their eyes. But the new story behaved like Kali, the Hindu goddess of time and change, whose many seductive limbs and endless promise drew men towards her deadly embrace. *Chaos* is the word that comes to mind. But chaos in the sense of a riot of opportunities, of paths to be taken, of drinks to be drunk to the full, of extreme sensations to be indulged — of energy unconstrained. Action, that was the thing, and destruction of the old the only consequence that mattered.

Emmeline Pankhurst, whose movement to secure votes for women had been suspended before the war and whose members had handed white feathers to any young man found in civilian clothes, was touring America and Canada lecturing about venereal disease. By 1928, women in the United Kingdom had won equal voting rights to men. The war could not have been won without their work in the factories. But with the vote came a life of spinsterhood for many. The corpses of those they might have married lay scattered across the battlefields of Europe.

There was a fault-line developing around the world. The goddess of change revealed a split personality and people were drawn to one side or the other, even within the same family. When 'Emily' Pankhurst returned from America, her views had crystallized and she stood as a Conservative parliamentary candidate. Her daughter, however, remained a staunch Socialist. In Italy, thirty-nine year old Benito Mussolini, who had given up on Socialism as being no more than a recipe for class struggle and divisive weakness, marched on Rome at the head of his National Fascist Party. Across the country people were fearful of the communist anarchy disrupting daily life and King Victor Emmanuel III handed power to the young adventurer in 1922.

Japan's fledgling democracy was dealt a blow when Hara Takashi, the first commoner to serve as Prime Minister, was assassinated by a disgruntled railroad worker in 1921. Concerns about the disruptive influence of Communism and Western influence generally were feeding Japan's sense of nationalism. In neighboring China, thirty-nine year old Mao Zedong's attempts to rally industrial workers to the cause of violent revolution were successfully subdued by the government, leading him to refocus his efforts on the feudal peasantry, a far larger part of his country's population.

> When one story loses its potency in the face of another whose potency is in the ascendant, the instability in the matrix caused by shifting allegiances and uncertainty magnifies random events and opens up opportunities for ambitious and ruthless individuals.

In the new Soviet Union, the civil war that had broken out after the 1917 revolution was drawing to a close. In spite of opposition from France and Britain (Winston Churchill, who was Britain's Secretary of State for War in 1919, felt that Bolshevism should be *strangled in its cradle*), the Bolsheviks had gained control of almost all the country by 1922. On April 3 of that year, a 43 year-old Joseph Stalin, who had been one of the original members of the Bolshevik party, was made general secretary of the Central Committee of the All-Russian Communist Party, a position he would build up into one of unchallenged power.

Between 1925 and 1926, the two volumes of 37 year-old Adolf Hitler's *Mein Kampf* (*My Struggle*), written partly in jail following an unsuccessful coup three years before, were published in Germany. Over the next eight years, around 240,000 copies were purchased. As in Italy and Japan, the story unfolding was being built around the idea of a centrally-controlled nation, in which every individual would play an equal part, according to his or her ability. Nationalists had no more time for Socialists than did Lenin, Stalin or Mao Zedong, a symmetry many Western intellectuals either failed to see or were reluctant to admit.

* * * *

Most Americans (or their immediate ancestors) had come to the New World to get away from the problems of Europe. With the war over, America turned inward. Tariffs were raised and taxes lowered. The union movement was crushed. American industry prospered. For the first time, the mass of people could afford a glittering array of consumer goods from cars to primitive washing machines. Radios broadcast shows that became favorites, along with the new jazz music popularized by black entertainers like Louis Armstrong and Duke Ellington. Women threw away the Victorian corset and became flappers, dancing the charleston in Art Deco dance halls, and attended co-ed colleges and universities.

Prejudices there remained aplenty, against Jews and Blacks and Spics and Drinkers (prohibition against the manufacture, sale, import and export of alcohol was introduced in 1920), but where there was a buck to be made, the rules were bent and large fortunes made. Alphonse Gabriel Capone (1899–1947) dominated the illegal Chicago liquor trade (and just about everything else that was illegal) in the 1920s, and if he did pray, he must have blessed the Puritan temperance movement every night before falling asleep.

For one man, a beneficiary of old money with no need to struggle for new, the early 1920s were not so good. Having received a drubbing as candidate for the vice-presidency on the Democratic ticket in 1920, he found himself crippled from the waist down by a mystery illness while on vacation in New Brunswick the following year. Determined never to be seen in the wheelchair he used from then on, Franklin Roosevelt was elected Governor of New York in 1928 (when the incumbent became the Democratic nominee for President), and re-elected in 1930, despite being attacked by his opponent for the rampant corruption in the Democrats' Tammany Hall political machine. With his characteristic flair for scaling the moral high ground while still keeping his feet firmly anchored to the often dirty floor, he initiated an investigation into the sale of judicial offices and won by over 700,000 votes. But that was still to come.

As the carefree stardust of the 1920s scattered its uneven bounty, those who could, made hay. At a time when inside knowledge was the only knowledge available, Joseph P. Kennedy was making his millions on Wall Street, moving skillfully into real estate and liquor imports, and F. Scott Fitzgerald was publishing his novel *The Great Gatsby*, about a man who had amassed a great fortune, although nobody quite knew how. The Broadway Musical, *Cabaret* (1966), depicting the high life that energized even Berlin during the last days of the liberal Weimar Republic, captured the mood. *Money, money, money*, was making the world go round and for many, money was about to stop.

* * * *

As the 1920s drew to a close, you would have to say that very few parts of the world were in control of themselves. And by 'in control' I don't mean in some slavish mechanical sense (because attempts in that direction are ultimately impossible and always self-defeating), but in the sense of having a stable tension matrix. And to repeat what this entails is that the individuals within it share essentially the same story about how the structure will dynamically meet their objectives. It also requires that its boundary condition can engage constructively rather than destructively with forces outside it.

The most coherent structure in the world was the relatively new United States of America, which had been constructed from scratch by its founding fathers based upon the best political, social and economic intelligence available in the 18th century. Its story was essentially the Puritan story of self-reliance, hard work and a belief that material success, here on earth, was a right and proper reward for the righteous life. But even America had had to fight a brutal civil war to ensure that this story won out over a different one, in which society relied upon an embedded class system, just as the ancient Roman state had done. All tension matrices, however, contain elements of the *Wizard of Oz*, simply because they can only ever be incomplete expressions of our human aspirations. The important thing, though, is for their attendant stories to be more believable than any other stories at the time. But that doesn't mean that there isn't an element of hokum about them.

In America's case, the hokum was that the land of opportunity distributed its largesse on the basis of individual merit and hard work alone. Compared to the old atrophied structures in Europe, it seemed close enough to this reality to satisfy most people. A steady stream of immigrants and the exploitation of the continent all the way to the West Coast ensured a positive dynamic (unless you were a North American Indian), in which booms and busts generally followed an upward trajectory in terms of material prosperity. If you couldn't make it in one area, well, you could just gather up your belongings and go try your hand in another.

But by the start of the 20th century, America's scale, increasing urbanization and growing involvement in the global economy meant that individuals were no longer independent operators, dealing with mostly local concerns, but were part of a system that was not well understood. The boom years after World War I had been something of a mirage in which easy credit had stimulated consumption, over-investment (to meet it) and enthusiastic stock market speculation (because companies seemed to be doing so well). When it started to dawn on the money men that loans would have to be repaid and that individuals could not go on borrowing to consume, or borrowing to purchase stocks, for ever, the credit elastic snapped back with a vengeance.

After increasing fivefold in five years, the stock market peaked on September 3rd 1929. By July 8th 1932 the Dow Jones Industrial Average had lost 89% of its value. It would not reclaim its September high until 1954, a wait of almost 25 years. There had been speculative excesses before, but the thing that marked this one out, in addition to its scale, was that it heralded what became known as The Great Depression, a human disaster that followed on the heels of The Great War. We humans clearly like to disguise our failures with superlatives.

As Chancellor of the Exchequer in 1924, Winston Churchill — in a misguided attempt to put the clock back to the world before the war, which he later regarded as his biggest mistake — anchored the British pound to the gold standard at the pre-war parity of £1=$4.86. All this did was to cripple British exporters and depress trade. The coal industry was badly affected and a General Strike followed in 1926, prompting Churchill to praise Mussolini for showing the world how to *combat subversive forces*. Luckily, Britain's political system was more robust than Italy's and Churchill's Conservative government was voted out of office in 1929.

The post-war world was simply unstable at many levels. Politically, there were two stories vying for people's attention: Fascism and Communism, although in reality these two extremes were opposite ends of the change goddess's personality. Economically the world was integrating, but with no boundary condition to regulate its behavior. Socially, large numbers of individuals were feeling politically and economically disenfranchised, because hardships were blighting their lives that they felt powerless to ameliorate. In such circumstances, people's natural inclination is to circle their wagons and listen to whatever voice gives them hope.

So when two senators, one from Utah and the other from Oregon, cobbled together a bill to further increase tariffs so as to protect farmers and domestic manufacturers in a labor market that was already showing signs of weakness in 1927, President Herbert Hoover signed the Smoot-Hawley Tariff Act into law on June 17th 1930, over the objections of 1,028 economists — or, as the President probably saw it, at the risk of losing a mere 1,028 votes. Countries around the world had their fingers poised on the protectionist trigger and enacted their own legislation. By the end of 1933, US imports had dropped from $4.4 billion in 1929 to only $1.5 billion, and exports had fallen from $5.4 billion to $2.1 billion, a pattern reflected everywhere.

US unemployment had risen from 7.8% in 1930 to 25.1% by 1933. In 1939, John Steinbeck published *The Grapes of Wrath*, a novel about a family busted out of their Oklahoma farm who head west in an old jalopy, worldly goods attached, lured by the promise of rich pickings in the California vineyards. They are shunned en route and abused when they get there, but for them and millions like them, the American dream somehow manages not to die. The story remained intact, with a little help from Franklin Delano Roosevelt, elected President in 1933. Much of his *New Deal* may have been smoke and mirrors but it was believed, that was the point, and his improvements in social welfare and financial oversight were real enough. But as would be the case in Germany under Hitler, it was rearmament that finally pulled America out of its slump.

Across the Atlantic, the great event of the 1930s was the Spanish Civil War, which drew idealistic young men from all over Europe to fight for what would be the losing side. Spanish politics had been destabilized by the Napoleonic wars of the 19th century and the last years of King Alfonso XIII's reign (1887–1931) were sustained by a military dictatorship under general Primo de Rivera. He was ousted in 1930 and a Republic was declared the following year. Agrarian reform, military cutbacks, and anticlericalism angered the old elite. The Right fought back and won most votes in the 1933 election, but not enough to form a majority. The atmosphere in the Cortes (parliament) became poisonous. In the 1936 elections, a coalition of Socialists, Communists and Liberals won 34% of the popular vote as against 33% for the right wing coalition government.

The Soviet Union actively encouraged the left wing extremists and the right wing coalition fractured, leaving moderates on both sides high and dry. In July, right wing nationalists under General Francisco Franco moved to take control of the country. The civil war was brutal, with atrocities committed on both sides, and did not end until February 1939. France, Britain, Italy and Germany all lent varying degrees of support to the nationalists, while the Soviet Union supplied the republicans with tactical advisors and sub-standard equipment in return for gold. Although some 200,000 had their lives snatched by the execution squads on both sides, and several hundred thousand sought exile, Spain was, at least, spared the horrors of the Second World War.

The failed struggle, however, became a symbol for the Left. The great Chilean writer, Pablo Neruda, who, as special consul in Paris, arranged for 2,500 Spanish refugees to be shipped to Chile on the battered old cargo ship, *Winnipeg*, described it as the noblest mission he had ever undertaken. But I somehow doubt that a Soviet-style Spain would have been to his or anyone else's liking. Kali's seductive smile lives on, though, to this day. What failed in Spain, as elsewhere at this time, was disciplined moderation — and how boring is that!

Germany had been struggling to pay the reparations demanded by the treaty that ended World War I and the American loans she had been taking on to do so, dried up. Inflation had already rocketed skyward by 1923, as the Weimar government had been printing money to pay government employees and settle reparations. By 1933 the government had lost all credibility and, against a backdrop of unrest stirred up by his party thugs, Hitler was sworn in as Chancellor. By 1938 he had crushed all political opposition, annexed Austria and become Führer — absolute dictator of Germany.

> At about this time, Lansdowne's young grandson, blessed with Hollywood good looks, was in California, marrying his twenty-year-old American bride inside a timber-built church called All Saints by the Sea. The story that would come to dominate the world after the war was already being built.

* * * *

Between 1930 and 1950, a period of only twenty years, the human world went through wrenching change. At a guess, somewhere between 100 and 200 million people lost their lives prematurely. World War II accounted for around 60, mostly civilians, the post-war Soviet Union can probably lay claim to 20 and the People's Republic of China to 40 million more. The precise accuracy of the numbers is less important than their order of magnitude. And death on an industrial scale has continued in places like Cambodia, Rwanda and most recently, Darfur. By my reckoning, these deaths were a consequence of our biological drivers doing what they do best: establishing boundaries between species, save that in these cases the species are particular kinds of human organization which we think of as nations or protonations. Every time our cerebral structure fails (consciousness cannot grasp the magnitude of the problems facing it), our biology takes over. And as I have said before, biology is a numbers game, with no interest in morality, other than the survival of its type.

There is no point in us wringing our hands when we hear about Japanese soldiers burying Chinese soldiers alive, or about Germans gassing Jews by the thousands, or about British and American bombers burning 60,000 Dresden civilians to death in one night. If we rely on our biological drivers to tell us what to do, those are exactly the sort of things that we will do, and will have to do. Unless we can build robust, dynamic structures, without the threat of those things being done to us, we will have no alternative.

The power of *a story* should never be underestimated — or ridiculed. We **all** live within one and the danger of our scientific age is that we will imagine that we do not. To repeat, a story is the template we use to make sense of the world around us and it naturally governs, to a large extent, what we see and how we see it. It influences our actions by being tied to our feelings.

> Even the Roman Catholic Church (which was a remarkably robust structure, although not a very dynamic one) was built around a most un-Christian concept — the threat of eternal hell and damnation (the biological driver of pain). When the threat didn't work, the holy fathers were quite prepared to engineer a little holy fire, as a salutary corrective, right here on earth.

* * * *

A core of the Germanic tribes that had humbled the mighty Roman Empire and populated much of France, Britain and northern Europe was bottled up inside what had been part of the old Holy Roman Empire. They had only recently attained an identity as a nation. Their rivalry with France was long-standing, but it was with their fellow tribesmen who lived in countries to the east, such as Czechoslovakia and Poland that they felt a particular bond. The idea of a Greater Germany was real and had roots.

In Japan, like Germany, the idea of fighting for survival was stronger than the idea of democracy, and one should not forget that Athens, where the idea of democracy in the ancient world was most thoroughly developed, eventually suffered defeat at the hands of Sparta, an overtly military state. As the cowboy was to become in popular American culture, the warrior had been central to Japanese imagery for centuries. When the era of warlords finally evolved into a unified nation state, the military ethos remained powerful. Japanese heavy industry enjoyed rapid growth after 1930, drawing heavily on the coal and iron deposits in Manchuria, an area she was seeking to colonize, sandwiched between China (that claimed it) and the Soviet Union she had wrested it from.

For many in Japan, building up their country's industrial and military strength was a paramount objective, overriding a democracy that was having to embrace a multiplicity of often-conflicting ideas, including those of the new Communism. In 1932, anxious to destabilize China, the military attacked Shanghai without authorization from the civilian government, and in 1936 the country signed the Anti-Comintern pact with Germany, under which both countries pledged to work together to oppose Communism. The following year, Japan launched all-out war against China, as well as against the Soviet Union to the north.

Following the collapse of China's Imperial Qing dynasty in 1911, the republican Kuomintang party (the KMT) attempted to unify the country, but in 1927 the communist faction (the CPC) within the KMT broke away. From then on, China was locked in both a civil war as well as a war with Japan. Chiang Kai-shek, who had taken over leadership of the KMT after its founder Sun Yat-sen's death in 1925, had less interest in keeping the Japanese out of Manchuria than in trying to defeat the CPC. In October 1934, almost encircled by KMT forces, the CPC, under its forty-one-year-old leader Mao Zedong, made a break to the north-west, eventually covering 12,500 km over the following year. This was to become the *Long March* of Chinese communist legend.

From 1937 until the Japanese surrender in 1945, the KMT waged war against the occupation, with intermittent help from the CPC, while at the same time trying to outmaneuver its ally. But from 1946 to 1950, the KMT and CPC waged all-out war with one another for control of the country. In spite of considerable financial help, principally from the United States, the KMT was eventually driven off the mainland onto the Chinese island of Taiwan and on October 1st 1949 Mao Zedong proclaimed the People's Republic of China, with its capital at Beijing. The KMT defeat contained a lesson as old as human history itself: a people unified by an idea are harder to defeat than a people unified by money. That said, the KMT had borne the brunt of the fighting against the Japanese and was exhausted.

But we have moved ahead. In the 1930s, in both Japan and Germany, the idea of the warrior nation was attracting far more support than the often-confusing idea of democracy with — as in the clear case of Germany and lesser case of Japan — its dismal performance record. Even in Britain at this time, a country with a long history of evolved democracy, the paramilitary British Union of Fascists was attracting a following with its plea that Britain should be for the British, not a dumping ground for goods produced abroad with cheap labor, and that Jewish bankers, who were seen as profiting from the world's financial turmoil, should be sent packing. Rampant democracy, its leaders often argued, was a luxury Britain could ill afford.

> When people have to choose between democratic mismanagement (with the disruption it brings) and the rigid order of a centralized state, they will invariably opt for the latter. Without order there is chaos, and there is nothing more terrifying to the human psyche than that.

Japan's vision was of an Asia controlled by Japan and freed from Western influence. The idea of Western-style democracy had lost its appeal following the onset of the Great Depression, when high tariffs were erected to keep Japanese goods out of Western markets. When a group of junior naval officers and army cadets assassinated Prime Minister Tsuyoshi, successor to Prime Minister Hamaguchi who had also been assassinated two years earlier for agreeing with the Americans to limit Japan's naval power (the young assassins received fifteen-year prison sentences and much popular acclaim), Japan's system of party government came to an end. The unitary system that replaced it was never wholly dominated by the military, largely due to infighting within the military itself, but, from that point on, Japan was unified, from cradle to grave, behind the imperial objective.

Just as Japan was indoctrinating its young, especially its young men, in the importance of fighting for the imperial objective, so Hitler's Germany was doing the same. The Hitler Youth was established in 1922 as a paramilitary organization in which teenage males were schooled in the disciplines of obedience that would be crucial to the armies they were expected to fill. By 1936, the movement had over five million members and it was almost impossible for a boy not to join. If one didn't, the consequences for him and his family would be about as unpleasant as they had been for Britain's pacifists in the First World War.

This clarity of vision, uncluttered by doubts, was seen as being central to the strength of a nation, an objective Mao Zedong and Joseph Stalin would each have recognized and applauded. A difference, which would ultimately undermine both Germany and Japan, just as it had Napoleonic France, was that militarism can only be expressed in terms of conquest, whereas Communism is concerned with totalitarian control over a nation itself. The first is driven outwards until it is defeated. The second is driven inwards until it defeats itself. Even the democracies, once committed to the struggle, would have to suspend disbelief and turn themselves into one-dimensional systems, if they were to win.

> The militaristic structure must harness all energy and thought towards external conquest. The totalitarian structure has to focus all its energy on maintaining absolute control from the top, but in doing so blocks creative thought which, by definition, is non-standard. By contrast, the adaptive structure must allow some of its energy to be used in ventures that will be unsuccessful. Biology suppresses adaptive mutations when the biosphere is in equilibrium because there is insufficient space left for the mutations to establish new structures. Unlike a species, however, human organizations can re-form around a new story and a new matrix and this allows cerebral structure to evolve more rapidly than its biological precursor.

* * * *

I sometimes think that men fight wars in order to discover what they are, and that women let them for the same reason. It is, I suppose, the most extreme of extreme sports in which collateral damage, to use that soothing American expression, is assumed. The Japanese had launched all-out war against China in the summer of 1937. In the autumn of the following year, the British Prime Minister, Neville Chamberlain, signed an agreement with Hitler (the Munich Agreement) in which it was asserted that the two countries would settle their differences peaceably, and that Germany would take the Sudetenland, with its Germanic population, away from Czechoslovakia. On his return from the meeting, and to the relieved applause of the British people, Chamberlain announced that he believed the agreement represented *peace for our time.* The following day (on October 1st), German troops occupied all of Czechoslovakia. Rarely has the triumph of hope over experience been so quickly exposed.

Having secured Austria (forced into accepting annexation in March) and now Czechoslovakia, with little more than a furrowed brow from Britain and France, Hitler moved to neutralize his Eastern flank the following year and authorized his ambassador Joachim von Ribbentrop to enter into an agreement with the Soviets, in which Eastern Europe was divided up into German and Soviet spheres of influence. Signed in August 1939 by the ambassador and Soviet foreign minister, Vyacheslav Molotov, and announced to the world simply as a German-Soviet non-aggression pact, the agreement dumbfounded Communism's anti-fascist admirers.

On September 1st, Germany invaded western Poland and on the 17th, in accordance with the Molotov-Ribbentrop pact, the Soviet Union invaded eastern Poland. After a ferocious struggle, the Poles finally capitulated on the 28th. At World War II's eventual end, some six million Poles would have been killed, half of them Polish Jews. Britain declared war on Germany and in the east, Soviet forces inflicted heavy losses on Japanese positions along the Manchurian border, even as Japan pushed south into China. In May 1940, just when Winston Churchill was replacing Neville Chamberlain as Britain's Prime Minster, Germany launched a lightning strike towards France. The French surrendered and the British were forced to evacuate their army from Dunkirk in an armada of private and government boats that chugged determinedly across the Channel to collect them, turning defeat into a peculiarly English sort of victory. Clearly impressed by the Führer's success, Benito Mussolini declared war on France and Britain in June.

If Hitler had had any ideas beyond conquest he would have stopped. With Spain and the Soviet Union neutral and Italy an ally, Germany had achieved control over central Europe in the space of two years, and with remarkably little loss. But so twisted, malignant, bitter and narrow-minded was the man, that only conquest made sense to him. Oh, and of course there was a sub-plot. Dubbed *The Final Solution*, with all the rationality of a lunatic, it allowed his puffed-up henchmen to demonize one group of their fellow citizens and process them through ghettos, train stations, camps, gas chambers and furnaces with every ounce of efficiency the dehumanized mind is capable of.

> Having spent most of World War I in the trenches as a private — one of the closest approximations to hell on earth the human race has yet devised — it is small wonder that Adolf Hitler and those who had shared his experience nurtured a distorted view of human life.

That the cerebral structure of a great nation can be turned in this way should be a lesson to all of us. First and foremost, it demonstrates the power of a tension matrix and its accompanying story. It does a lot of our thinking for us. By all accounts, the leadership structure in the Third Reich was extremely loose and simple, centered on the Führer himself. His key aides, Heinrich Himmler (SS-Gestapo) and Joseph Goebbels (propaganda) carried out what they believed to be his wishes, as did the heads of the Army, Airforce and Navy. Industry processed orders, much of it for either rearmament or the eventual war effort, as efficiently as it could, using whatever labor was available to it.

The mass of the German people got on with their daily lives, which — by the end of the 1930s — were much improved. They imagined, no doubt, that they were part of a normal, functioning state. If some of their number were being roughed up, it was no more than they deserved in light of the fact that such people were not really Germans, and were part of a conspiracy against the German people (as they had been told and were happy to believe). In America, later in the war, Japanese Americans were removed from their homes and interned in camps, so what the German people accepted was not unusual.

> Scapegoating — the biological equivalent of ejecting a mutation — is as old as the hills in human history. It is simply a way of solidifying the essential identity of a structure so that it can act unambiguously and with all the force its character can muster.

No, the remarkable thing about the Third Reich was the absolute simplicity of its structure. It was designed to implement, and not to reflect beyond how to get the job done that the man at the apex of its hierarchy had reflected upon and authorized. Its imagination was the imagination of the Führer. Somehow 70,000,000 people had suspended all critical thought. They had bought into the idea of a Greater Germany, a promised land their beloved Führer would lead them to. Their task was to obey, to record and when called upon to do so, to fight — and fight they did, often with incredible skill and tenacity.

> There could hardly be a better example of how a large number of people within a tension matrix, defined by a clear story, can become what amounts to a species with the character of a single organism. All opposition — and there was opposition — was ejected like the mutation it was deemed to be. With cerebral judgment suspended, the Third Reich was governed by its biological drivers alone.

If there were people who wanted to question and express different ideas, the tension matrix of the Third Reich had long since been stripped of any means that would enable them to do so. Responsibility for this vandalism lies squarely with the German people as a whole. But before any of the rest of us feel too self-righteous, remember how hard it was, even for a man like Lansdowne, to get his letter published in 1917. The cerebral capacity and so morality of a tension matrix is best judged by how it accommodates minority views. This is because human truth is a composite. Pandering to a majority may ease decision-making and help focus action in the short run, but it is likely to be at the expense of the quality of decisions over time.

* * * *

Luckily for European democracy, there was a rather eccentric man across the Channel who, only nine years earlier, had narrowly avoided being killed while attempting to cross New York's Fifth Avenue. An unemployed trucker from Brooklyn unintentionally hit him a fair wallop as he was pacing the streets, trying to come to terms with the fact that his hard-won earnings had just been eviscerated in the Wall Street crash. Like Hitler, he was fearless. Like Hitler, he understood his people. And like Hitler, he was a superb orator — a master storyteller. But unlike Hitler, he had a wonderful sense of humor, and a good heart. He also knew his history.

Winston Spencer Churchill was something else besides. He was the product of a democracy. The 1930s had been a wretched decade for him. Turning sixty, beset by financial troubles and concerned that he would lose Chartwell, his beloved home, his political career seemed over. But though the government and the British people were passionate for peace — memories of the last war had been seared onto the mind of every Briton — there were a growing number of men, like him, who saw the signs in Germany and feared the worst. When Hitler's evil intent could no longer be wished away, Chamberlain was among the first to recommend that Churchill replace him as head of an all-party government. Because the future can never be known, a plurality of views is a mighty strength, provided, of course, reason and discipline are respected.

If you want to understand England, visit Chartwell and look down at the wealds of Kent and Sussex laid out below like a green quilt of squares edged in hedgerows, and then imagine the Battle of Britain being played out before you. The air assault was launched by the Luftwaffe on the 10th of July 1940 and effectively ended on the 15th of September when Air Chief Marshal Sir Hugh Dowding ordered everything that could fly into the sky and repulsed Hermann Göring's final throw of Germany's aerial dice. There would be many years of fighting still to come, but just as the rout of Spain's Armada in 1588 had persuaded Philip II to give up on his attempt to foist Catholicism on England, so the Third Reich's first defeat persuaded Hitler to turn his attentions elsewhere. Almost as important, it undermined the assessment of America's ambassador to London, one Joseph P. Kennedy, that Britain was doomed, and persuaded President Roosevelt to prepare his own country for war.

> Cerebral structure is not some abstract thing that exists 'out there' waiting to be grasped, but is the product of an interaction between real people with real abilities and real character, struggling to make sense of the world and to steer a sane course forward. And they must do this within the tension matrix that exists and against the background of a story that is often pervasive.

* * * *

How do you disentangle the rational from the irrational, the opportunistic from the deliberate? When the treaty of Paris was signed in 1783, ending America's war of independence from Britain, could anyone have imagined that only 158 years later the thirteen colonies would have become part of an industrial powerhouse and Britain its junior partner? The United States had constructed itself deliberately. Its cerebral structure, made manifest in its constitution, had empowered its people and the North American continent had been their opportunity. The civil war had cemented in place one vision — one story. Business and the business of business had flourished, as waves of immigrants had provided both labor and markets. But the Great Depression reminded America's leaders that they were part of a wider world, whether they liked it or not.

Roosevelt was elected President for a third term in 1940 on an anti-war platform and on the promise of more intervention in the economy. As it happened, his New Deal was having a rather limited effect on the economy, but a most positive effect on people's spirits. His swipes at America's leading industrialists (the so called Robber Barons and makers of new money as against his old) went down well in the depression years. He even went so far as to set the Internal Revenue Service on Andrew Mellon (banker and industrialist), a man of impeccable integrity who was eventually fully exonerated, but not until after his death. If nothing else, this rather disreputable incident goes to show the temptations of power and the need to prevent any one person — however admired — from gaining too much of it.

Roosevelt didn't much like the English either, and liked what was left of Britain's empire even less. So it rather pleased him to be able to let Churchill twist in the wind, and to make Britain pay for the food and armaments he authorized his government to release in 1940. But in spite of his anti-war rhetoric and the public's distaste for war, he encouraged rearmament and by 1941 unemployment had fallen to under 1 million. *New Deal* may have been the label, but it was an old tonic in the bottle. Gradually he talked his countrymen round, although, like a good poker player, he wasn't about to bet his nation's assets until all the other players in the game had reached their limit.

Roosevelt worked the American political system with consummate skill, but it is hard to say that as an individual he was wholly admirable (hypocrisy in both his private and public life being his stock-in-trade). What differentiated the leaders in World War II (Roosevelt, Churchill, Hitler, Stalin, Emperor Hirohito and Mao Zedong) were the tension matrices each led and the stories that underpinned their legitimacy. The old adage ***cometh the hour cometh the man*** may embody some truth, but the type of man or woman the hour calls forth will reflect the cerebral structure they represent.

The structure of the Third Reich had no purpose other than to do its Führer's bidding, and he had no vision other than external conquest and internal purity. Having been thwarted against Britain, he turned east and in late June 1941, to the complete surprise of Joseph Stalin, one of the most suspicious of men (who had even been warned), Germany invaded the Soviet Union. In late 1940, Japan had already occupied much of French Indonesia (Vietnam, Cambodia and Laos) and Roosevelt was increasing aid to Chiang Kai-shek's Chinese Republic. When Hitler's armies marched east, he offered aid to the Soviet Union also and in July, when Japanese forces continued their advance into Indo-China (towards Burma in the west and down towards Singapore in the south), he curbed the sale of oil to Japan, which then amounted to most of its supply.

On December 7th 1941 the Japanese launched a pre-emptive strike against the American Pacific Fleet, damaging 16 warships and killing over 2,400, including many civilians. The following day Roosevelt declared war on Japan with his outraged people now fully behind him. (In February of the following year, he would authorize the internment of first-generation Japanese Americans and their children). After their success at Pearl Harbor, the Japanese moved quickly to take over the Philippines from America as well as the remaining Dutch and British colonies in the region (Singapore finally fell in February 1942). On December 11th 1941, Germany and Italy declared war on America.

While the British gradually pushed the Germans and Italians out of North Africa, and the little Island of Malta (then a British colony) earned a George Cross for its resistance to repeated German air attacks, the Americans planned for what would be the Normandy landings. In the east, Soviet forces slowed and then stopped the German advance. If you want to read an account of desperate men, fighting eye-to-eye, in appalling conditions, you could do no better than Antony Beevor's history of the battle for Stalingrad.[11] Hitler threw all that he could into a struggle that might have gained the Reich Russia's oilfields, but the Soviet leader poured in enough men to stop him and the Russian winter did the rest. The battle was fought between July 17th 1942 and February 2nd 1943. Combined casualties may have reached 1.7 million. I have said it before and I will say it again. In the end, biology is a numbers game.

As the Soviet armies pushed west, British and American troops fought their way up Italy, and in June 1944 the allied invasion of France began. Whatever else one might say about the infamous Third Reich, the German soldier exhibited all the tenacity and courage of his forebears. But by the end of August, Paris had been liberated and on May 2nd 1945 Berlin surrendered to the Soviet army. In Indo-China, British Commonwealth troops were starting to regain lost territory and the Americans were working their way across the Pacific, island by island, against Japanese soldiers intent on fighting to the end.

But by then, three of the war leaders were already dead and one was about to be dismissed from office. Franklin Roosevelt had died on April 12th, Benito Mussolini had been killed by some of his own countrymen on April 28th, and on the 30th Hitler had shot himself. In July, Winston Churchill was defeated in a general election by Clement Attlee, leader of Britain's Labour Party, and on August 15th Japan surrendered after the new American President, Harry Truman, authorized two nuclear strikes, the first against Hiroshima on the 5th and the second against Nagasaki on the 9th. World War II may have been over, but war in Indo-China was not.

* * * *

---

11. Stalingrad (1998), Viking Press.

China's civil war did not end until December, 1949 when Mao Zedong's communist forces finally evicted Chiang Kai-shek's American-backed nationalists from the mainland. Japan had annexed Korea in 1910 and, at the end of the World War, Russia occupied the north of the country and America the south in accordance with an agreement reached at the Potsdam Conference, held in August 1945 between the Soviet Union, Britain and the United States, primarily to decide how to administer occupied Germany. Between June 1950 and July 1953, the Communist north, now backed by China, pushed south and the American-backed south countered by pushing north. After heavy fighting and many casualties, the two sides ended where they had started and an uneasy truce has remained in place since. During the campaign Truman contemplated using the atomic bomb and General Douglas MacArthur had barely been restrained from trying to march on Beijing.

After a stunning defeat by the communist-backed Viet Minh in May 1954, the French pulled out of Indo-China, granting independence to Cambodia and Laos, and leaving a puppet government in the south of Vietnam, pending elections. They never took place because the Americans, who had taken over the puppet regime from the French, were convinced the Communists would win. So much for democracy! Between 1959 and 1975, the communist-backed north fought an unrelenting campaign against the American-backed south, finally achieving victory on April 30th. It is estimated that 1.4 million soldiers died (58,209 of whom were American) and up to 2 million civilians. In 1961 and 1962, President John F. Kennedy authorized the extensive use of chemicals to destroy crops and their residue is still undermining the health of Vietnamese people today.

It is hard to know where to end what has become a catalogue of human folly or, as I would prefer to put it, repeated examples of our biological drivers at work. Britain granted independence to India in 1947, and when it became apparent that Muslims and non-Muslims were not going to be able to live with one another (a result, in part, of Britain's imperial policy of divide and rule), the country was partitioned and some 500,000 were killed in the resulting recriminations.

After the First World War, Britain had been given responsibility for administering Palestine where Jewish groups had been buying up land with a view to establishing their own state. By 1947, Britain had had enough of trying to keep Arab and Jew apart and had been unable to find a solution that would satisfy both parties. On May 14th 1948, one day before the British mandate expired, David Ben-Gurion declared Israel to be an independent state. High-level and low-level conflict has continued between Jew and Arab ever since.

The attachment of present-day Jews to their land in Palestine attests to the power of a story. Ancient Judea and Israel were tribal areas variously controlled by the Egyptians, Persians, Greeks (under Alexander the Great) and Romans. For at least 2,000 years, there had been no independent Israel and yet the story of an ancient homeland persisted. The modern Israeli state consists of a tension matrix that evolved in Europe and now relies on American support. It was transported to the Middle East against the advice of General George C. Marshall (author of the Marshall Plan to resuscitate Europe after the Second World War) who saw it causing nothing but trouble.

Arab Palestinians came under the influence of Islam in the 7th century, with Jerusalem falling to Muslim control in 636 after the Roman garrison there capitulated. Jews and Christians in the city were allowed to continue in their faith however.

Following the collapse of the Ottoman Empire after the First World War, its many parts have been struggling to establish independent Arab-Islamic structures in the face of persistent Western interference. Even when we do not know our history, its residue influences us greatly.

* * * *

Today the countries that were once part of the Ottoman Empire, although excluding those in Eastern Europe but including Morocco in the far west of North Africa, have a total population of some 300 million people. If you add Saudi Arabia and Iran you are close to 400 million. Their faith is predominantly Muslim and a majority are Arab. When the Ottoman Empire came to an end after the First World War (by backing the losing side), its territories, except for Turkey which became a secular republic, were divided up between the victors. The spheres of influence were as follows: France — Morocco, Algeria, Tunisia, Lebanon, Syria; Italy — Libya; and Britain — Egypt, Palestine, Jordan, Iraq. All these countries (except for Palestine) are now independent nations, although each has experienced a high degree of European and American interference.

Islam is a very complete religion and it is probably fair to say that most people were happy to lead their traditional family-structured lives and to leave it to their princes to build courts of earthly splendor. The idea of a world which an individual could access, change and build up for himself, outside his traditional arrangements — the idea at the heart of Protestantism — was (and to some extent still is) alien to Islam. It wasn't that these things couldn't be done, it was just that they were not seen as being particularly important. Islamic Fundamentalism, a movement that exists, in varying degrees, across the Muslim world today, is a reaction against Western values seeping into Muslim culture as well as a reaction against Western interference in Arab affairs.

As in any loosely-connected group of people, there are factions whose own story is stronger than the national story they are part of. In Iraq, Sunni and Shi'a have been battling it out for power ever since the Americans and British, in a particularly cack-handed intervention, almost destroyed the idea of Iraq as a nation. In Lebanon, Western-backed Sunni, Druze and Christian factions seem eternally poised on the brink of civil war with the Shi'a Hizbollah and Amal factions backed by Iran (the previous one lasted for 15 years and destroyed the country). The Palestinian people are not only split geographically between the Gaza strip and the West Bank, but politically between Hamas and the Palestinian Authority.

When young men have scant employment prospects and factional loyalties are the only game in town, it is hardly surprising if they expend their energies in that direction. The idea of the nation state is still fragile in much of the Arab world, and is probably a flawed model in any event. All self-interested Western meddling does is to give the disaffected a focus away from where it is most needed — on building up the infrastructure that will improve their lives.

The Arab world must find its own way to modernity. Islam is central to its story and empowers individuals far more effectively than any crude overlay of democratic structures will do. Many in the West often seem to forget that what we call democracy did not spring out of thin air, but is the outcome of a long process in which Christian (and pre-Christian) values vied with secular necessities to create the cerebral structures we possess. Cerebral structure is felt. It does not exist apart from us. There are undoubtedly principles that should be applied (and, indeed, it is these I am arguing we must learn), but whenever human beings place form before substance they reap a bitter harvest.

* * * *

> Our tendency to ignore other people's history because we take our own for granted, is one we should vigorously resist. A brief look in the following section at the way in which the countries of South America evolved shows, rather clearly I think, how cerebral structure, even when it is rebuilt, is a product of its past.

An intriguing question is why did North and South America develop in such different ways? The simple answer, which also may be the right answer, is that South America (in its modern guise) was the child of Spain and Portugal, whereas North America was the child of Northern European Protestants. What Spain and Portugal brought to the New World was the Catholic Church and aristocratic elites. In Argentina, the great landowning families and the Church ran the country until the mass of the people demanded a voice. However, when the people found their voice they didn't know what to say, other than to call for mass programs that were often economically indefensible. Unlike the Puritan families, who settled along the east coast of North America, they were economically illiterate.

At over 380 million, South America has a similar-sized population to the Arab world. 180 million of them live in Brazil and of those, a majority are under 25 years old. South America is a region full of young people. There was a time, between about 1880 and 1916, when Argentina was one of the world's ten richest countries. But left-wing populism took hold and the nation ground to a halt. The standing joke was that Argentina had a great future behind it.

It seems to be one of the truisms of revolutionary change that a people embarking on it will invariably install a harsher version of the system they are trying to get rid of. Napoleon was more absolute than Louis XIV, Stalin was every bit as terrible as Russia's Ivan and Mao Zedong could have stood side by side with any of China's great emperors. And as for Juan and Eva Perón, what a parody of kingship were they. The reason for this is that evolution is creative and will produce new solutions, whereas revolution is regressive and will just put different people in the same chairs because no one can conceive of anything else. In a perverse way, revolution keeps the story intact, whereas evolution subtly changes it in ways no one could have anticipated.

Modern South America started as a reflection of Spain and Portugal, where there was no habit of individual self-government. The aristocracy attended to business, which was mostly agriculture and warfare, and the Church attended to morals. In the New World, after the initial invasion, the aristocracy was happy to get out from under the thumb of the king and to leave aside warfare for making money and spending it. The army was the most effective secular hierarchy in the various countries, and as in Spain in the civil war of 1936–39, Church and aristocracy and army (and very often a sizeable portion of the population, who were far from convinced by radical ideas) invariably ended up dominating South American politics.

Whatever one's romantic view of the *Left* might be, or how great one's detestation of *the generals*, few South American countries possessed a cerebral structure capable of combining multi-party democracy with effective government. Beneath the surface, however, evolution was taking place. Right and Left were both learning lessons. Chile after Pinochet became an exemplary multi-party democracy, just as Spain did after Franco. Brazil has had a left of center government for many years now, and is flourishing. If *the generals* were responsible for abuses, the Left must take its share of the blame. Populist ideologues, peddling promises they could never fulfill, have been the cause of much misery in the world and they should be ashamed, rather than thinking of themselves as injured beauties.

> These conflicts between conservatives who put the order they represent above all things and radicals who believe that change can only come about by a complete dismemberment of the order that exists, are truly dialogues of the deaf. Each behaves like a competing carnivore, dependent on the flesh of the other to keep itself alive.

* * * *

The most recent aftershock arising from the demise of the old European order, and yet another example of how our past can be ever-present, was the collapse of Yugoslavia. Originally a federation of Slavic states, it was once part of the Hapsburg Austro-Hungarian Empire. Broken up by Italy and Germany in the Second World War, it was reformed under the control of the Communist faction, led by Marshal Tito, whose charismatic and effective leadership managed to suppress the federation's national divisions. In the 1970s, however, a recession in Europe and bad economic management in Yugoslavia itself led to the IMF imposing strict conditions on the country. By 1984, these had been tightened further in the hope that *Shock Therapy* would push the country towards a capitalist system. By 1989, this tough love resulted in some 600,000 workers losing their jobs and a further twenty percent of the workforce going unpaid.

All this was going on at the same time as negotiations to adjust the relationship between the various republics that made up the federation, with Serbia resisting fragmentation and the other republics moving towards independence. Tito's death in 1980 had already removed an important symbol of Yugoslavian unity. Civil war broke out in 1990 and the world's television sets were treated to scenes of ethnic cleansing, as Serbs ousted Albanian Kosovars from territory they considered theirs, and the Kosovars reciprocated in kind, but with far fewer resources. Kosovo had once been part of the Ottoman Empire and borders largely-Muslim Albania to the south, the only country occupied by the Third Reich in which the Jewish population actually increased (Jews and Muslims have a long history of rubbing along together, although usually with Muslims occupying the dominant role).

The international community did not cover itself in glory, although the European Union did try to make amends, after peacekeepers had finally brought the conflict under control, by hauling Slobodan Milosevic, the Serbian leader, in front of the Hague Tribunal on war crimes charges, but he died before the case could be concluded. They have recently arrested the Bosnian Serb leader, Radovan Karadzic, and doubtless hope to find this man guilty before he, too, dies.

> Judicial activism runs the risk of becoming crass empire-building however egregious the case to be tried, particularly when its reach goes beyond its statutory boundary. Throwing a boundary condition around a structure that was not party to the formation of that boundary condition is a form of cerebral imperialism we should guard against.

* * * *

We have almost completed our forced march through history. I will have dwelt too long in some places and moved too fast in others, and I have certainly been very selective. But what I hope I have shown is some of the often unintended and frequently violent steps that have brought us to where we are. My argument, of course, is that we have largely been following a biological script, albeit one that has steadily been augmented by our conscious intent — or as I am calling it, by cerebral structure — as we have moved rather haltingly from the biological to the cerebral system state.

This new evolutionary system state, as I believe it to be and have said, consists of the thought patterns we have embedded within our structures (the tension matrices) that are given their potency by the stories we have evolved to provide the context (or to establish the boundary conditions) within which we exist. The tension within this state, and which underpins its evolutionary dynamic, arises from each individual's reaction to the collective dictates of the structures he is part of and which make up the whole.

Unlike the species that populate the biological system state and must evolve in the direction of their specialty until they achieve an equilibrium, cerebral structures can re-form themselves around a new story and an adjusted tension matrix. This has substantially speeded up the evolutionary process. However, because our understanding of cerebral structure is still undeveloped, our organizations have assumed many of the characteristics of species. Individuals whose identity is largely defined by the boundary condition they are part of, such as the members of trades unions or particular industries, will act to defend that boundary condition, thereby inhibiting adaptation and change.[12] Nations, in particular, have behaved a little like dinosaurs. Their justification has invariably been their predatory relationship with other nations and their means has been internal control.

Differing from biological species that contain many individuals, a portion of whom must be lost to predation, human organizations function like the members of a species but grow by increasing the number of individuals they can coordinate, while being able to shed a portion of these individuals whenever they compete. Although warfare, the most basic form of competition between human structures, has been extraordinarily profligate in its expenditure of individual life, the dynamic arising out of this competition has spurred productive efficiency to such an extent that our cerebral structures can now sustain over 6.7 billion individual souls.

The challenge we face is how to evolve with intent rather than as a product of our biological drivers. The reason this seems to be so hard is that, as soon as an individual functions as part of a structure, he or she sets aside his sense of personal morality in favor of whatever morality is

---

12. In his superb analysis of this phenomenon in *The Rise and Decline of Nations: Economic Growth, Stagflation, and Social Rigidities* (published by Yale University Press in 1982), Mancur Olson (1832-1998) described how groups form within economies around particular activities and then exert political influence to protect their interests. These at first small structural rigidities accumulate over time to such an extent that a nation saddled with them eventually loses its ability to adapt and goes into decline.

embedded within the structure itself. If you are a member of an army your mission is to destroy your enemy; if you are a torturer your task is to extract a confession or information from those at your mercy, and so on. Naturally the structures within a tension matrix will attract those whose characters and skills suit them to the roles that make up the structure.

That Plato (c428–348BC) was discussing such things as the nature of justice, the state, government, democracy and tyranny over 2,000 years ago and we are still feeling our way and making the most heart-wrenching mistakes, should give us cause for concern. And for anyone who imagines that Communism as practiced was better than Fascism, on account of its seemingly more moral story, Archie Brown's *The Rise and Fall of Communism*[13] should serve as a salutary corrective.

If this historical perspective has suggested anything, it is surely that cerebral morality can only ever be the product of an interaction between individuals who have equal power. By contrast, biological morality can only ever see the individual members of a species as being a means to the end of that species' survival. This is the fundamental and absolute difference between the biological and cerebral system states.

Although a crucial innovation, the heart of the problem lies in the fact of hierarchy, the means by which particular functional skills are levered up within a tension matrix. Plato's distinction between the productive, protective and governing classes (which he associated with appetite, spirit and reason, respectively) has held sway from his time to ours, in one form or another, and has been at the heart of many ills. It separates individuals from the whole they are naturally part of, and in so doing undermines the morality that cerebral structure must rely upon if it is to detach itself from biology.

---

13. Published by Bodley Head, 2009. A masterly account of Communism's appeal to intellectuals in spite of that belief system's wholly immoral practice is *The Passing of an Illusion* by François Furet (University of Chicago Press, 1999).

A question worth asking, I think, because of Ancient Rome's place in history, is this: if the disposition of the Roman Empire was really so excellent, why did two monotheistic religions (Christianity and Islam) supercede it? The answer, I believe, is because these religions sought to make the individual whole again. Within the boundary conditions each provided, people were no longer just components of a mighty state but shared equally in a universal morality.

Secular life had to continue, of course, and an hereditary model was adopted for the very sound reason that it coincided with people's personal experience and seemed the least disruptive way of allocating power. But it was not the only game in town. High-handed they often were, but the high-born were subject to the same moral standard as the lowly-born. With the advent of Protestantism, the secular power that the Roman Catholic Church had accumulated was challenged along with the idea of heredity. A more complex social organization was evolving that required particular talents not associated with birth. An aspect of this complexity was an increase in diverse hierarchies: the traditional pyramid shape gave way to one that was shaped more like a bell.

As we saw, however, this transition proved to be highly destabilizing. With the demise of the Ancien Régime, a veritable proliferation of opportunities appeared to open up, not dissimilar to the Cambrian explosion.[14] Unfortunately, what were no more than ideas, some good and many bad, served to undermine the old story and the order it sustained, such that national boundary conditions assumed ever greater importance. As protospecies, the bizarre logic of these drove great swathes of humanity, as mindless sheep embedded within national flocks, into a self-destructive orgy of conflict.

We are still, I believe, far too ignorant about the moral nature of the structures we build. America's Founding Fathers did a good job in trying to create a moral tension matrix, where one structure countered the immoral tendencies of another and the freedom of the individual to pursue

---

14. The evolutionary biologist, Stephen J Gould (1941–2002), believed that evolution was characterized by long periods of relative stability, interspersed by periods of rapid change, of which the Cambrian explosion was one.

his happiness, under a law that applied equally to all, was set as the overriding objective. But even America is not immune to the moral blindness of structures. President Eisenhower's farewell speech to his people in 1961, in which he warned that America's military industrial complex had become so large a part of his nation's fabric that it might lead the republic astray from the values of its birth may focus on only one aspect of the problem, but it remains a salutary reminder of liberty's fragility.

> Until the latest of our world conflicts, the United States had no armaments industry. American makers of plowshares could, with time and as required, make swords as well. But now we can no longer risk emergency improvisation of national defense; we have been compelled to create a permanent armaments industry of vast proportions. Added to this, three and a half million men and women are directly engaged in the defense establishment. We annually spend on military security more than the net income of all United States corporations.
>
> This conjunction of an immense military establishment and a large arms industry is new in the American experience. The total influence — economic, political, even spiritual — is felt in every city, every state house, every office of the federal government. We recognize the imperative need for this development. Yet we must not fail to comprehend its grave implications. Our toil, resources and livelihood are all involved; so is the very structure of our society.
>
> In the councils of government, we must guard against the acquisition of unwarranted influence, whether sought or unsought, by the military-industrial complex. The potential for the disastrous rise of misplaced power exists and will persist.

It is an old problem. Julius Caesar was murdered on account of it. All too often a polity looks outwards because war seems an easier option than trying to solve its problems within. The projection of nationhood has proved a beguiling story precisely because it plays to one of our deepest biological drivers. The urge for conquest is no more (and no less) than a species' drive to colonize what it can.

Somehow we must elevate empathetic thought above blind biology as the principal driver behind human action. To achieve this and to blunt the myopia of boundary conditions that for functional reasons must be narrowly drawn, thoughts, and the feelings that generate them, need to be linked to some concept of the whole — hence my insistence that we see ourselves as part of the universe overall. We have concentrated almost exclusively over the centuries on individual morality. While clearly important, it will be in the context of the tension matrices we are part of that our evolutionary potential is expressed. As the tragedy of Communism has demonstrated, merely falling blindly behind a good-sounding story is not enough.

This makes it essential that we pay great attention to the morality of the structures we build, recognizing that change is to be welcomed and acknowledging that order is often an individual's only protection. The central question for us is surely this: do we need to go on slugging it out with one another militarily, and exploiting one another economically, in order to continue evolving?

If we compete to enhance life, rather than competing to exploit it, surely not.

In ***Part 3*** I will draw attention to some of the issues I believe we must think through in order to do this. We will consider the role of the human brain, how we function as individuals and how the relationships we build give rise to institutions that reflect our humanity. We will look at how new ways of doing things — new technologies — upset the status quo, and we will consider the process of change itself. Finally, we will examine how the political process reacts to change, sometimes managing to amend the dominant story and tension matrix to accommodate it, but at other times being overwhelmed by it. In ***Part 4*** we will contemplate the road ahead.

Chapter 10 – Historical Perspective

Part 3

HERE, IN PART 3, I will set out how I believe the dynamics we are subject to affect us. I adopt a building-block approach, starting with the human brain. As the organ most closely associated with cerebral structure, how it works is clearly important. In a few pages one can do little more than paint a picture, but hopefully this will suffice to show how the brain fits into my larger argument.

I then consider the position of the individual. Although in isolation we are insignificant things, save in our own eyes, the individual must be cherished as the only window we have into the universe. My daughter recently had her third child, a daughter named Pearl after my great-aunt, a wonderful lady who campaigned tirelessly to make life better for her fellow man.[1] Shortly after the birth I asked her elder sister, aged three, what Pearl's name was. There was a considered pause followed by the announcement: *Baby Jesus!* The symbol of the individual human child is one we should never lose.

1. There was nothing Pearl Chase didn't campaign for, from native Indian rights to the environment. Without position or elected office she got things done by the force of her personality and good sense. There is a lovely memorial to her and her brother near the beach in Santa Barbara where they lived. She was selected as their woman of the year by the Los Angeles Times in 1952. She died in 1979.

From the individual I move to relationships. It is extraordinary to think that out of that between a man and a woman the entire elaboration of our present social structure sprung. The tension between these two independent individuals, drawn together by a need that often confounds both, reflects the tensions that drive our human systems generally. What each of us strives for must be expressed through others against the cycle of birth, life and death. The tension matrix we are locked inside governs how we interact with each other and is justified in our conscious minds by a story. Consider, as just one example of this, the rich and changing imagery that has accompanied marriage.

I then go on to discuss institutions, arguing that each of those we now have draws its legitimacy from the issues that had to be dealt with by members of our earliest social groups. In effect they generalize and formalize those same feelings that give rise to relationships. The New Oxford Dictionary defines the word as a society or organization founded for religious, educational, social or similar purpose and gives a country's banks, Church or parliament as examples.

I will use a broader definition to encompass all formally-constituted organizations, while recognizing that we tend to think of institutions as being those associated with particular concerns we hold dear - law and order, justice, religion and governance in particular. They are, if you like, part of the essential grammar that we have evolved in order to live together. I suggest that the scale of modern society has separated many of us from our institutions, making them things out there, rather than part of our everyday lives, an unhealthy gap we should use technology to bridge.

Next, I consider technology itself, but probably not in the depth some might like. It is a big subject. But from my point of view technology is the man-made environment that is steadily separating cerebral structure from the biological world it is evolving from. I don't get into the debate about whether technology is going to leave man behind, because I think it is based upon a false premise. Technology is simply part of evolving cerebral structure and at the heart of cerebral structure are human brains. In *2001 A Space Odyssey*, the errant computer, *Hal*, was interesting because of its effect on crewman Dave, and so on us.

Trundling alone through space, *Hal* would not have been interesting at all. Technology's relevance lies in what it allows us to do. That said, we still have to learn how to manage it.

I then discuss the process of change which over the centuries has caused us such grief and brought us such rewards. ***Notes*** is about the dynamics of man precisely because change is a constant, even though all parts of the universe, including us, struggle to attain equilibrium. Although a simple-sounding word, change leads us down a long philosophical corridor. Should we be passive, and just go with the flow? Or should we seek to influence change by conscious intent? And if we should, to what end? Consciousness, I believe, demands that we put evolutionary change into some context, and it is this that I am attempting to do.

The engine of change, at least in so far as we are its motor, is politics — the ongoing conversation we have with one another about what we are doing and why we are doing it. In the final chapter of ***Part 3*** I suggest that we should see politics solely as the process whereby the story that justifies the tension matrix we are part of is built, maintained and amended, and that it should be separated more clearly than it is from government.

11

The Human Brain

I HAVE SUGGESTED that the next phase in evolution is the creation of cerebral structure. As cerebral structure is a creation of the human brain, we need to consider what the human brain is. This can be approached from four directions. What is the physical nature of the brain? What is the role of consciousness? What is the relationship between the brain and individual behavior? How do individual brains interact and give rise to collective behavior? Philosophically and practically we need to try to understand whether individual brains, acting in a loosely coordinated fashion within a tension matrix, constitute a creation that is bigger than the sum of its parts. If the answer is yes, as I believe it must be, then evolution depends upon how we manage this interaction.

The physical nature of the brain.

Anatomically, the human brain is about 3 lbs in weight (1.5 kg) and 1.6 liters in volume, consuming some 20–25% of the body's energy (although nearer 60% of an infant's). Males and females have the same ratio of brain weight to body weight and we seem to have reached an upper limit in brain size because anything larger would require the female to possess an even larger pelvic opening than at present, which would be structurally challenging.

Much of the brain is taken up with monitoring itself and the rest of the body and the biological basis of consciousness has so far eluded description. Some one hundred billion neurons (specialized cells) communicate chemically and electronically with tens of thousands of nerve cells. The increase in the size of the human brain, over the last 3–4 million years, was mostly associated with the neocortex (accounting for around 76% of the brain's mass), which is the part of the human brain most closely associated with language and consciousness.

A typical human brain is dealing with hundreds, probably thousands of tasks every second. Mostly these relate to maintaining a balance within the body — blood, oxygen, water and a whole host of chemicals that evolution has arranged into the functioning system that is us. All of this could take place without what we call thinking. Even our response to extreme positive and negative stimuli could be left to the autopilot within us, and to an outside observer it would appear that our actions were self-directed.

It was once thought that the brain evolved like any other physical component — such as a lobster's large claw or wasp's sting — but it appears that a large number of mutations, over a comparatively short period of time (only some tens of millions of years), was necessary to bring the human brain to where it is today. As one moves up the evolutionary chain, the ratio of brain size to body size tends to increase, but the acceleration in respect of the human brain, after humans parted from chimpanzees, is marked.[1]

It seems that the brain starts with a jumble of interconnected neural pathways, which are rapidly cut down early in life as specific associations are formed. Different parts of the brain appear to be associated with different functions, with the right side associated more with creative tasks and the left side with establishing order. The forebrain, which includes the general lobes of the cerebral cortex, controls the higher functions, such as thought, reason and abstraction, while the

---

1. Follow the work being carried out by Bruce Lahn and his team at the University of Chicago.

mid- and hindbrain are more involved with the unconscious, automatic functions. As already stated, the neocortex, accounting for some 76% of the human brain's mass, is involved with communication and awareness.

Brain-related genes seem to have evolved faster than other genes, and in humans certain genes relating to brain size and brain behavior appear to have evolved faster still. This suggests that the brain was a medium (like the ocean or the air) into which a new class of biological components (a new class of protein structures) could form opportunistically (like the Cambrian explosion, for example[2]) and be whittled down, through the process of selection, on the basis of their usefulness.

Recent evidence[3] suggests that the rate of change of brain-related genes in humans may be slowing. The complexity of the brain is now such that mutations are less and less easy to accommodate. This is not an unusual pattern in biological evolution. As a structure becomes increasingly refined and specialized, its ability to adapt declines. I have called this the evolutionary cul-de-sac. Homo sapiens, as biology's great generalist, has so far avoided this fate. How we continue to avoid it, if the physical ability of our brains to evolve is diminishing, will be considered towards the end of this chapter. We turn, now, to the relationship between the brain and consciousness.

The role of consciousness.

Interest in the role of consciousness has grown apace over the last decade or so and a fierce debate has developed between those like Daniel Dennett (1942 –) who argue that the subjective quality of our sensory experience (the *ooh!* factor in a sunset, or sweet smell of a cinnamon roll as examples, and called *qualia* in the business) is the result of the evolved material correlates inside our brains (the dispersed neural networks that fire up and fix the content we are aware of at any given time) and others like David Chalmers (1966 –) who argue that subjective experience is more than the sum of its parts.

---

2. That time, 530 million years ago, when fossil records suggest the ancestors of most complex animals evolved, probably in response to a life-supporting improvement in the environment.
3. Work by professor Chung-I Wu, University of Chicago.

And of course the problem with the first person point of view (that which I have in my head and you have in yours) is that it must remain partly inaccessible to the scientific, third person point of view. This is the essence of subjective experience: *I know how you feel. No you bloody well don't!* For Dennett, what any of us feels will eventually be accessible (from a third person point of view) when we have worked out how that extraordinarily complex organ, the human brain, works. What I think David Chalmers would say is yes, we will surely be able to point to the synaptic and neural structures that fire up for a split second when a particular feeling is experienced, but this will still not fully capture a person's unique subjective experience.

Before I show my hand in respect of this debate there are other aspects of consciousness we need to consider. One I particularly like was put rather nicely by the biological psychologist, Petra Stoerig: 'the self/non-self distinction is the most basic in biology; it is really the first thing you have to have if you want not to digest yourself.'[4] From my point of view this is just another illustration of the ubiquitous nature of boundary conditions in the evolution of the universe. Our sense of 'self' also happens to be at the root of what Daniel Dennet believes is our distorted view of consciousness. We place a boundary around our point of view which causes us to see it as being distinct from what it has evolved from.

And it goes deeper still because we do not see trees and houses and cars and all the stuff that streams into our visual cortex every day, but electromagnetic waves which we interpret to be these things. Experiments into what has been called change blindness demonstrates that if we are shown two images of essentially the same scene but that are, in fact, slightly different, we are unlikely to notice the difference if we blink between them. In other words, we are not storing a detailed image but recreating an approximation in accordance with our expectations.[5]

---

4. From *Conversations on Consciousness* by Susan Blackmore, Oxford University Press 2005, p.220.

5. Experiments by Stephen LeBerge (1947 –) and his colleagues revealed that only 25% of 150 people shown Luis Buñuel's film *That Obscure Object of Desire* noticed that two different actresses played the central role in alternating scenes.

Unexpected things happen at the subconscious level too. Research has shown that people with brain lesions that blank out their visual field can still respond to images without being aware that they have seen them.[6] Enough is entering their brain for them to be able to react to the image, but not through the normal channel that would enable them to be aware of it.

From my point of view, consciousness must be put into a fresh context. There is the individual, certainly, because we are windows into the universe. It is not just 'out there' but in us. In this sense I'm with Dennett and we do need to see ourselves as something 'really big' not just as a point of consciousness around which everything else revolves. But my argument goes beyond that because what I am saying is that consciousness is an integral part of cerebral structure and, as a new evolutionary system state, will have its own rules. And this takes me closer to David Chalmers' point of view (I'm hedging my bets) in that it elevates consciousness to a plane above the biological (and all prior systems states) so that its rules (and all prior rules) will not capture this new structure, this new matter, call it what you will, in its entirety.

The point of view we have to adopt, I believe, is that of the universe as a whole. As individuals, what we perceive is partial, even though what we are part of is the whole, and we need to interact with the perceptions of our fellows in order to expand cerebral structure towards its potential. In Francisco Varela's (1946–2001) language, the phenomenology of the subjective, its wonderful intimacy, is embodied within the structure of the universe and we must learn how to 'see' it. From his perspective we would do well to try and integrate what Buddhism has learned about states of consciousness over thousands of years into our approach.

As for the mechanics, I am very much drawn to Roger Penrose (1931 –) and Stuart Hameroff's (1947 –) suggestion that if, as David Chalmers believes, consciousness is a fundamental property in the universe, then it must have existed (in some manner) at the outset. For

6. Research by Petra Stoerig at Heinrich-Heine University, Düsseldorf.

them the quantum state (in which conjugate variables, such as position and momentum, cannot be calculated with arbitrary accuracy) is the obvious candidate on account of its non-computability (in the conventional algorithmic sense). In my language this is the manner in which creativity can occur, the manner in which understanding fires up inside the brain by interpreting the stimulus it must contend with in a new way. Obviously the bulk of such 'firings' come to nothing because they are local to the individual. Some, however, will be reflected collectively, leading to incremental change, and a few, if given sufficient leverage, will lead to fundamental change.[7]

As we go forward, the problems we must overcome are that we are aware of only a portion of what is around us and are directed in what we do see by our biological drivers and the structures we ourselves have built. From my perspective, consciousness should be looked at not just as an individual phenomenon but in the context of the tension matrix and the story within which it functions and through which and by which it must evolve.

The brain and individual behavior.

A distinction needs to be drawn, although it may be an artificial one, between what goes on inside an individual's brain (the concern of psychiatry) and what goes on when individual brains interact collectively (psychology). When one individual behaves in an abnormal fashion, he or she might be consigned to a madhouse, although it is not often called that now. But when a whole nation exhibits collective madness all the rest of us can do is shrug helplessly, unless we are forced to go to war against it, as was the case when Germany fell badly off the

7. As a result of his work in anesthesiology, — and after reading Roger Penrose's book *The Emperor's New Mind* (1989) which suggested that consciousness was more likely a quantum process than a Newtonian one — Stuart Hameroff was drawn to the view that protein structures called microtubules, which make up the internal structure within nerve ends, might be the place where quantum effects were manifest. So far the jury is out on this, with critics branding the association of quanta with consciousness as pixie dust and the Penrose/Hammeroff side branding the computational approach of their critics as unprovable one way or the other.

rails in the 1930s. In this section we will concentrate only on relationships between an individual's behavior and that individual's brain. This inevitably takes us into the realm of extreme behaviors, because the relationship between 'normal' brains and 'normal' behavior is largely invisible to us.

Take schizophrenia, associated with genes on chromosome 6, and bipolar disorder associated with genes on chromosomes 18 & 21. Schizophrenics have a distorted view of reality compared to the rest of us and, although the state is associated with certain biological markers, the relationship is not yet clear. Some drugs can bring on the condition and social processes may also be a factor. Those with bipolar disorder are prone to wide mood swings, alternating, in extreme cases, between mania and depression. These conditions are not considered socially useful, or pleasant for individuals, and in time we may choose to screen out these variations by preventing embryos with them from being born, even if their link with behavior is not direct.

Brain scans of individuals with unusual skills, such as those with savant syndrome, reveal an unusual pattern of neural activity. Work carried out by Professor Allan Snyder and Dr. Elaine Mulcahy shows that when the left side of the brain of normal individuals is subjected to magnetic pressure (shutting it down somewhat), they exhibit some of the characteristics associated with savants, such as an ability to assess quickly and retain large amounts of data. Snyder believes that shutting down the left side of the brain allows individuals to access early brain processing associated with hand-eye coordination, which enables a person to 'know' the trajectory of a ball. In the 1988 film Rain Man, Dustin Hoffman plays an autistic savant able to 'know' how many toothpicks have fallen to the floor from a packet. In real life, Kim Peek, whose unusual ability spurred Barry Morrow to write the film script, can recall over 12,000 books from memory.

The capability of the human brain is undoubtedly greater than we realize. Some people with head injuries discover that their brain reconfigures itself, enabling them to perform different functions, occasionally at a higher level. It is as if the organ, relieved of performing some functions, compensates by drawing energy into others. The greater sensitivity of blind people to sound and touch is an example. That the brain can be trained to operate in certain ways seems clear. Indeed, there would be little point in education otherwise.

Studies of child prodigies suggest that their unusual talents (for their age) are probably a mixture of genetic propensity, nurture (often from a parent) and the child's own desire to excel. However, one of the problems child prodigies encounter, apparently, as they grow older and their abilities become less unusual, is that they are not necessarily able to convert raw ability into creative excellence. This suggests that the ability to be mechanically competent and the ability to create are separate. It also underscores the fact that the interplay between a brain and its body is contextual and holistic. A great diva is a physical manifestation which a brain develops in response to growing external appreciation. Without the voice box it couldn't happen. Without the applause, it wouldn't.

Should the era of designer babies ever dawn, the dilemma we will face is that the creativity and dynamism of cerebral structure depends upon the diversity of individuals which, of course, helps to put the tension into the tension matrix. We might well conclude that, after screening out mutations that cause (or are strongly associated with) severe physical and mental disabilities, it would be best if we left the rest to the lottery of gene mixing and circumstance that prevails now.

That said, substantial moral issues will have to be addressed. Psychopathic behavior (behavior that is amoral and antisocial in the extreme), may, for example, be at the far end of a continuum that includes those vital (and often irritating) individuals who are not easily swayed by the consensus, and occasionally prevent us from behaving like lemmings. And if our prisons are full of individuals with certain identifiable characteristics and situational backgrounds, it behoves society to improve the environment its citizenry grows up in before even thinking about screening for what might be, under certain circumstances, unhelpful characteristics.

But we shouldn't be too squeamish either. Men and women who have murdered and harmed in an unprovoked and predatory manner should probably be kept out of harm's way for good. There is no evidence I am aware of that justifies parole boards reaching a contrary conclusion. It seems far too easy for the authorities (in Britain, at least) to persuade themselves that an individual is a changed person, on the basis of that person's behavior in a prison environment. With the constraints of prison removed it is rarely explained, with any rigor, why the individual won't revert to his or her prior behavior. The time may come when we can offer individuals procedures that will alter their behavior more effectively than the frontal lobotomy ever did.[8] But until then, we should be cautious.

Prison time is an aggressive intervention, supposed to protect the public from the socially dangerous. It is also supposed to deter antisocial behavior and rehabilitate those caught straying from what is deemed to be the straight and narrow. As part of the criminal justice system, prison, one of mankind's great institutions, grew out of our desire to banish from the tribe those who simply did not fit in. But thanks to the notion that *the punishment should fit the crime*, it has, I think, become something rather different: a validation of certain behaviors. For many it would seem that committing the crime and doing the time are perfectly rational considerations. This hardly seems like a smart way to manage voluntary behavior. And when crimes are committed as a result of largely involuntary behavior, it may not be so smart either.

---

8. A procedure, popularized in the 1930s, that entailed cutting the connections to and from the prefrontal cortex. Used on some 40,000 people in the United States, 17,000 in Britain and over 9,000 in the Scandinavian countries, many of whom were in mental institutions, the procedure involved pushing an ice pick into the brain via the orbital cavity and moving the point around to dismember the cortex. Justified on the grounds that it made many mental patients easier to handle, it was savagely criticized in 1948 by Norbert Wiener, who suggested that killing the patients would make handling them easier still. Joseph Kennedy submitted his 23-year-old daughter, Rosemary, to the procedure, on account of her moodiness. The lobotomy reduced Rose to an infantile state, including incontinence and incoherent babbling. Her sister, Eunice, founded the Special Olympics in her honor in 1968 and the film *One Flew Over the Cuckoo's Nest*, based on Ken Kesey's 1962 novel, rammed home, to a wider public, the horrors that can ensue when the hubris of the medical profession is left unchecked.

We will consider in a later section whether rehabilitation wouldn't be better-placed within a different institution, such as education. The extent to which some behaviors are involuntary, given a mix of background, circumstance and genetic profile, is far from clear. What we do know is that individuals can be trained to commit acts in times of war that in peacetime would be considered criminal. The link between brain structure and individual behavior is still largely opaque and the mechanics behind volition little understood. What is surely beyond reasonable doubt, however, is that most of us, most of the time, act on the basis of perceived consequences. If the reference point against which we measure consequences is simply ourselves, or a small group with whom we identify, the rather clumsy threats of the criminal justice system are unlikely to influence our behavior very much. We will consider the role of peer pressure next.

Collective action and the interaction between individual brains.

From an evolutionary standpoint, one would expect brains to exhibit mutations from time to time and for these mutations to affect individual behavior. If a mutation improved an individual's life chances, then theoretically at least every time that mutation appeared it would give the individual possessing it a better chance, so that over time, those with that mutation would swamp those without it. With humans and other social animals, however, the most potent evolutionary mutations are likely to have been changes in collective behavior.

The demise of Neanderthal man, who existed in Europe 130,000 years ago and seems to have been eclipsed by Homo sapiens (who probably moved north from Africa) 100,000 years later, remains a mystery. The cranial capacity of Neanderthal man was, if anything, greater than that of Homo sapiens. In Europe's harsh northern climate, the self-sufficiency of Neanderthal man (who appears to have relied on a diet of meat) may, like the wolf, have depended upon small hunting groups. It is possible that Homo sapiens, blessed with the more benign African climate, evolved larger and more complex social structures, and that these simply overwhelmed Neanderthal man when Homo sapiens migrated slowly north, as Europe's climate improved.

Much of what happens to our brains, as they are tuned by experience into the prevailing cerebral structure of the societies we are born into, is the destruction of potential, an ordering, almost a normalization, if you will, which recasts a rather malleable organ into one adapted to its surroundings. This obviously has many advantages (not least, that it enables a child to function within his or her society), but carries dangers as well. Prejudices and misinformation are transmitted from one generation to the next (along with vital information) and unusual abilities or propensities tend to be suppressed.[9] There is also a presumption that whatever society deems it necessary to do is what should be done: a potentially dangerous circularity that will lead, ultimately, into an evolutionary cul-de-sac.

The herd instinct is a fundamental biological driver in almost all brain-directed animals, be it towards prey or away from danger. It is a coordinating mechanism that has ensured survival. An elaboration of this is hierarchy. The most able in a group, in terms of survival criteria, tends to be followed. The divine right of kings was built around the same driver, although in the human sphere the office became more important than the individual. And it was the office that both Cromwell and Robespierre were anxious to murder.

In war, the game is to lose fewer men than one's opponent, but when a soldier goes into battle his brain is not calculating the odds of survival and measuring them against some quotient of expected gain. Like each fish in a shoal, he is programed to act so as to give his group, his shoal, the best chance of survival. Sacrificing members of the group is part of the strategy, which every country's memorial day tries to reinforce. The soldier has to try and close his mind to the possibility that he will be one of those given up (in this, the unthinking fish has a distinct advantage), and take comfort at being thought a hero if he is.

---

9. In her book *The Meme Machine* (1999), Susan Blackmore suggests that replication is a fundamental process in the universe and that we can usefully look at social constructs (such as altruism) as replicable memory structures she calls *memes* (following a suggestion by Richard Dawkins) which are spread by individuals on the basis of their perceived utility.

The tension matrix, within which we all function, is — first and foremost — a coordinating mechanism. Each of the system states through which the universe has evolved has been contained within a boundary condition defined by the laws that pertained to it. Like the others, the biological system state has displayed an opportunistic elaboration of possibilities, constrained by the boundary condition that is life-sustaining, no different from the temperature threshold within which subatomic particles were able to form. The evolution of consciousness elevates reasoned intent above such blind drivers as the herd instinct, which has operated so successfully within the biological system state. However, reasoned intent must establish a shared boundary condition in order to be effective.

What this means is that in place of the herd instinct which operates within a biological tension matrix, we are building (although evolving is really a better word) a tension matrix that reflects our reasoned intent about the sort of world we individuals want to live in, and is described, in general terms, by a story depicting that world which each of us carries in our head. As an evolutionary strategy it is far quicker to adapt than anything biology has to offer. Using reason and experience, groups of individuals can coalesce around new ways of adapting the matrix and attempt to influence the story each of us carries to that end.

The tension in the matrix, therefore, that underpins what I am calling cerebral structure, is generated by competing ideas, as opposed to the competition for survival that generates the tension within the biological matrix. The trick we are going to have to master, and which we are slowly mastering by a process of trial and much error, is how to build a matrix that can both generate and then synthesize competing ideas, without recourse to our blind biological drivers.

The future of the human brain.

I am drawn, repeatedly, to the idea developed by Noam Chomsky and others that the human brain has evolved a basic sense of grammar that underpins all language. This seems wholly logical to me, in that human brain size, human organization and human language all appear to have expanded over the same comparatively short (in evolutionary terms) timescale. And I think we can take this idea about how the human brain is evolving quite a bit further.

If the brain, as an organ, does not appear to be evolving much at present, then it is to how the brain is used that we should look. What is clear, I believe, is that the average human brain has a great deal of underutilized potential. Although an ability to count instantly the number of toothpicks that fall from a box onto the floor is not very useful in the context of our lives as they are currently constructed, and so in most of us has been suppressed (as the research of Snyder & Mulcahy and others implies), this strongly suggests that our evolving matrix can access capabilities within our brains that are largely hidden from us at present. It also lends weight to my contention that more than a trivial amount of what we do collectively is driven by biological processes of which we are similarly unaware.

Along with the essential grammar of language, the most fruitful areas to consider, I think, are those procedures I discuss in the chapter on institutions, that enable the members of a tribal community to function together, and which, over time, I believe, have evolved into the institutions we have today. I argue that the members of all human communities possess an inbuilt sense of what those institutions represent. However, there has often been a trade-off between the consensus evident in well balanced communities and the use of force apparent in those facing a crisis, real or imagined. In such circumstances, so as to prevent community collapse, distorted structures often evolve that revert to the brutal matrix of biological survival.

An example of such a structure is the evolution of a secret police. In a tribal situation, the forerunners of such a police are the eyes and ears of the community as a whole, which serve to keep the tribe's members singing from the same hymn sheet and in touch with one another's feelings. Fast-forward to Nazi Germany and the communist Soviet Union of the 1900s, and you find communities of such scale, whose traditional institutions (for all their faults) have effectively been lobotomized with the sophistication of an ice pick (see note 8 on page 181), that a structure, such as a secret police, was about the only way the new story (the new ideology) could be forced into people's heads, so that the majority of them functioned in some sort of harmony. Even the poor Jews in Nazi Germany and refuseniks in Soviet Russia shuffled off to their horrible demise in a more or less orderly fashion, cowed by the idea of a community of which they felt themselves part.

The great challenge for humanity has been to evolve scale-supporting structure at the same time as preserving what it means to be human. The only way we can do this is by engraving the meaning of our institutions, which reflect our deepest feelings, onto the brains of each of us, and by making sure these institutions are the possession of us all. I suggested earlier that the use of prison in our criminal justice system may have become counterproductive. So let me elaborate.

Criminality is an artificial construct, in the sense that what behavior is or is not deemed illegal is decided by a community, under some process, and then defined in words. Attached to each illegal behavior is a punishment, usually expressed as a range of penalties, which a court can apply according to circumstance, in recognition of the fact that the seriousness of an illegal behavior should be judged in its context. In countries with an Anglo-Saxon legal system, evidence of illegality is presented to a jury of the accused's peers, who must decide if the individual is guilty as charged, beyond all reasonable doubt.

In many respects, the process sticks closely to what one imagines went on, although with less formality, in tribal communities. The urge to steal would have overwhelmed some people occasionally, and no doubt jealousy would sometimes have caused others to injure those they thought responsible. Most of the time, antisocial behaviors would have been dealt with by a severe look or harsh comment, but occasionally a formal meeting of the whole community would have been needed to decide upon a matter over which there were conflicting views. Very occasionally, in instances of extreme behavior, a community member might have been banished.

The problem that arises when scale and structural elaboration enter the equation is that the boundary condition which defines what is socially acceptable for an individual may become separated from that which defines what is socially acceptable for the community as a whole.

The reference point for the gang member is likely to be the gang. The reference point for the career criminal is likely to be the criminal fraternity. The reference point for the terrorist is likely to be his or her ideological cell. In short, for some people, the criminal justice system will lack any moral authority, which is the bedrock of community justice. For such people the calculation is simply between the perceived benefits of the crime and the inconvenience of getting caught.

Whenever criminality, as opposed to justice, becomes institutionalized in this way (becomes part of the structure of the community), society loses its most effective sanction (people acting in the 'right' way because they *believe* it to be the right way) and must fall back on harsher punishments or higher rates of interdiction, or both. Such measures are not only expensive but serve to exaggerate the already divided nature of a community.

Unfortunately, the disconnect between our evolved institutions and what people feel is not restricted to the criminal justice system, but almost certainly applies to them all. Education does not always educate; democracy often leaves whole groups out in the cold; our military does not always concentrate on defense; our medical establishment often fails to deliver adequate health care; executive power is often distorted by the few things it can do; our regulatory system is often crisis driven; our economic system is often hampered where it shouldn't be and unhampered where it shouldn't be; our media often feeds on the sensational and neglects the important; government is less accountable than it should be; our universities try to answer the small questions they are paid to answer, rather than the large questions society needs them to answer; our family lives are often subject to extreme pressures; and in the past, our spiritual lives became a battleground for religious power and we are the poorer for it.

All of this might seem to have taken us a long way from the human brain, but if our institutions are the guardians of our freedom and the foundation of our evolutionary potential, then we need to reconnect what they mean with those feelings that underpin them. Communities defined by distinct boundary conditions tend to look at each other with great hostility. That is how biology is designed to work. But we need to get beyond that. We need to talk to one another in the shared language we in fact possess. Cerebral structure is the grammar that allows us to do so. Our respective institutions might appear distinct, but they draw on feelings we all share, and we can learn much from each other's experience. It is essential that we train our brains to recognize substance over form, not just in others, but in ourselves and in the structures we jointly build.

12

The Individual

GIVEN THAT there are over 6.7 billion human beings, it is remarkable that each of us considers himself special. In terms of the overall population, we are not special. As far as our attributes go, whatever lights we may have will most likely remain hidden under a bushel. Not only will the universe be unaware of our brief existence, but even the other nobodies living in the adjacent street to ours will likely remain similarly ignorant. *Body of man found in home. Had been dead a month* makes the headlines because we are convinced we should matter. The mindless chatter of care workers around the old, infirm and dying (*Come on, Rose. Let's have a smile from you*) attests to our conviction that life without social intercourse is not life at all. It is almost as if we are terrified of being alone. To be part of the herd, in whatever capacity, seems to us essential, and still we imagine ourselves special.

2,500 years ago, give or take, Siddartha Gautama abandoned the life of an Indian prince in search of truth. Having experienced one extreme, he subjected himself to the other and almost died from his privations. With these outer boundaries established, he went on to commit his life to teaching moderation and self-awareness through contemplation. Buddhist monks today continue his tradition and almost all religions have orders dedicated to spiritual awareness. Regardless of denomination, the purpose of these is to re-engage the individual with the universe, rather than have him blow this way and that on the capricious winds of sensation and passing sentiment.

Unfortunately, the quest for truth at an individual level can translate very badly at the collective one. Weak reeds, when wrapped around an ideology of certainty, become binding chains. When some of Mussolini's Black Shirts bundled Giacomo Matteotti (1885–1924), leader of the Socialist Party in the Italian parliament, into the back of a car and stabbed him several times with a carpenter's file while he was struggling to escape, they acted with the strength of belief. Mussolini justified the killing on the grounds of bringing order back to the country (although in reality Matteotti was silenced because of his attempts to expose fascist tricks). And although happy to be spared the gory details, many Italians, disgusted (and frightened) by the chaos communist and socialist strikes were causing, applauded Mussolini's justification for the act.

Probably the only Russian leader who has genuinely believed in democracy, Boris Yeltsin (1931–2007) — the first to be popularly elected — ended his time in office reviled because the free-market reforms he pushed through caused a great deal of hardship for ordinary Russians. The individual can only see the food on his plate and pay in his pocket, and generally supports whichever leader and program he thinks will ensure that those two staples keep coming his way. Unlike Christianity, Communism offered the prospect of well-being in this life, and Lenin was shrewd enough to realize that at a time of great uncertainty (which the Bolsheviks, like the Fascists, helped stir up) the most ruthless leader was likely to win. Yeltsin's successor, Vladimir Putin, has placed order above democratic niceties (such as a free press), and seems very popular in consequence.

* * * *

In just two pages we have moved from a mass of nobodies to a Buddha, then to a murderer, hero of the Right, and on to his victim, a hero of the Left. We have mentioned a great Russian democrat, whose predecessors included the first Communist Tsar and whose successor defies political description. Each one an individual, certainly, but an individual who represented a story. So does the word *individual* mean what we think it means? And I have yet to mention a single celebrity from the world of entertainment. We need to back up a little.

Sigmund Freud (1856–1939) may have been eight tenths flimflam — most of his assertions are unprovable — but he did capture the spirit of his age and he did resuscitate an interest in the subconscious that goes back beyond biblical times. In accordance with his era, he tried to give it a scientific gloss, which is odd considering that he saw his work as running counter to the cult of objective rationality which was so popular at the time. I have talked about each of us having a moral compass — that is a set of simple values, which seem to be widely shared, about how humans should behave. I have also said that we are subject to biological drivers, the result of evolved survival criteria. Finally, I have suggested that we have conscious intent and that it is this which we are slowly using to build cerebral structure.

Freud's rather neat characterization (which shows why he was so good at marketing his ideas) was *ego*, *super-ego* and *id*, where the *id* was our impulsive selves, the *super-ego* was our sense of right and wrong and the *ego* was our synthesis of the two. His obsession with an individual's sex life and parents overwhelmed much of his work. He documented numerous cases of childhood abuse amongst his patients, which he subsequently had to recant and put down to fantasies. Psychoanalysis has moved on a long way since then, but you only have to watch old soldiers recount their battlefield memories, with tears in their eyes, as if it were yesterday, to appreciate that stored experiences sit, at some level, within every human mind. But it would be odd if they did not. How else could an individual human gain experience?[1]

We still know remarkably little about how the interaction between our biological character and experience affects our subsequent behavior. We know that soldiers can be trained to kill. We know that kids left to

---

1. Teams at the Brain and Behavior Discovery Institute at the Medical College of Georgia School of Medicine and scientists at East China Normal University in Shanghai, believe they have isolated a 'memory molecule' in a mouse and used it to remove its painful memories. With this, brainwashing has taken on a whole new meaning!

their own devices in rough neighborhoods work it out for themselves. We know that some businessmen will resort to what subsequently is considered unethical behavior when the pack is in full cry. We know that the children of parents who fight suffer. In fact we know that just about everything it is possible to imagine a human being doing, some human will have done.

In the natural environment, a self-directed organism is disciplined both by the constraints of its structure (its physical boundary condition) and that environment. Only mutant behavior that aids survival is likely to persist. In the human environment, a wide range of behaviors seems to exist. Liberalism is predicated on the assumption that all behaviors should be tolerated save those shown to be harmful to others. A benefit of such an approach is that it will probably encourage diversity, and a diverse environment should be a richer one for us all. Unfortunately it is not always clear how harm to others follows from individual behavior, save in obvious instances such as when one person stabs another with a carpenter's file.

No human individual can function without a cerebral as well as a physical boundary condition. A person's interaction with the natural world provides a physical boundary. Extreme sports, and perhaps warfare, do so, for men at least. For women, having children and nurturing children do the same. In such circumstances the dynamics of the situation discipline, restrict and channel behavior. But because we are conscious, reflective beings, we also need to be able to establish what we are in the context of some cerebral framework. The word *individual* therefore means more than just our particular characteristics (we all are different to some degree). It also means how we develop these characteristics in conjunction with the cerebral structure we are part of.

* * * *

The function of hierarchy, within a tension matrix, is to lever up, and so make more potent, certain attributes that are held to be beneficial to the matrix and its story. The pomp that surrounded kings, for example, was designed (or rather evolved) to solidify a people's sense of community as well as reduce the likelihood of power struggles. Regicide was therefore deemed to be a crime against the community, and not just an assault against the person of a king.

As revolutionaries, bent on regicide, both Cromwell and Robespierre had to convince their followers using quasi legal argument in public court that the person of the king they sought to murder had somehow become a threat to the very community that king represented. By contrast, as he had already passed the point of no return when they were captured, Lenin was happy to have the Romanovs murdered without the benefit of a show trial and their bodies disposed of in unmarked graves.

We have not found it easy to distinguish between an individual — as an individual — and an individual as an exponent of a particular attribute of our tension matrix and its story. As our consciousness has elaborated, and the hierarchies within our tension matrices have multiplied to reflect this, we have become better at seeing the role an individual occupies within a hierarchy as something separate from what they are as individuals. In other words, we are beginning to learn the grammar that underlies cerebral structure. The fact that we often now occupy positions in several hierarchies has made this easier. The problems faced by the leader of a small discussion group, for instance, are not entirely dissimilar to those faced by a president.

We are also becoming more aware of, and interested in, the overall character of the individuals who occupy positions at the top of these hierarchies. We believe that they represent aspects of ourselves and so should reflect what we think of as our better characteristics. This has given rise to the minders of such individuals running behind their luminaries, be they politicians, film stars or golfers, with the equivalent of pooper-scoopers, in the event that their charges are caught doing something distastefully human.

While it is undoubtedly healthy that we are coming to appreciate our similarities, and it certainly enriches our lives mightily to be able to enjoy the unusual talents of our fellows (which multiple hierarchies have made possible), we must avoid slipping into old habits and according to great golfers, famous film stars, or even our best-known politicians, attributes of general divinity they do not possess. When we do this we are only expecting them to reinforce our prejudices anyway, thereby sparing us the effort of having to think about things for ourselves.

* * * *

The problem we face in our largely man-made environment is that we have to institute those constraints the biological world previously provided, even though we cannot be sure about outcomes because of the creative nature of the universe. The youth movement that gathered pace in the 1950s and '60s, for example, was frowned upon by many in the adult world. But luckily commerce came to the rescue as the great change agent. When Elvis Presley was finally invited onto *The Ed Sullivan Show* on September 9th 1956 (Sullivan having earlier vowed never to have him on), the camera crews were under strict instructions to keep away from his groin.

Even though the show was a smash hit, attracting around 60 million people, Jack Gould began his review in *The New York Times* by observing that Elvis Presley injected movements of his tongue and indulged in wordless singing that was singularly distasteful, adding that over-stimulating the physical impulses of the teenagers was a gross national disservice. One can only hope that his own tongue was stuck firmly to at least one of his cheeks. Of course, looking down, or up, at our drug-fueled world today, he is probably saying *I told you so.*

* * * *

A significant evolutionary breakthrough on the road to cerebral structure was the appearance of two great monotheistic religions (both offshoots of Judaism) within a short time of one another. For large numbers of people in the Mediterranean world, a common moral framework suddenly became available. Inevitably, I suppose, both Christianity and Islam established boundary conditions and sadly the greatest sin, according to the most strident advocates of these religions, was to deny their sect's omnipotence. A little rape or pillage, even the occasional murder, could be forgiven, but blasphemy — Oh no! Such flagrant double standards might not have upset the ignorant poor, but in today's better-educated and more curious age such shoddiness has cost the Catholic Church dear (and will probably do the same for Islam).

What these two religions did provide, however, across each of the Muslim and Christian worlds, was a common story that tied together a large number of relatively independent secular structures. A Muslim or Christian individual could move around his world with a set of expectations about how he and others should behave that was independent of the secular power structures he might encounter. Naturally this made the fault-line between Christendom and Islam quite distinct.

The great problem with morality is not its rules, which can often be expressed quite simply, but how to interpret them when the situation one confronts is new and the issues opaque. This follows from the fact that life is not a deterministic enterprise but a creative one. When 6.7 billion less one say that such and such a course of action is the correct one, and the lone holdout says it is not, where will the moral balance be thought to lie? I have always had a fascination for martyrdom since I saw gruesome woodcuts at school of men and women being tortured for their beliefs. How could they, I wondered, put up with such pain on account of an idea?

In time, my question was answered by my own revulsion at the spectacle. Those responsible for the atrocities were not worthy of the exalted status they had accorded themselves. But then when I hear about some good citizen being needlessly killed by a drug-crazed youth, my blood rises and I can see him being pulled limb from limb, quite slowly, in front of his compatriots. And this is the dilemma we face. The boundary condition that enables an individual to function is expressed in terms of felt imagery. Just as the Gautama Buddha found it necessary to experience extreme hardship in order to make sense of his easy start in life, so each of us has to construct a felt model that delineates a range for our behavior.

Rites of passage are part of this process, of which warfare may be an extreme example. It seems remarkable to me that so little of education is directed towards helping our young to build these models. Naturally they will build models as a direct result of felt experience because none of us can exist without them, but to allow this process to be solely the result of playground encounters at best, or back-street encounters at worst, seems to me a valuable opportunity missed. And this has got nothing to do with prescriptive morals, but everything to do with allowing our young to role-play, in a constructive environment, so as to discover, for themselves, where certain actions lead. Television and film have taken the place of the pulpit in portraying situations and their consequences but, like the pulpit, these have their limitations.

* * * *

During the First World War a rather remarkable thing happened. On Christmas Day 1915, troops all along the line started to call out to each other from their trenches, on opposite sides. Hey Frenchie, Tommy, want some schnapps? Bit by bit, here and there, small groups of soldiers walked onto the no-man's-land between them. This bit of chocolate was exchanged for that bit of sausage. Then Christmas carols were sung, with each line trying to outdo the other. It was a brief moment of humanity in an otherwise inhuman war. Most of the men at the front that year were volunteers. After only a few months they had come to question what they had so eagerly signed up to. If one ever wanted an example of how our structures think for us, the events surrounding that foul war will do well enough, although when it comes to examples, we are spoilt for choice.

The point is that neither the soldiers, nor the commanders, nor the politicians who sent them to battle, nor the national populations who cheered them on could have acted differently. The Kaiser was prisoner to a military tradition. If he had failed, he would not have been thought a man. Germany was a frustrated empire stuck in the middle of Europe in an age when empire was believed to matter. France was Germany's old adversary — a sort of standard football fixture. There was no realistic long-term prospect of Germany running France or of France running Germany, regardless of who won. Even Britain was stuck with its long-standing balance of power model — she would ally herself to any group of European powers so as to prevent any one becoming dominant.

If Britain had stayed out of the conflict, what would have been the result? Germany would have beaten France and both countries would have been bled dry. Britain would have emerged with its finances and empire intact, although the components of that empire were straining at the leash and starting to cost more than the empire was generating (just as the Western Empire had for Rome). WWI certainly accelerated social reform in the country, but there is every indication that would have taken place anyway. So was Lansdowne's *Entente Cordiale* with France to blame for getting his nation and the body of his son into the mud of Ypres? The hostility to his *Peace Letter* suggests otherwise. No, the cerebral structure of Europe was perfectly designed for conflict, and conflict is what it got. The entrance of the United States into the game in 1917 was wholly opportunistic, in spite of the grandiose language about peace and democracy and a League of Nations, and it heralded the American age.

So is the individual just a helpless cork, adrift on structural currents that will go where they will? No! But by heaven, we do make it difficult for ourselves. For any individual to change any aspect of cerebral structure is incredibly hard. Only very recently have we come to appreciate — and acknowledge — the value of the entrepreneur (the man or woman who sees how to do something better and pushes his idea forward), and this is true only in the specific field of business and markets. In most other areas, the change agent has to suffer greatly for his efforts, and martyrs still abound. For the individual to be motivated in the face of such odds means that he will have had to endure great privations. But unlike the way it was for the Gautama Buddha, these will not have been self-induced, but imposed, as the lockout and its attendant hardships were on Carnegie's workers. The martyr reacts to a sense of injustice, he does not normally engineer it.

What this means, unless humans start designing cerebral structure better, is that we will have to go on learning from our mistakes. In other words, only when a sense of injustice has built up sufficiently to persuade individuals that the cost to them, personally, of taking action is worth it, will they attempt to overcome the barriers to change that are currently built into cerebral structure. This becomes a messy and often confrontational process, warfare being an extreme example.

* * * *

There are obviously two aspects to improving the design of cerebral structure as it affects the individual. One relates to the configuration of the tension matrix and the other relates to how individuals react to the tension matrix, the two combined being the essence of cerebral structure.

A question I do not know the answer to is whether each of us needs to experience trial by fire in order to clarify our stand on issues. Based upon my own experience and what I have read about that of others, I believe we do. The creative process — which simply means the process whereby one sees something in a new light — almost always entails a fair degree of angst, because one is having to override existing preconceptions which have a comforting certainty about them. However, artists have not had to go to war to paint great pictures nor have entrepreneurs in order to create wonderful new products, so do we really need to go on fighting one another in order for cerebral structure to evolve?

One of the things I think was going on in the 18th, 19th and first half of the 20th centuries was that large numbers of individuals were feeling that they should have greater control over their lives. This was partly the result of urbanization and industrialization and partly the result of more rapid communication and rising living standards. The old rural model in which the Church supported a structured aristocracy (which pretty much had to be largely hereditary as there was insufficient wealth being produced by the mass of toiling farm laborers to maintain a sizeable middle class) could no longer cope. Power was moving into the factories and towns. Religion was becoming a consumer durable and the old safety valve of a little war here or a little war there, to mop up and entertain underutilized farm labor, was taking on industrial proportions, the more so as improvements in health and welfare had stimulated a sharp rise in population.

Change was in the air, but no one knew where it was going, and how could they? The old model was buckling at the joints, with some countries, like Britain, adapting better than others, such as Russia, and one in particular — America — with a population of independent-minded souls, in the enviable position of being able to design for itself new structures based upon the experience of others. Into this charged atmosphere ideas flowed like kerosene.

The First World War was almost like a massive social convulsion in response to stresses the system could no longer handle, with the Second World War its devastating aftershock. The boundary condition of Church and class that had once defined the outer limits of people's lives was melting in front of them. And this was as much the case for the 'haves' as the 'wanna-gets'.

In Russia, rather than reinforcing the old order, the war went badly and served to undermine it. A conflict with a common enemy turned into a civil war. As in England in the 1640s, the country was divided along ideological lines (White Russians versus Red Russians in place of Royalists versus Parliamentarians), with the same anti-establishment outcome. What tipped an individual into one camp or the other? Probably no great depth of thought in most cases. A bias here or there, a chance encounter, but neutrality was hardly an option. As one American president was prone to say, when a close examination of the issues would have been uncomfortable, you are either with us or against us.

The art of polarization is designed to prevent an individual from adopting a boundary condition other than that of friend or foe. By closing down a person's options to just two, he is made an object to be controlled, either as a 'friend' who must do as he is told to show that he is a friend, or as a 'foe', in which case he is beyond the pale and anything done to him is within bounds.

When the English were colonizing Ireland in the 14th and 15th centuries, they established a Pale around Dublin, with a radius of some 20 miles, which they gradually fortified against Gaelic incursion. If you were an Englishman in Ireland at that time, you did not want to live beyond the Pale. The Third Reich, of course, divided its population into them and us. It is a leadership trick as old as the hills, but what 'friends' often fail to realize is that they are as much its prisoner as their 'foes', although there may be substantial short-term compensations.

What this strongly suggests is that we need to look at the nature of boundary conditions as they affect both individuals and the larger social groupings they define. Biologically — and this is the key, I think — boundary conditions establish competitive synergies: everything feeds off everything else. A nation state (a large, elaborated tribal structure that defines itself as being different from other large, elaborated tribal structures that define themselves in the same way) is a boundary condition almost designed for war. Mercantilism, the notion that trade is a zero sum game (what one country gains another has to lose) was widespread in the 17th century. By the 19th, the idea that the state, as the formal embodiment of what had once been the tribe, should control the lives of all within a nation's borders was in the ascendant. With rapid industrialization, mass communication and rising populations, such toxic definitions virtually guaranteed the miseries of the 20th century.

Only very slowly have we come to realize that trade can benefit all who participate in it and that a whole host of problems cannot be solved at the national level. And yet how are individuals defined? Try traveling without a passport. With an increase in the perceived threat of terrorism, individuals are becoming subject to scrutiny as never before. Eye scans, DNA data banks, mass fingerprinting, internet surveillance, the monitoring of credit card use, and the widespread deployment of CCTV in city centers, all serve to recreate the eyes and ears of the tribal group, but on a bureaucratic scale.

The common justification for these innovations is that modern technology enables terrorists to do unimaginable things that only the use of modern technology can prevent. If you have done nothing wrong, the reassuring mantra goes, you have nothing to fear. But at the flick of a switch, any one of us could be declared a non-person, and placed beyond the pale: no credit, no useable bank accounts, no state benefits, no right to work or to travel. And if you are the young Brazilian electrician, Jean Charles de Menezes, living lawfully in the Tulse Hill area of south London, you can expect to be shot in the head seven times while sitting in a carriage in Stockwell station on your way to work, after the security services misidentify you as a suspected terrorist.[2]

The dilemma we face, as individuals, is that we are very reliant on the tension matrix we are part of. We know it sustains us. And just as the plains Indians of North America once revered the buffalo they had become dependent upon, so we have elevated *the state* to almost godly standing. But this is just a subtle expression of our biological drivers. The state is like an ancient forest. From time to time it will take one of us. And if that is the sacrifice *we* must make in order for *it* to keep sustaining us, so be it. We mourn for Jean Charles — and we do — but if his death is the price *we* must pay in order to keep terrorists at bay, so be it. Strangely, I do not know the name of even one of the 52 killed or 700 injured when Islamic radicals detonated bombs inside London's public transport system on July 7th 2005 — the event that led to Jean Charles's death.

Freud suggested that individuals follow dictators because they yearn for a father figure. I think that it is more certainty people yearn for and that dictators take advantage of that need in troubled times by being ballsy enough to persuade us they can provide it. And there may be a twist in this tale, because individuals clearly like stimulus and prefer not to be bored, especially when young. This likely makes dynamic certainty particularly attractive. The communist covenant with all its thrills and spills on the way, just like the promise of salvation for the Christian soldier, or the assurance of heaven for the Muslim jihadi, is a powerful motivator, and an addictive draught once tasted.

* * * *

All this leaves us with a very troubled view of the individual. Whatever our respective capabilities, they must be expressed within a

2. Jean Charles was murdered by the state on Friday July 22nd 2005. In spite of numerous inquiries the only charges that have been made to stick against the Metropolitan Police (whose officers were directly responsible) were violations under the Health and Safety at Work Act. As George Orwell would have enjoyed telling us, it is very hard for the state to prosecute the state.

tension matrix which goes a long way towards defining them. Take a professor, a Nobel laureate at the top of his game, or a singer known around the world, with millions of records to his name. Each possesses a mixture of physical, mental and emotional attributes that produced an outcome which was recognized and promoted by the matrix. The tension matrix represents aspects of ourselves and we turn those who reach its pinnacles into gods as a way of worshiping what we are. This has even resulted in celebrity being applauded for its own sake, without the need for it to be attached to any notable individual qualities.

Of course we should express joy in the tension matrix we have created. Never before have so many aspects of the human character been developed to such a pitch. We are creating a wonderfully rich tapestry for ourselves. But neither should we be fooled. We are celebrating one-dimensional aspects of the human character. Taken together they do express what we are and what we are capable of. But there is a very real risk, I think, that the bright lights will blind us to the true nature of individuality.

And what is its true nature? Well, I don't want to say weak, although we are very easily led by the boundary conditions that sustain us and are prone to assume that the tension matrix we are part of is a given, beyond understanding and redesign. I don't think it unreasonable to say that most of us, most of the time, do not feel responsible for the decisions the tension matrix directs, day in, day out. And after all, that is the point of the tension matrix. It is supposed to synthesize all our little aspirations and shortcomings in such a way as to produce outcomes that are better than we could achieve on our own. And it undoubtedly does — most of the time.

But no tension matrix is cast in stone, handed down like the Ten Commandments, but a man-made construction that requires constant maintenance and improvement. This task falls on the shoulders of each of us *as individuals* — not as great golfers, great movie stars, great businessmen, or even as plain vanilla celebrities. To execute that task we need to see ourselves as part of a boundary condition separate from that which defines the state. But why?

Throughout history there are copious examples of individuals becoming so identified with their role in the tension matrix that they execute their allotted function without any regard to its effect on those they are dealing with, beyond its prescribed purpose. Indeed, that is what Weber's bureaucracy called for and what the Fascist and Communist states demanded of their citizens. Even democracies have to turn individuals into cogs that drive killing machines if they are to win wars. Individual worth is measured by the skills, talent and dedication a person brings to their allocated task. But we *know* that this only reflects one aspect of what we are.

What I call our moral compass requires that we see ourselves in a context separate from that which the matrix defines for us. To bolster this ability, individuals have used a variety of strategies which all entail a shift in the reference they use to define their identity. As a junior officer in the Second World War, a playwright I once knew refused to attack a French town occupied by the Germans on account of the civilian casualties that would result. He was duly cashiered and sentenced to a year in Wormwood Scrubs prison. Clearly no army could function if it were made up of such men — but he was the most lovely individual and later wrote around 50 plays.

Another very special man I had the good fortune to know, and who had the misfortune of being my minister for many years, served as chaplain to an SAS group operating behind enemy lines in the same war, for which he was awarded a Military Cross. This individual had no compunction about seeing enemy soldiers killed, convinced that the war he helped to win was wholly justified. What both these men shared was deep humanity and a compunction to act in accordance with their beliefs, regardless of the consequences for them personally. Their sense of self, of what they felt themselves to be part of, went well beyond the narrow confines that their role in the matrix defined. Although neither was in any way boastful, I've no doubt that the playwright looked upon his time inside Wormwood Scrubs with as much pride as the minister looked upon his medal.

The tension matrix had bestowed an honor on both men — one intended, one not, which demonstrates, rather nicely, the dynamic tension inherent in the relationship between the matrix and the individual. Just as the Roman symbol of domination became the Christian symbol of hope, so the civilian suicide bomber has upended our comfortable assumptions about the actions of our government abroad (about which we are generally unconcerned, save in a jingoistic, boundary-reassuring sense) and our security at home.

On the face of things, it certainly did seem absurd to imagine that all 6.7 billion of us were special as individuals. Were we not just a product, and a rather successful product, of biology's numbers game? Well to some degree that must be the case. But it is the degree to which we are not that matters. What evolution has come up with in us is a *perpetual mutant*, because that is what being an individual amounts to. Each of us, if only to a small degree, can react to what the tension matrix foists on us in a unique way. Over time this dynamic has changed both the matrix and its story and contributed to the evolution of cerebral structure. The extent to which individuals can develop an identity, separate from that which the matrix bestows upon them, will determine the level of their contribution.

13

Relationships

THE RELATIONSHIPS I want to consider in this chapter are those 'natural' bonds that are formed between individuals, their environment and each other. The word 'natural' here is simply meant to denote 'naturally occurring' in the sense that they were not mandated by any conscious laws. In the following chapter on institutions we will discuss some of these same relationships, but in an altogether different context. The institution of marriage, for example, grew up when a large number of laws were applied to the natural relationship that can form between a man and a woman. In this chapter I want to concentrate only on relationships that occur regardless of law.

The word natural is derived from 'of nature', meaning that which occurs in the biological world as a matter of course. In other words, the relationships under consideration here are those which are the result of our biological drivers. And although I am arguing that cerebral structure is a new system state beyond the biological, I want to repeat (and will repeat often) that no matter how sophisticated cerebral structure becomes, it will always be grounded in feeling, NOT abstract intellect, because it is feeling that ties us to the universe we are part of. That said, we need to understand what these feelings are and where they come from.

The simple answer to the questions *what are these feelings that cause us to establish relationships and where do they come from*, is that they come from our evolutionary past as sensory survival scripts we are now aware of as feelings. Biology has evolved countless stratagems, or feedback loops, that have allowed a range of varyingly autonomous structures to develop, reproduce and adapt, forming an interdependent whole that has resulted in the biological system state that now exists here on Earth.

To go against these feelings means to go against these survival scripts, which clearly have been successful in that we exist. We should be careful not to ignore this success, or to put our full faith in it, because biology is programed to maximize first the survivability of the biological system state as a whole, and after that, to maximize the survivability of a species rather than any of its members, although it is within the members of a species that these survival scripts reside. With the evolution of consciousness and analytical thought, we are — as individuals — able to override both positive and negative stimulus (pleasant and unpleasant feelings) if we *think* that doing so might be to our advantage. This process of being able to elevate thought and its accompanying expectation of pleasant and unpleasant feelings over blind reaction represents a concrete step in the evolution of cerebral structure.

If we concentrate only on humans, while recognizing that many of our characteristics can be found in other species, the family unit constitutes the basis of most interpersonal relationships. The sex drive brings men and women together and results in children. The slightly different proclivities of the male and female have led to divergent roles, with females remaining closer to dependent children and males ranging farther afield, often to hunt. The slow development of a human child made it impossible for a female to mate and then head off on her own to rear her young (as the female bear does). The communal life that resulted, augmented by extended families, stimulated social evolution.

A relationship needs to be thought of in the context of a boundary condition. Sexual attraction is what it is: an evolved script that is supposed to augment the propagation of a species. Female deer cluster around a dominant male so that their offspring will benefit from his superior genes. Young female humans are known to cluster around male pop stars (the groupie phenomenon), no doubt for the same reason, although they almost certainly have no idea why they are doing so, and may be taking the contraceptive pill in any event — an example of thought overriding biological imperative. The sex act opens the door to a relationship, but it is what happens afterwards that defines it.

In human arrangements, like those that have evolved in apes, the family dynamic (as a consequence of the sex act) has resulted in group structures. This evolutionary strategy has proved successful in that it has utilized collective action to ensure survival, and group learning to adapt and transmit successful strategies from one generation to the next. For these reasons, group identity has evolved to take on considerable importance. The family, and the group to which a family belongs, almost certainly represent the earliest boundary conditions to which individual humans were subject. Its only competitor might have been a sense of *place.*

In thinking about relationships, it is easy to overlook the one we all have with the environment that surrounds us. Our brains, like those of other animals, create pattern maps that inform us about where we live: its opportunities and risks. Over time, what is familiar generally gives us a positive feeling, particularly if the familiar provides us with what we need, from our mother's breastmilk to the apple that falls from a tree at the end of our garden.

It is no exaggeration, I believe, to say that the millions who have marched to war over the centuries have done so, in large part, because of their evolved relationship with their group and their locale. Throw in what seems to be a need in many individuals, particularly male ones, for adventure, and you probably have trapped most of what lies behind human warfare. Behavioral psychologists argue that everything we do can be described in terms of evolved stimulus-response scripts. My own view is that this accords quite well with the biological system state.

The process by which a positive stimulus-response script (doing x gives me a pleasant outcome, so I keep doing it) leads to a change in behavior when that same stimulus-response script turns negative (doing x starts to give me an unpleasant outcome) describes a structure's ability to adapt. Biological structures tend to adapt quite slowly, unless starting in a fluid state within an environment where there is little competition and many stratified regions to colonize (the conditions that probably prevailed at the start of the Cambrian explosion). The specialized structures that evolve to occupy environmental niches are likely to be up against it if their niche changes (the evolutionary cul-de-sac). So the behavioral framework probably does not apply in all circumstances, even in the biological system state.

None the less, there is enough evidence of individuals being trained to act contrary to initial relationships, such as children being educated for ideological reasons to turn against their parents, to support the relevance of behaviorism in the human sphere. But if the idea of cerebral structure means anything, behaviorism cannot be the whole story (or even its principal theme). Cerebral structure requires that an evolutionary process is taking place inside the human brain that will affect how each individual's brain interacts with the brains of others.

Cognitive psychologists have gone beyond the behaviorists in that they allow for an intermediate state (such as belief, desire or motivation) to exist between the external stimulus (the pleasant or unpleasant outcome mentioned above) and the individual act (the *x*), such that the relationship between the stimulus and the act is not a foregone conclusion. A case in point might be how different people react to torture. Debate between the two camps can become sterile, with the behaviorists suggesting that the intermediate state is mechanical and measurable, and so predictable: alter the torture, for example, to take account of belief, desire or motivation, and you will get the desired result. Certainly politicians try to do this all the time (although not through torture, generally, unless you count having to listen to their platitudes as such), so there may be some truth in the argument.

The essential question is whether humans behave in response to stimulus in a hard-wired fashion, like Ivan Pavlov's dogs whom the Russian physiologist noticed beginning to salivate at the sound of a bell he rang before feeding them, or does some creative process occur in the brain that influences how an individual will react to any given stimulus? I think the answer is both, for one very practical and one more complex reason. The practical reason is that individual humans have to process thousands of stimuli every day[1]. If each of these had to be thought about from first principles, our brain would just freeze up. Instead, we build up a library of standard responses that appear to have worked previously and apply them. This means we only have to identify the type of stimulus and apply the matching response from our collection, a much easier and quicker task.

The more complex reason has to do with the nature of creativity, a subject we understand all too little about. We know when we experience something new — a painting, a piece of music, a product — that it *is* new, partly because it unsettles us by forcing us to address familiar territory in a different way. It must be sufficiently familiar for us to recognize it, and yet different enough to make us recalibrate the map we carry in our heads. The creator — the artist, composer or entrepreneur — has already challenged his or her own preconceptions to produce what he has. The recipient experiences some of the same dissonance as he attempts to come to terms with what is before him. The new has to be approached from the standpoint of the old. We still apply an interpretive framework from our library of standardized responses, but find that, fully to come to terms with it, we must add a new book to our library.

If, as I have suggested, relationships arise out of what becomes familiar to us on the basis of the positive and negative stimuli we have experienced, they are likely to act as a drag on creativity because creativity is about change. This underlines the importance of trying to understand the grammar of such relationships (what it is about them that gives us pleasure or pain), so that change can be expressed in terms of augmenting what is pleasurable and negating what is painful. All too often change initiatives are poorly thought through. They are then foisted on people in a callous manner that offends a string of cherished relationships and utterly fail to achieve their purpose as a result.

* * * *

1. And this is at the conscious level. At the sub-conscious level, our brain has to deal with hundreds of thousands of stimuli each day as it monitors and runs our body.

When we are young, the importance of a 'best friend' can be considerable. Our first relationship is likely to be with our mother and then with our father, and then with our siblings, if we have them. But that moment when we find ourselves away from the familiarity of our home and discover another individual, as lost as we are, with whom we can interact, is probably remembered by many of us. In part, we are seeking confirmation of our own identity. Our best friend reflects our self back to us, and replaces, in part, the responses we became familiar with while we unbudded within the bosom of our family.

At this early age we are comparing the responses we get from different individuals with our own developing feelings, and building up a sense of our own identity and of how the world around us works. At least as far as each individual is concerned, it seems to me that a process, similar to the creative one generally, is taking place. In other words, to some probably very small degree, we are developing a unique map of our world. This arises directly out of the relationships we form. What this means is that evolution in the human mind continues after the biological matter has been constructed and is a function of our interaction with others. So while many of our responses are likely to be hard-wired or, as I would put it, biologically driven, some have the capacity to be unique to ourselves and to be the product of our conscious minds.

A further distinction needs to be drawn, however, between what is hard-wired as a direct result of our biology and what becomes hard-wired as a result of our particular make-up and experience, which we call a person's character. That still leaves a small amount of leeway in which we can override both our biology and character in response to any given situation and produce a new synthesis that changes the previous pattern of our actions. In Charles Dickens' *A Christmas Carol* (1843) Ebenezer Scrooge is shaken out of his miserly habits by the ghost of his ex-partner, Jacob Marley, who appears before him in a dream and points out how barren Ebenezer's life has become.

The tension matrix may be externally visible in the form of physical structures, customs, formal relationships and laws but it exists within our heads. Ebenezer Scrooge was so wound up in the business of money-making that he had lost sight of life's other dimensions. These, though, were lurking deep within him and when the tension between what he had become and what his moral compass told him he might have been reached breaking point, the conflict burst from his subconscious mind into his conscious one in the form of Jacob Marley.

In Roman Polanski's film *The Pianist* (2002), based upon Wladyslaw Szpilman's autobiography, a Polish musician who has witnessed the full horror of Nazi atrocities against the people of Warsaw is finally discovered by Wilm Hosenfeld, a captain in the German army, as the war draws to its pitiful end. Learning that the Jew he has stumbled upon is a musician, Hosenfeld asks Szpilman to play on an old piano that has survived in the bombed-out building where the two men meet. Lifted out of the degradation that surrounds them by Chopin's *Ballade in G minor*, Hosenfeld rediscovers his humanity, and rather than turning Szpilman in, brings him food. The pianist endures but Hosenfeld later dies as a Soviet prisoner of war.

In both *A Christmas Carol* and *The Pianist*, men are locked within a tension matrix that directs their actions in certain ways and defines the relationships they have. In Dickens' world, the poor are held to be always with us and are mostly ignored. In the world of Nazi Germany, anyone not deemed to be a pure German was treated with varying degrees of contempt and hostility. Through his stories, Dickens was attempting to prick the consciences of the middle class into changing the tension matrix that regulated everyone's lives. He was suggesting that there were poor because of a systemic failure, not because that was they way it had to be, even though he did not really know how to fix it. In *The Pianist*, the story is attempting to show that human beings share an identity (which music can express) that transcends the narrow definition of self to which a tension matrix often confines them. This does not mean, of course, that at one level many individuals don't thoroughly enjoy the often bestial roles they are given.

As a boy, I well remember a day out hunting with a friend. We finally managed to shoot a bird, I forget what kind, and to assuage our still unsatisfied bloodlust we took it in turns to throw the dead creature into the air for the other to shoot — again and again! There was little left of it by the time we had finished, save for an uncomfortable feeling of guilt that has stayed with me to this day. We had acted as a cat does when it tosses a mouse back and forth before killing it. Our bird was quite dead and all we had done was waste some ammunition, so why the guilt? I think it had something to do with the fact that we had lost control of ourselves to a deep feeling whose presence troubled us. In the mood we were in we could easily have shot any number of unarmed opponents, had we been grown men.

The ability to project not only thoughts but feelings — that is to say the ability to look back at ourselves and experience outcomes that have not yet happened — is the essence of cerebral structure. But it doesn't stop there. Cerebral structure is not something private to ourselves. It involves conscious interaction with others. The wife beater and the beaten wife have a symbiotic relationship that is quite well documented in psychiatry. She finds it hard to escape him and he finds it hard not to abuse her. They are stuck in a biological relationship based upon dominance and submission. The urges they are subject to are so powerful that they find it all but impossible to project an alternative relationship with sufficient force so as to evoke feelings stronger than those they are subject to.

* * * *

How we form relationships and maintain them must be intimately connected with how we communicate. Starting with our home life and building out from that, all of our experiences will combine to form a map of positive and negative stimuli into which our relationships have to be slotted and through which our unique propensity to act must be filtered. The linguist Noam Chomsky has proposed that we all start life with an innate sense of grammar that enables children to learn language quickly at an early age. This is very suggestive of the cerebral structure I am proposing, because it implies we have evolved (and are still evolving) a sort of sense-making syntax that helps us to order and construct *and reinterpret* the relationship we have with each other and the world around us.

Psychologists talk about *cognitive dissonance* to describe a situation in which an individual is forced to grapple with two conflicting stimuli.

An example might be this: you find yourself dealing with a person whom your in-built script tells you to be wary of, let us say, on account of their race, but you discover that they are, in fact, quite agreeable. Your library response is predicated upon the assumption that those who appear to be demonstrably different from you might do you harm, and yet your actual experience of them suggests that a different reaction is warranted.

Resolving such incidents of dissonance is not particularly straightforward, as anyone who cohabits with a partner from a different background will know. In a neutral environment (one to which neither partner belongs) the external pressure on the arrangement might be minimal. But in an environment which favors the preconceptions of one partner, the external pressures on the other can be acute. And this need not be a question of blind prejudice, but a recognition that people with different background experiences find it far harder to bond than those whose background experiences are similar.

It seems to me inconceivable that there is not a genetic (that is to say, a biological) component in such distinctions. In other words, the reason people tend to cluster in similar types, which of course gives rise to them having similar background experiences, likely owes its pedigree to biology's tendency towards species differentiation. Now this might sound like a contradiction in terms — surely a tendency towards differentiation should encourage mixing? — until you give weight to how important it is for a species to maintain its boundary condition (it is what defines it, after all) and eliminate mutations.

And if you step back a little and look at liberal Western society as being one that favors a certain type of individual with a certain set of characteristics (let's summarize these as being liberally-educated agnosticism), it is not hard to imagine that individuals who might be described as conservatively-educated believers (and I'm not sure it matters what the nature of their belief is) feel marginalized, because they are. What we have here is akin to the process of species differentiation. Let us call the first group (the currently dominant group) the Liberati and the second group the Fundamentalists. The biological imperative calls upon the Liberati to neutralize what they see as the mutation in their midst, whilst at the same time calling upon the Fundamentalists to assert their distinctive characteristics and find a space within which they can flourish.

Turn the clock back five hundred years and in place of the Liberati imagine the Roman Catholic fraternity, with its lock on education and the many sinecures that followed from it, and in place of the Fundamentalists imagine the Protestants, and you have a good example of the process of species differentiation as it has been interpreted by Homo sapiens. If you looked inside the heads of Roman Catholics and Protestants, or inside the heads of the Liberati and Fundamentalists, I do not know whether you would find any genetic or physiological difference, but you might find evidence of heightened mental activity in the asserting group that was less prevalent in the dominant one.

I suggest this merely because individuals in an asserting group (like early Christians in the Roman state) would be constantly needing to reinforce each other's emerging identity in an environment that sought to crush it. Such dissonance would likely lead to higher levels of stress in general, and perhaps to greater focus than you would find amongst individual members of the dominant group as a whole.

All this might seem to have taken us a long way from relationships, the subject of this chapter, but relationships, it seems to me, are at the heart of evolving cerebral structure. The crucial difference between what humans do and what occurs in the biological system state is that species differentiation in the latter leads to structures (animals, plants, etc.) that can no longer interact actively (by breeding with each other), whereas in the cerebral system state, differentiated thought structures (and let's take Protestantism and Catholicism as examples of these) have the capacity to fuse into entirely new thought structures, such as those which gave rise to the Liberati.

One of the outcomes in Britain of the First World War, in which people from the working class, middle class and upper class mixed in the most horrendous circumstances, was a growing feeling that the thought structures that underpinned these distinctions were no longer appropriate. The often-close relationships formed in the trenches did not lead to an alteration in Britain's political disposition overnight, but it undoubtedly encouraged individuals in each of the classes to question the arrangements they had grown accustomed to, making political reform, when it came, appear more *natural*.

Today, company managers and their advertising agencies talk about creating relationships with their customers. Indeed marketers define a brand as a promise kept. The idea behind these relationships is that of reciprocal benefit and predictability (the promise kept). It draws from exactly the same well as did our having a best friend: positive reciprocity. Now here's the thing. What happens when circumstances change? Our friend gets accepted by university la-di-da, whereas the best we can manage is college nuts-and-bolts; or the bank that has nurtured our business for years suddenly gets caught up in a credit crisis and cuts us adrift without even a goodbye.

Relationships, ultimately, are about belonging and reassurance. Even relationships that embody negative reciprocity, such as warfare and battered wife syndrome,[2] offer a perverse sense of belonging and reassurance. Conscious man is a lonely man, unless he attaches himself to what is familiar. Indeed the reason I am writing ***Notes*** is to embrace the universe I find myself in, so that I and it can become one and its immensity my own. Of course the idea of God seeks to do the same.

But is there not something pathetic about the way we imbue inanimate objects, such as a crucifix or book of stories, with special powers? Some might think so, but iconography is not about the object but about what the object represents, and what it represents is a thought structure with which we have a deep, intimate and personal relationship. The wedding ring on our finger; the poster on our wall depicting the first pop concert we ever went to, in which we got to see those whose music opened up a part of ourselves we didn't know existed.

---

2. Technically known as battered person syndrome and classified by the World Health Organization as ICD 995.81, it describes how people can develop a psychological dependence on their abusers. ICD stands for International Classification of Diseases.

My argument in ***Notes*** is that we do have a relationship with the universe, in every way as real as that between a child and its mother. But mothers die and children have to grow up. The nature of this relationship is to be found within us and the active agent, at least in so far as it affects mankind, is ourselves. Whatever it is, we are. Whatever it is trying to move towards, it is trying to move towards through you and me.

One of the ideas associated with God that I particularly like is that he never lets you down — that he's a best friend that beats all best friends. Cynics, of course, say that if God was any more real than Elwood P. Dowd's imaginary rabbit Harvey,[3] he would *do something* about this world of ours! Well, I think that rather misses the point.

The relationships we form with our physical and human environment often constitute our strongest boundary condition. Those who build armies know this well. You may not fight for a general, or even a country, but you'll fight for your buddies. Team-building within corporations follows the same dynamic. The immediate and the familiar, that is what is likely to impact us most. But there is a real danger here because it is this dynamic that lies behind the herd instinct. Our nearest neighbor runs so we run.

In 1841, Charles Mackay published his still-popular book *Extraordinary Popular Delusions and the Madness of Crowds*, in which he described the history of various fads or manias, such as alchemy, witch-hunts, and financial bubbles. As I am writing this (at the start of 2009) the world is experiencing the after-effects of a major financial bubble bursting. Over a decade's worth of cheap credit, brought about when developing countries ran up huge export surpluses which had to be recycled into the developed countries because the developing countries were unable to invest all the money they were making, led to some increasingly imprudent lending practices by the banks.

---

3. *Harvey* was written as a play by Mary Chase and premiered on Broadway in 1944. It was later adapted for film, starring James Stewart and Josephine Hull, who also played the lead roles in the stage play. Chase received a Pulitzer Prize for Drama in 1945.

The head of one of the world's biggest explained in an interview in July 2007 that so long as the music was playing you had to keep dancing.[4] Seventeen months later the company he ran had lost 90% of its market value and he had been 'retired'. The financial products invented by his and other leading banks to recycle the exporting countries' surpluses — essentially anyone who wanted a loan was given one and these loans were then packaged up and sold on — suddenly became unsaleable when it was realized that a lot of the folk who had taken out loans were not going to be able to repay them.

These toxic assets, as they came to be called, had to be written down in banks' books to reflect their market value, which no one could work out, because no one was prepared to buy them. This decimated bank balance sheets, and as banks lend a multiple of their capital, the great lending boom was suddenly thrown into reverse, denying money to companies around the globe and giving a whole new meaning to the expression *relationship banking*.

If bankers and borrowers and regulators, who had all been happy to party while the music played, had had their own invisible rabbit warning them that the world might not be as it seemed, perhaps more would have left the festivities early. But as every religious non-conformist (and every owner of an invisible rabbit) knows, swimming against the tide is hard work and often personally unrewarding. As will be discussed in the chapter on change, events invariably move in cycles for the simple reason that it is easier to go along with a trend that is benefiting those with whom we have relationships.

Relationships are not only fundamental to what it means to be human, they are also one of life's great joys. But if we are serious about strengthening the individual, we must help him to develop a relationship with an integrity greater than the day-to-day by giving him a parallel story that will act as a counterpoint to the mood of the moment. And if it helps to call that counterpoint Harvey, or even God, so be it.

---

4. Chuck Prince, the CEO and Chairman of Citibank until November 2007, commenting on his bank's lending practices.

Because the purpose of a tension matrix is to coordinate the actions of many individuals for the general well-being of them all, people are slotted into functional roles that exaggerate aspects of their character. Indeed the idea of merit is predicated on just that. The roles we occupy in a matrix should be those best suited to our character and abilities. The basis of relationships is altogether different.

Whereas a matrix reflects only certain aspects of ourselves, our relationships reflect something deeper. Their potency, which can be as easily expressed in hatred as in love, suggests that their source should be tended deliberately and with care. And what is this source? I cannot describe it in any way other than it is the complex set of feelings that infuses our conscious selves and makes each of us what we are. Its dynamic nature needs an anchorpoint.

I recently visited a man in hospital. He had led a very constructive life and was deeply committed to the Roman Catholic faith. Instantly we both knew we were saying goodbye. The feeling we shared was not one of sorrow, but one of rejoicing in a life well lived that was coming to its proper end. Although on paper our beliefs were utterly different, what we shared was the certainty that we were part of a whole from which death could not separate us.

Each of us needs to have such a relationship because without it we will not value either our environment or our fellow man, nor will we have the strength to resist the selfish siren calls the tension matrix can sometimes augment. In the following chapter we will examine how we have built on these natural relationships to create those formal structures that make up the visible tension matrix. Although these structures are designed to meet what we perceive to be our needs (such as external defense, internal order, interpersonal justice and mutually beneficial exchange), they sometimes serve to exaggerate our biological drivers in ways that run counter to any notions we might have of what human morality should be.

14

Institutions

IMAGINE EARLY MAN, wandering in small groups, hunting, and settling for the evening, probably around an open fire. We can only guess at the form conversation took, but that of stone age tribes in existence today must give us an idea. Events would have been recounted and stories told. Comfort would have been drawn from their familiarity. This seemingly informal gathering would have given individuals an opportunity to air tensions and to arrive at decisions about what they should all do. It would have served to reinforce their shared sense of identity.

If you travel to central Australia, you might come across Ayers Rock, a solitary mound of spectacular sandstone sitting squat in a wide, featureless landscape of scrub and baked earth. A remnant of a mountain range pushed up in the early Cambrian period, over 500 million years ago, it is also known as Uluru, after the local people, who connect it to their Dreamtime when Creators walked the Earth and made it what it is. In 1873 Europeans came upon the rock (and renamed it[1]) but the area has been inhabited for over 10,000 years.

1. After Sir Henry Ayers, Premier of South Australia in 1872–73.

Wherever you look, across the centuries of human history, you are likely to find evidence of two things that have been important to us: community and place. The first is personal and intimate, extending outwards from the family, the second, like the rock, anchors us in some special way to the enormity we are part of. Both serve to create a boundary condition within which we can establish our identity. And we build stories about them as a way of expressing, in our conscious minds, their importance to us. These, it seems to me, are the first institutions we created, the first structures that represented, and in some way ordered and made explicit, our deepest feelings. For the political economist, John Stuart Mill, what shaped the character of a people was not so much what was purposely taught *as the unintentional teaching of institutions and social relations.*[2]

My argument here is that the institutions we have built are all expressions of feelings, manifest as tensions, that exist in the simplest of our human communities. And by simple I do not mean to imply something qualitatively inferior, just fundamental. Biological life, as a whole, is built around the same two distinctions. A species must be able to recognize its own type as well as the environment with which it has to interact. Because of consciousness, these two sentient boundaries must be explained. It is this that gives rise to cerebral structure.

The tensions that exist within a small tribal community arise from the fact that individuals possess a conscious sense of self. The tensions within an ant colony, by contrast, arise because of the interaction between the functional characteristics of the ant types and the environment within which they exist. The social order of the ant colony is hard-wired as is the physiology of each ant, adapting only when some accidental change in behavior or some physical mutation improves the colony's prospects. While a good deal of what a human tribe does is also hard-wired (the distinction between a male and a female, for example, is a given as is their need for so much food and water), an individual human's conscious sense of self introduces an additional element into the mix.

---

2. An observation he made in an article in the Morning Chronicle in 1846 on *The Condition of Ireland*, as quoted in Richard Reeves' biography of him (Atlantic Books, 2007).

Consciousness requires that the members of a tribe explain how they relate to each other as well as how they relate to the environment on which they depend. Over time these explanatory stories become augmented by customs and rituals, all of which serve to reinforce a people's sense of identity as well as to reinforce the habits that sustain them. Like so many of Mill's observations, the one quoted above is astute and draws attention to the interplay between an individual human mind and the evolved customs and habits — precursors of our more formal institutions — that make community life possible.

The tension matrix, which I described in Part 1, is really a loosely interlocking set of what were once informal arrangements that we evolved to regulate our lives together. Over time we categorized these into such things as the transition from childhood to puberty, and the way in which disputes were settled, embedding them within formal rituals. Because of a change in climate, I suspect, some of our ancestors found themselves having to compete for resources. This would have put pressure on communities to strengthen their boundaries and improve their productivity by differentiating their activities, a dynamic leading to increased scale. To accommodate this, our forebears would have had to reconstitute their informal, ritualized arrangements within distinct structures.

So at the heart of these structures, that we now call institutions, lie some of our deepest feelings. The difficulty we must often overcome today is how to reconnect them to the sentiments that gave them legitimacy. As a means of tracing the progression from where we have come let us imagine life as it would have been in the beautifully preserved roundhouses at Skara Brae on Orkney, off the west coast of Scotland.[3]

These physical structures brought what one imagines were family groups inside around a fire. Local stone was used to line the walls and make some simple shelves and storage places. An eye for the practical is evident, with attention to detail and order. Sunk into the ground, probably with an earth-clad roof and a hole in the center for the fire smoke to

---

3. A Neolithic settlement of ten stone-built roundhouses, occupied from around 3100–2500 BC, and found on the island of Orkney off the west coast of Scotland. The village had been buried beneath sand dunes until 1850 and was not properly excavated until 1925.

escape, these homes would have felt solid and secure. Each could have accommodated around 10 people, and although 5,000 years separate us, it is not hard to imagine the life they led.

Although a fire was a means of keeping warm, the idea of the hearth as a place where people gathered is still evident. But the fact that there were ten houses, where ten sets of ideas could be exchanged, suggests that a process of social elaboration was under way. Resolving tensions within the community could no longer occur naturally, through informal discussion at the end of each day, but would have required a more formal set of arrangements. And it is the evolution of such institutions that have made the large scale of our societies possible. They are very particular structures which we have imbued with ideas about how we should live together.

The people of Skara Brae will occasionally have had to deal with individuals whose behavior threatened to undermine the community. Today, we have a criminal justice system. In Skara Brae there would have been quarrels to resolve. Today we have a body of contract law and civil courts within which disputes are settled. In Skara Brae collective decisions would sometimes have been needed. Today we have political parties, through which individuals are selected to run for elected office in legislative chambers, and an executive. In Skara Brae collective decisions would have been implemented by agreement. Today we have government agencies. How to feed, clothe and shelter themselves would have exercised the people of Skara Brae greatly. Today we are part of a complex commercial system that seeks to do the same. In Skara Brae the community would have had to deal with illness. Today we have an extensive medical establishment. In Skara Brae knowledge would have passed naturally from one generation to the next. Today we have an education system and specialized training.

In Skara Brae they might have had to defend themselves from outside attack. Today we have the armed forces. When something concerned the inhabitants of Skara Brae they would have discussed it. Today we have our debating chambers and media. In Skara Brae they would occasionally have dwelt upon the meaning of life and wondered how it would affect them. Today we have our great universities. In

Skara Brae they would have had rituals to celebrate and reaffirm what was important in their lives. Today we have our religious and civil traditions. In Skara Brae the eyes and ears of the whole community would have watched over things. Today we have our regulatory agencies and oversight bodies. In Skara Brae the people would have had to work out who did what and who got what. Today we have our economic and democratic systems.

These then, broadly, are the institutions that have evolved out of the tension matrix that defined our earliest communities, with some inevitable overlaps: the Family; Courts of Law, Criminal and Civil; the Executive and Legislature; Government Agencies; the Business Community; the Medical Profession; the Education System; the Armed Forces; the Media; Universities; our Religious Structures; Regulatory and Oversight Bodies; our Economic and Democratic Systems. The story that underpins them generally is that each represents an issue which concerns us collectively. An integral part of this general story is that all will conduct themselves in a manner we consider fair. The story that underpins them individually is that each is competent to perform the task allotted to it. In a practical sense, our institutions reflect the grammar of evolving cerebral structure.

The journey from Skara Brae (and the many similar communities that existed 5,000 years ago) to today has been a rocky one, to say the least. As I have argued, what seems to have happened is that competition for resources between communities put pressure on those affected to increase in size. This forced them to evolve specialized structures out of the previously implicit tensions that could be resolved naturally within them when they were small. In light of the dynamic affecting these communities (the more isolated ones that still exist today were clearly not subject to such pressure), the initial emphasis was on governance, particularly as it related to military and productive efficiency.

A consequence of structural elaboration was that individuals were separated from the whole, the whole previously being a small tribal community that was accessible to each individual in its entirety, and whose tension matrix underpinned natural morality. The actions of individuals who became soldiers, for example, were no longer governed by the whole, but by a specialized boundary condition that was now part of a whole that some governing function was empowered to direct. The drive behind such elaborated structures was akin to the competitive drive which lies behind the predatory interdependence of species. In large part, human communities' reliance on their biological drivers at this time was down to the fact that their new structures were designed for conflict, and individuals could see no alternative.

While there is no doubting the stimulative and evolutionary effect of this process, certain characteristics were greatly exaggerated. The most marked was the association of government with warfare. This was mirrored on the economic front, with pressure placed on farm work to produce increasing amounts in support of the government and military structure. Because humans are not like hard-wired ants and require a story that makes sense of their existence and justifies their daily round, the government function was invariably allied to a spiritual dimension as well. Over time this elaborated into three powerful institutions: a secular hierarchy that embraced both a military and a priestly one.

Notwithstanding attempts by the Athenian Greeks to elevate the status of justice through law, governance by consent, truth through reason, well-being through commerce and to a lesser degree, education by training and example, dimensions recognized by the Romans, the triumvirate of church, state and army, often with a single, unifying individual at the head of all three hierarchies, surfaced repeatedly as being the most potent. In our own times, even those two social pustules — Communism and Fascism — operated to the same script.

Of course the reason for their predominance is grounded in the nature of coercive power and the belief that conflict between tribal structures that evolved into nation states was the natural order of things. Driven by this biological logic, tens of millions of individuals in the 20th century were willing to sink their identity into structures that then functioned like single organisms, but with the brains of a pea. Those individuals able to see the madness of this were completely overwhelmed, as were those other institutions that might have arrested people's collective amnesia. The raw urge to survive at the individual level translated at the national one into a collective blind fury that rippled through every substructure and boundary condition, determining its moral trajectory. Total war seems to be a massive release of the tensions that ineffective peacetime structures cannot resolve.

One of the most gratifying developments to take place over recent years has been a decline in the perceived need for competition between nations as the boundary conditions to which our identities are most often held hostage. I may be imagining this, and if I am not it could easily be reversed. To counter my optimism, deep-seated tribal animosities are evident across Africa and religious fundamentalism is once again a force in world politics. But I believe the change is real and we owe it to the level of economic empowerment that has spread to at least most individuals in the world's more prosperous countries. It may be fashionable to mock consumerism, but never before have so many individuals been able to build a world of their own choosing, undirected by those in charge of that over-mighty triumvirate: army, church and state.

Consider for a moment the tribe tucked away in the Amazon delta and imagine what a great release of tension it must be when an individual can just wander off, sustained by the munificence of the rainforest. The Australian Aboriginal had his *walkabout.* We all need this: the ability *not* to be part of the collective. Only if we do will its necessary strictures be acceptable to us. We are then part of it because we choose to be part of it and for no other reason. The anonymity of the city appeals to us, I think, because of this.

Now this takes us into some difficult territory, but it is ground we ignore at our peril. The worst possible situation, one into which I fear our hubris and laziness are inclined to lead us, is when we convince ourselves that we have engineered a structure that will cater for everything, such that we give it our complete trust. When it fails us, our anger knows no bounds and we cast around for scapegoats and easy solutions. The different reactions of Americans and Germans to the privations of the Great Depression illustrates what I mean.

The American story had promised individuals freedom, no more and no less. The assumption in 1920s Germany was that the state owed its people prosperity and when it failed to provide it they blamed everyone (from Jewish bankers to communist infiltrators) but themselves. And where did they look for salvation? To the very state that had failed them. Americans, by contrast (many of whose ancestors had been Germans), drove and walked and hopped on trains in what was all too often a forlorn quest for work. Their state had certainly failed them too, but they looked to themselves for a solution.

Not only must our institutions be balanced so that the triumvirate is cut down to size, but they must promise no more than they can deliver and be truly accountable to the communities they serve. But more than that, we must stop trying to build structures that purport to control everything. Firstly, it cannot be done and so will only lead to disappointment and bitter recriminations. Secondly, we all need a degree of freedom within which to build our lives. A society awash with unenforceable rules will drive the good into a state of apathy and the bad into overdrive. And besides, it is out of our freedom to interact with one another that we will create new solutions to the problems we share. This is also how cerebral structure will evolve.

An ongoing predicament we face arises out of our inability to see problems, let alone their solution. This is because our story and tension matrix govern, to a considerable extent, what we see and how we address what we see. If the difficulty arises because of faults within our tension matrix and its story we are likely to find ourselves stuck in a *catch-22* dilemma.[4]

---

4. In Joseph Heller's novel, *Catch-22* (1961), set on an island airbase off the Italian coast during the Second World War, bombardier Yossarian seems to be the only person able to see the war in personal terms. Resentful that his life is continuously being put in danger by officers anxious to advance their military careers, he struggles to find a way out. But every ruse he attempts traps him in circular logic. On one occasion he pleads insanity but is told that only a sane person would know he was insane. Eventually he refuses to fly any more missions and is offered a choice between being court-martialed or being given an honorable discharge, just so long as he gives his superiors' tactics (which include flying black-market food around Europe) a ringing endorsement. As this would condemn his fellow pilots to even more suicidal missions, he chooses to desert instead, and in this way finally regains control over his life.

This suggests that we need to invent a new institution (and I will outline a form this might take in the last chapter, *The Road Ahead*). Its purpose would be to examine our evolved structures in order to determine (a) whether they are performing the function they were intended to perform, (b) whether they possess moral integrity in that they produce outcomes individuals with equal power would voluntarily endorse, and (c) whether they encourage diverse approaches to the solution of problems. Even if we can agree on what are desirable outcomes, in a creative universe we can never be certain what will be the best means of achieving them.

This, of course, is a massive task and would represent a frontal assault on all those vested interests that populate our institutions as they stand. It would be like saying to the Catholic hierarchy in 1500, we need you to accept the possibility that your power and influence might have to be greatly reduced in order to bring Christian practice back down to the community level where it started. You don't have to imagine the reaction of such a body to such a request. You only have to look at what happened after Martin Luther posted his suggestions onto the door of his local church. Europe then plunged into 200 years of conflict as a new expression of Christian practice was established outside the boundary condition of the Roman Church.

And if that wasn't enough, this was followed by a further 200 years of conflict during which the Christian religion itself came under sustained attack from a miscellany of individuals attracted by scientific determinism (the idea that there was no mystery in the universe, but only facts that needed to be ascertained). This, of course, was a false god in that determinism denies our evolutionary potential by removing all moral responsibility from us as individuals, while at the same time denying the universe its creative potential. If the choices we make are irrelevant, we are irrelevant and the universe we are part of is irrelevant, a ridiculous position to take at best.

There was much to criticize in the way Roman Catholicism evolved. Here is just one example of how the Church confused the wonder it sought to represent with itself. In 1640, during the Counter-Reformation against the rise of Protestantism, Pope Urban

VIII felt compelled to keep Gregorio Allegri's magnificent choral composition, *Miserere Mei, Deus,* locked in the Vatican because it was spiritually so powerful. He insisted that it be performed only once a year during Holy Week by his personal choir in the Sistine Chapel.[5]

In laying claim to a composition that captured something universal, Urban displayed the hubris that drove so many from his church. Luckily, in 1770, a child prodigy called Wolfgang Amadeus Mozart heard the piece and was able to write the whole thing down later from memory. It is certainly easy to poke fun at Urban's myopic vision of a world dominated by a wealthy, self-centered, man-made church in which anything that was spiritually uplifting should only be experienced through it. But a far bleaker vision was hatching, in part, I think, because the Roman Church had traveled so far from its roots that it could not adapt.

By the end of the 19th century a godless universe had come to haunt mankind. The triumvirate of church, state and army had been recast with the first of those gone and the idea of nationalism elevated in its stead. To his credit, Pope Urban VIII did at least recognize the difference between the sacred and the profane. But because of the tension matrix he was locked inside he was unable to see the creative potential of the universe in any other context save that of the Church he loved.

Only the new United States of America tried consciously to create a tension matrix and a story that rebalanced those feelings which lie at the heart of our institutions. The Founding Fathers, in effect, played the role of the new institution that I feel we need. The idea of a universal God was central, but religion was put in its correct place. I won't rehearse the other aspects of their construction, other than to say it gave individuals the freedom to build their lives within a framework of universal laws whose application they were given the power to oversee.

---

5. This from Howard Goodall's lovely book, *Big Bangs — the story of five discoveries that changed musical history*. Vintage, 2001.

But no construction remains adequate for all time. Circumstances change, our knowledge increases, technology makes things possible that were not possible before, and all institutions fall prey to their own interests. If a man like Dwight Eisenhower, who had been an accomplished general and the leader of his nation, saw his country's greatest problem as being one he himself had been part of, tinkering around the edges is unlikely to help. Our institutions belong to us — to *we the people* — and we need to remind ourselves of their purposes and then we need to ensure that they are achieving them. Responsibility for doing this is ours, but only by appointing some of our number to a body whose task it is to keep them both grounded and up-to-date, will we be able to identify any problems that exist and start doing something about them. Leaving it to the structures that are in place just won't do, and it is simply stupid to wait for these to fail.

15

Technology

THE GREEK WORD from which our own technology comes is *tekhnologia* — 'systematic treatment'. *Tekhne* means art or craft and *logia*, the study of. For many of us, I think, technology is a black box. We know it is important. We know we use it. We can readily point to examples of it. But somehow it seems a little mysterious, almost threatening. Will it run away with us? That is what we wonder. And with good reason, because the evolutionary dynamic I have described, as it has affected human beings, can be boiled down to a competition between groups for a 'better' way of doing things that has frequently translated into warfare and the domination of one group over another. The more benign association with art or craft has been lost. Even our expression *high-tech* denotes something slightly racy.

And yet the entire tension matrix within which we all live is a consequence of systematic treatment. It is the result of knowledge we have accumulated through trial and error applied for practical purposes. As I have said, the forest we now live in is one of our own making and its 'trees' and 'shrubs' and 'flowers' are expressions of thought applied to problems we have wanted to solve, and each, to some extent, is defined by its own language and boundary condition. How did this creep up on us?

* * * *

Archeologists have unearthed evidence of simple tool-making in the Great Rift Valley of Ethiopia that dates back more than 2.3 million years, so even before the evolution of Homo sapiens, which is put at about 200,000 BC. But 50,000 years ago a quicker pace of change seems to have begun, with evidence of more sophisticated stone tools, more complex behaviors and an increased brain size, perhaps by as much as a third. The speculation is that this coincided with the evolution of language. To me, of course, this represents hard evidence of the emergence of cerebral structure, in that human consciousness appears to have been constructing a network of meaning which could be manipulated by intent. In other words, evolution was beginning to create a new kind of matter out of the biological system state.

Evidence of humans employing fire has been dated to 500,000–400,000 BC, with the use of clothing and the construction of temporary dwellings placed as early as 380,000 BC. The development of agriculture appears to have gotten underway in earnest only around 12,000 years ago and would have required a marked change in behavior and more sophisticated tools. Copper has probably been used for 8,000 years. The ore was quite common and the metal easily extracted even in a wood fire, although more easily still in a hotter, charcoal one. The discovery, 2,000 years later, that by mixing two soft metals, copper and tin, you could produce a far harder one, bronze, was a major advance.

At about this time (say within a range of 5000–3000 BC) there is evidence of settlement along the Nile, use of the wheel in carts and of wind to power boats. The first pyramids, built as burial chambers for the Pharaohs to help them on their journey into the celestial afterlife, date from 2600 BC, clear evidence that human society and the imagination of individuals could create a tension matrix of extraordinary sophistication and beauty.

The use of specific knowledge to make specific things is always embedded within a tension matrix and its explanatory story. If we turn the clock forward by 4,500 years, and move from the Nile to New Mexico, we find 130,000 individuals, each with specific knowledge, bent on the creation of the first atomic bomb. Whereas the Pharaohs had only wanted to send themselves to kingdom come, by the 1940s man was making a pretty good stab at sending every member of his species there.

The interplay between technology, a tension matrix and its story is rather well illustrated by the cold war, in which two nuclear powers, capable of destroying not just each other but the whole human species, had to design systems that would lessen the chances of them doing so inadvertently. Stanley Kubrick's classic film *Dr. Strangelove: How I Learned to Stop Worrying and Love the Bomb* captured the madness of the time. An American president attempts to persuade a Russian premier that a renegade bomber heading his way armed with a nuclear bomb and piloted by a mad Texan is not an all-out attack.[1]

---

1. Made on a budget of just $1.8 million, Kubrick's black comedy was released in 1964. Suspecting a communist conspiracy to sap the potency of America's sacred bodily fluids, delusional Brigadier General Jack Ripper orders his fleet of B52 bombers to attack the Soviet Union, using a special code to be deployed in the event of the US High Command being obliterated by a first strike. He and his UK counterpart, Group Captain Lionel Mandrake, are holed up at the airbase which comes under attack by troops sent in by US President Merkin Muffley to bring the renegade Brigadier back into line. But only Ripper has the recall code and is shot before Mandrake can get it out of him. In the Pentagon War Room General Buck Turgidson tries to convince the President to take advantage of the situation and let the attack proceed (*and those commie bastards have it!*), which he thinks will knock out 90% of the Soviet missiles and result in only 10 to 20 million US dead—*depending on the breaks*. Instead, President Muffley insists on calling in the Soviet Ambassador, and contacting the Soviet Premier, Dmitri Kissoff, on the hotline. Meanwhile Mandrake, who has deduced the call-back code from doodles on Ripper's blotter (*purity of essence*), persuades Colonel 'Bat' Guano, who has taken him prisoner, to let him call the Pentagon. But with the phones on the base knocked out in the attack, they have to use a pay phone in a nearby convenience store, after Colonel Guano has shot up a Coca Cola vending machine for the money. Kissoff, who is the worse for drink, takes some persuading but eventually agrees to accept the bomber coordinates from President Muffley so that any not recalled can be taken down. One, piloted by Major T J 'King' Kong, is damaged and its communication disabled and so continues on its run. Only then does the Soviet Ambassador tell Muffley that his country has just built a Doomsday device which will destroy the world in the event of an attack. *Not much good if we don't know about it, surely?* complains the President. *We were about to tell you*, the Ambassador

I have outlined the complete story in the note for two reasons. The first is that it does actually show how hard it is for two opposing entities, whose tension matrices and stories have been built around confrontation, to reverse course. We now know that at least once the world came perilously close to nuclear annihilation when Soviet spy satellites mistook sunlight distorted by high altitude clouds for a US missile launch. If it had not been for the action (or inaction) of Lieutenant Colonel Stanislav Petrov, who suspected the satellite alarm was false and did not immediately inform his superiors whose protocol called for massive retaliation, there would likely have been a nuclear exchange.[2] As I have said, in large part our story and tension matrix tell us how to think and how to act. That, after all, is their job.

The second reason is that when it comes to technology we often overlook what is in front of us. Kubrick's film, together with the distribution and production system that enabled it to be seen, was no less a technology than the bomb it caricatured. He and those who worked with him on the project were using humor to change the story that governed America's tension matrix. Indeed the use of tragedy and humor to depict the world we live in, which Shakespeare did so well, may be a way of subtly recalibrating the human brain. The word catharsis means the process of releasing, and so providing relief from, strong or repressed emotions. It seems likely to me that our brains reflect the tensions of the matrix we are part of, and that shared laughter and sorrow help us to put things into a broader context.

---

assures him. Muffley then calls in Dr. Strangelove, an ex-Nazi whose gloved hand makes involuntary Sieg Heil salutes. Strangelove advises that 200,000 of the nation's finest specimens, with a ratio of ten women to every man, be relocated in a deep mineshaft. General Turgidson rants that the Commies might have a deeper mineshaft, as the Soviet Ambassador takes pictures of the War Room with his spy camera. The film ends with Major Kong astride his bomb, which he has had to free manually from the damaged bomb bay, riding it to earth like a rodeo cowboy, while Vera Lynn sings her old World War II favorite *We'll meet again, don't know where, don't know when. But I know we'll meet again some sunny day. . . .*

[2] Lieutenant Colonel Petrov was aware that the system had experienced some problems and believed that the limited number of incoming missiles it identified was incompatible with a first strike. The incident took place on September 26th 1983.

Although in a general sense technology and the tension matrix are indistinguishable, there is one facet of what we call technology that does seem to be distinct. Going back to the forest analogy, and recognizing as technology all those man-made devices which make up the environment most of us now live within, it is clear that products as functional ideas (the cars and computers, for example, that make up our forest) can be used by people who have no idea how they work. This means that individuals can operate a product even though they were not part of the tension matrix that made the product possible.

At one level this is to be expected and as it should be. The whole point of specialization is that the majority can benefit from the concentrated labors of the minorities in its midst. We do not all have to be electricians to enjoy the benefits of electric light. This is why system integrity is so important. We have to be able to take it on trust that the things we buy and services we utilize will function as advertised. But technology is about leverage. It is about expanding, often greatly, what an individual can do. So it is also about power.

* * * *

An obvious example, within a tension matrix, is when a young man, either through exceptional earnings or inheritance, finds himself in a position to purchase a high-performance car. He feels immensely empowered. In no time he is pushing the car to its limit and himself beyond it, often with pitiable consequences for those he kills or maims. As it did for the young men in their jeep with their guns who came upon Shona's African village (the fictional situation described in chapter 6) and gave vent to the power that they had, technology exaggerates what he can do. Technology, in the sense of specifically applied knowledge, needs to be incubated within an appropriately nurturing boundary condition and, as a result, there is a chance that those within it will possess some notion of how it should be used. But once created it can, like a virus, jump from one boundary condition to another in which there may be no such constraints.

Place a gun in the hands of a people whose previous weapon has been a spear and watch their tension matrix rip apart. The argument that *if we didn't sell the stuff to them someone else would* does not smack of great moral vigor. Introduce into the buffalo country of North America's Plains Indians with their bows and arrows white hunters using repeating rifles, eager to sell bison hides into eastern city markets, and watch a way of life destroyed. All too often we have used technology in exactly the way biological evolution would predict. Secure an advantage and then use it to dominate anything and everything. But because specific aspects of technology can jump so easily from one boundary condition to another, allowing our biological drivers to rule the roost in this way is likely to prove extremely dangerous.

An obvious example of how technology can destabilize boundary conditions is the ease with which pornography can be delivered via the internet. Often generated in areas where exploitation is stimulated by poverty, the images can be sold into areas where such exploitation is no longer possible because the rights of individuals are protected. The biological urge in each of us to exert power over another is immensely strong when roused. The normal sexual relationship between a male and a female is predicated upon the power each has over the other (she to attract and he to deliver). But as soon as the relationship becomes unbalanced the consequences can be highly disruptive, as they were when those young men with Kalashnikovs came upon our fictional Shona's village.

By its very nature, technological innovation is destabilizing. Indeed it is differences that stimulate creative evolution. However, settled relationships are complex and unless new systems and products are introduced carefully they are likely to do considerable harm in the short run, even if their long-term effect is broadly beneficial. Globalization and the technology transfer that accompanies it are frequently held to be universally good. But when it undermines traditional communities by attracting individuals to elements of an imported tension matrix that recognizes them only as a low-cost resource, problems are created that economics tends to ignore. Logically the social technologies that evolve alongside industrial technologies should be exported as part of globalization, although they seldom are. Sexual exploitation may attract the headlines, but it is only a subset of economic exploitation generally.

* * * *

With the proliferation of a nuclear capability, the chance of rogue elements securing and using tactical nuclear weapons increases. As the events of 9/11 demonstrated, there are individuals who would be prepared to use such weapons if they could. On the face of it, America's response was entirely logical. Rogue elements have to be based somewhere, so put pressure on all countries where they might exist to eliminate them. Brand those countries unwilling to do so 'rogue states' and threaten them with direct action.

But in an age of mass communication, rapid technology transfer and asymmetric warfare, where one side fights as an army under the gaze of its own media and the other fights covertly on its home territory, using its opponent's media as a weapon, invasive occupation, particularly by a democratic state, is likely to be inconclusive and messy, simply because a commitment to total victory will almost certainly be lacking. Such a commitment would require an imperial power to absorb the subject power within its own boundary condition, and what, in today's economically integrating world, would be the advantage of that? This means that, ultimately, only a political solution will be successful and so one should have applied political logic rather than imperial logic at the outset. But to do that would have required America to wrap itself inside a different story before it invaded Iraq.

Watching governments struggle to control the internet, as it penetrates nation state after nation state, is like watching national health authorities try to control the spread of a virus. At least mankind has evolved the World Health Organization which can set standards and coordinate action. Technology, generally, needs the same supranational body to set standards and coordinate action. We are trying. The International Atomic Energy Agency, whose Director-General is currently Mohamed El Baradei, is such a body. But until we establish a relatively small number of geographically contiguous and culturally similar blocks embracing multiple nation states around which a new United Nations structure can be built (an approach discussed further in chapter 18, *The Road Ahead*) and develop a generally accepted protocol about how we handle the impact of technology, such bodies will lack the political potency they need.

The primary impetus behind globalization comes from corporations in one boundary condition seeking to exploit commodities, labor cost differences, or markets within another boundary condition. The first is the most troublesome because the revenue paid to the commodity-producing country will be under the control of whatever group dominates its tension matrix and so may only serve to distance its elite from the bulk of its population. The second involves more individuals, but apart from making them somewhat better off in money terms than their peers (and sexual exploitation can do that), it is unlikely, on its own, to improve the tension matrix they are part of. However one can expect the third (exploiting a market) to have real impact because it must interact with a large number of people who have a choice.

If we think of the technologies in products which have been developed to meet mass consumer demand as discrete clumps of cerebral structure (service technologies are more complex in that they require a higher level of interaction and so may have an even greater impact), it may be easier for us to grasp the enormous potential technology has for improving the human lot, so long as its use is life-enhancing. The wind-up radio, for example, has had a most beneficial impact on communities with no access to electricity.

The ideas contained within these products trigger a chain reaction amongst those who come upon them for the first time. The leaders of closed societies have everything to fear from such encounters. Their people say look, here is something we like that you have not given us. And this causes these people to wonder if their story and matrix, which their leaders guard with such jealously, is really so perfect? After a slow start, China's leadership grasped this logic and is now embracing free-market capitalism with a vengeance, albeit within a story and tension matrix that are uniquely their own. And we, in the West, should not carp about that. China's civilization is far older than ours and there will surely be things we can learn from them.

But selling arms to factions that control sought-after commodities is quite a different matter. It is about as moral as paying a gang not to vandalize one's car, and certainly as stupid as arming that gang into the bargain. How we can espouse democratic values, which can be reduced to the simple principle that the power of all individuals should be increased at the expense of those few who control a state, and still sell coercive technologies to national cabals who are no better than thugs, defies all logic. Of course our mental gymnastics in this regard are predicated upon the assumption that democracy applies only to our own boundary condition, and that all outside it must be judged from the standpoint of our 'national interest'. This is standard biological thinking, lacking even a shred of cerebral morality.

* * * *

We often talk today about technology transfer, as if it is just a simple matter of showing people who never came close to inventing an automobile, for example, how to build one. Factories can be built. People can be trained to work in them. But what has been transferred is often very little. The wages paid may be insufficient to purchase the item produced and the infrastructure of the country might not be suitable for it in any event. Instead of working on a dirt farm, or intermittently in the shanty town of some metropolis, the individual can work in a factory. Over time, his view of the world will be transformed — over time.

There is scant evidence that the blacks who worked down South Africa's gold mines, which were set up, organized and run by European corporations, took home much more than their low wages. No doubt they were grateful for these. But there was almost nothing in what they did that might have given them even an inkling of the nature of the tension matrix that conceived and utilized the mines. And frankly, that suited the Europeans very well. All they needed was the product (the gold) and the muscle power of the workers. As Britain industrialized in the 18th and 19th centuries, the individuals who streamed from the countryside into the burgeoning, smoke-filled towns found themselves in a similar situation, but with an important difference.

They were part of the tension matrix that was evolving. The factory-owning entrepreneurs and their workers were in the same boat, learning as they went along. It was messy, often fractious, frequently unfair, but bit by bit a consensus evolved about how an urban, industrial matrix, as opposed to a rural, predominantly agricultural one, should be organized. Towns learned to improve their governance. Unions of workers were formed and eventually recognized in law. The habits of the rural economy, such as whole families working in the fields at high season from dawn to dusk, often seven days a week, had been transferred into the factories, until factory acts put a stop to child labor and regulated hours.

Without the markets and distribution systems that had steadily grown up as farm products were shipped into towns in ever increasing quantities, and the expertise built up by the city trading merchants in capital formation and accounting, industrialization would not have developed as rapidly as it did. And it could not have happened at all if a spirit of enquiry and desire for progress had not excited the imagination of a growing educated class. The dynamic tension during this transformation was often extreme, but somehow the institutions of the country managed to adapt and engineer a new consensus.

So to think of technology in terms of the steam engine, the coal mine, or the semi-automated factory alone is quite misleading. It encompasses a whole mindset, in which the physical aspect of technology may be the least important. We need to distinguish between what a technology enables individual humans to do and the tension matrix that enables a particular technology to be conceived and used.

A tension matrix governs the way people within a boundary condition interact and seeks to contain their often competing aspirations. It is built up around reciprocal customs that may be formalized as institutions and must integrate into a functioning whole — what individuals do, and how they do it. Introduce a technology substantially more powerful than any they are familiar with, and expect the equilibrium of their tension matrix to be disrupted. A young man given a Kalashnikov can quickly undermine the village elder who has known only a spear. Drunk with power, like a French Revolutionary, he will tear down generations of tradition that gave rise to the existing tension matrix. In its place he will insert a one-dimensional matrix — centered around his own power — and all the checks and balances that people value and which lie at the heart of institutions will have to be reinvented.

* * * *

A technical innovation is cerebral structure's equivalent of biological adaptation. It can come about by happenstance (induction), or in response to reasoned intent (deduction).[3] But either way, the relevance of the change, in the context of the prevailing tension matrix, must be appreciated by at least some individuals. Modern corporations have been built as a result of both induction and deduction. The disruption brought about by the changes they bring is generally accepted as progress because they are sustained by individual customers.

By contrast, sending a fully-formed product (such as the arms sold to African nations) into a boundary condition whose cerebral structure could not have conceived it, is like lobbing in a hand grenade. And even when an entire tension matrix is imposed upon a boundary condition that did not conceive it, the apparent stability is likely to disguise deeper and more long-lasting disruptions.

The achievements of the Roman Empire have come to dominate Western history. But just as the United States owed everything to the European culture it grew out of, so did Rome owe everything to the rich Mediterranean culture of which it was a part. Rome's trick, like America's, was to pick the best examples of hard and soft technology (physical and organizational structures) from its neighbors, and incorporate them into a tension matrix that was dominated by a will to achieve imperial excellence (its story).

From government (taken from the Greeks), to seamanship (taken from the Phoenicians), to military organization and civic engineering

---

3. Deductive logic is when you start from a general principle (the more concentrated the application of a force, the more likely is it to disrupt the atomic structure of any object to which it is applied), and use it in a particular situation (a flint arrowhead, if thrown with sufficient force, should penetrate an animal's hide). Inductive knowledge is when a process of trial and error (repeated attempts to bring down a mammoth) leads to a general principle (large animals are best killed by driving them over a cliff — or the more massive an object, the harder the fall).

(based upon the best they observed), the Romans adapted everything they could to serve their ambition of conquest and control, all for the greater glory of Rome. S.P.Q.R. (*Senatus Populusque Romanus* — the Senate and People of Rome) meant something. Romans believed they had discovered a better way and forced it and their story upon the world.

But when the Western Roman Empire collapsed in the 5th century AD and the legions that had upheld Roman order suddenly left, what remained? As it was following the destruction of the Berlin Wall after the collapse of Soviet Communism's far shorter hegemony, people across Europe found themselves free. Free of the certainty of being ruled by another. Free of the security that others had provided. Free to run for themselves the infrastructure of roads, towns, aqueducts and markets that had tied them to a center which was no more.

Modern Europeans are recovering from their shorter enslavement more quickly than their ancient ancestors who entered into a period dubbed by the 14th century Italian scholar, Francesco Petrarca (*Petrarch*), the Dark Ages. From 476 to 1000, populations struggled, little was recorded, few things were built and cultural achievements were minimal. Out of all the technologies the Roman state had bent to its purpose, only the Roman Church retained any coherence, and it had evolved in opposition to the Roman ideal.

My guess is that people simply reveled in being free and collapsed into a state of mental indolence in which the thought of order, on anything other than the most local scale, was just too much to contemplate. Over time, warlords carved out little fiefdoms for themselves and their supporters, and over time, and after much infighting, these became bigger and fewer and civil life was gradually rebuilt. 1,500 years after Pax Romana, Pax Europa is looking like a real possibility — 1,500 years!

The truth is that boundary conditions are incredibly important, because they speak to our identity, and many in Europe today are still suspicious of the idea of Europe as a controlling entity. There are even Scots who do not want to be part of Britain and Catalans and Basques who do not want to be part of Spain.

In reality, we are part of a single boundary condition, called humanity, whether we like it or not, so our choice is between allowing our biological drivers to sort out the evolutionary discontinuities that will inevitably spring up between us, as we struggle to *master the craft* of expressing ourselves, or having the gumption to design structures that enable the process to unfold with the support of all those affected.

Eurocrats talk about the principle of subsidiarity (the theory that power should only be delegated upwards through the layers of government as appropriate), but have so far failed to persuade the average European voter that they know what it means in practice. And how right the average European voter is, because the very term *subsidiarity* reveals a complete misunderstanding of what is required. A subsidiary is something that is controlled from above and what we want is something that is controlled from below — from the level of the individual. This is an objective that is entirely compatible with structures designed to uphold a dynamic order, so long as they always have integrity and transparency as their guiding characteristic.

* * * *

Although the culmination of many ideas, the internet has, to my mind, been the greatest technological innovation of our age. For the first time, since we left the self-contained clan, we have found a way to communicate with one another that is instantaneous and informal, independent of social hierarchy and vested interest and dependent only upon proximity to a terminal — the modern equivalent of a shared fire.

That there is a great desire for such communication is clear. Internet traffic has grown rapidly, following a similar pattern of use to the telephone after it became generally available. In fact it is clear that mass consumer demand has stimulated technologies that are moving us back towards the kind of single boundary condition that was once enjoyed by the atomic tribe. The automobile, the telephone, cheap air travel, popular culture, the personal computer and, crucially, the purchasing power that our modern economy has given to ordinary men, women, teenagers and children, has shifted power decisively to members of the human community at large. The way in which the internet allows individuals to access and distribute a wide array of information to one another across every conceivable boundary condition (even the Pentagon is not immune to teenage hackers) is accelerating this healthy process mightily.

But — and isn't there always a 'but'? — the customary dangers still lie in wait, ready to hijack this process if we let them. Commercial interests, that previously enjoyed some monopoly over access to individuals or to specific knowledge, are being challenged, although mostly by other, newer, commercial interests that are themselves consumer-driven. More worrisome are all those entities that sit behind our democratic façade, those quasi-government bodies and the corporations that have developed a symbiotic relationship with them. Until these are brought under better public control (and this will be discussed in ***Part 4***), they will act to protect their boundary condition from examination. While all organizations are entitled to some privileged information (although none that is hidden from proper institutional scrutiny), attempts to hide behind blanket protections — such as on account of national security — should be strenuously resisted. As a general rule, allowing for patent protection and copyright, knowledge itself should be available to all.

This does not mean that the internet should be a free-for-all. We have learned the hard way that children can get lured into danger through it, and with new technologies there will always be outcomes that are impossible to predict. But this particular danger is a function of the success of the internet in enabling children to communicate more readily. While we should certainly subject every new technology to moral scrutiny, the emphasis should always be on reducing the dangers so as to preserve the benefits, rather than on outright bans that please some special interest. The dangers the internet exposes us to (the most obvious being image abuse[4] and fraudulent solicitation[5]) need to be and are being flagged up, and the risks reduced.

---

4. This would include using an individual's image in a way that was demeaning, degrading or patently false in terms of its suggestion about them.

5. This would include soliciting by encouraging false expectations — a few politicians would probably fall foul of this one!

There is, I think, a misconception about technology, namely that it is value neutral, the implication being that we can never get enough of it. But such an observation is as meaningless as saying that a rock or a forest is value neutral and concluding that we should have more rocks or more forests. Technology is at the very heart of cerebral structure, because it entails thought structures in action. And it will be through technological innovation, especially that which helps us interact more effectively with one another, that cerebral structure evolves. But the crucial difference between biological evolution and the evolution of cerebral structure is that while the former relies on blind trial and error, the latter is down to our conscious intent. This does not mean that we will always get what we seek. But it does mean that we should always be open about what we are trying to achieve.

16

Change

OVER THE VERY long term, it looks as though energy and mass (which are technically the same — see chapter 2, *The Universe*) will dissipate across an ever expanding, increasingly cold and lifeless universe. It is thought that even black holes, which feed on matter, will eventually dissipate as the small amount of structure they discharge becomes greater than the matter they are able to consume. All this is derived from the laws of physics, which are clearly incomplete as we do not know how the universe came into existence in the first place. So the dynamic that underpins us is not fully understood. However, through consciousness we feel a great urge to exist, which must reflect something endemic in the cosmos.

So although change has been a constant so, too, has been the impulse towards evolved life (if you assume, as I do, that the construct 'life' should be applied to the universe as a whole). And what is more (and what should give us comfort) is that change does not entail an abandonment of what has gone before (the fallacy of the revolutionary), but its reworking. Change is not a matter of what I win you must lose, but a creative process whose objective, in our terms, is to expand conscious life for us all.

It is not particularly straightforward to detach the process of change from the matrix, as it is the matrix that sets up the structure within which change has to occur and it is the matrix itself that is altered by change. This helps explain why revolution is usually less radical than evolution. Revolutions invariably put different people into existing positions within existing structures, and then give these positions and structures different names. Evolution, on the other hand, tends to alter the matrix in subtle, creative ways, which can have significant long-term consequences.

The easiest way to think about it is to go back to the beginning, to the interaction between matter and energy, total freedom and total order. This generates the tension from which everything else flows. Energy and matter work on each other to create a rich elaboration of structures. That this occurs suggests that asymmetry may be a fundamental property we should recognize. Matter would not have evolved if matter and antimatter particles had been distributed evenly. The galactic system state would not have evolved if atomic matter had been distributed evenly. The Christian idea of the angel, Lucifer, who fell from grace speaks to this same phenomenon. Without what the Church called sin, and we might now call behavioral mutations, the human dynamic would have been stillborn. Asymmetry is the grain that disturbs a structure and makes possible an evolutionary pearl.

Evolution, however, also depends upon order. If structures cannot establish a degree of stability, nothing much is possible. The advantage of thinking in terms of system states is that we do not have to go back to the quantum, the atomic, the galactic or the biological — all of which operate within their own broadly stable matrix — and each of which is a distinct elaboration of the dance between matter and energy. We can go straight to the human matrix (or, as I am arguing, to the matrix that pertains to cerebral structure), always remembering our Russian doll relationship to the others.

Each of us occupies something akin to a honeycomb cell delineated by those dimensions that draw on our deepest feelings and have given rise to our institutions.[1] The sense of them is defined by the story that

1. The family and friendships; our economic and democratic systems; the armed forces; our religious traditions; courts of law — criminal and civil; the executive

we carry in our heads about what we are, and it is the tension they place on us, as we fulfill our life cycle, that causes us to interact with others in the ways that we do. Ours is not a wholly passive reaction, however. It is moderated by our moral compass (our sense of fairness which arises out of consciousness) and by our ability to think about the whys and wherefores of our existence.

When Spartacus led his slave revolt against the Roman state, his own and his followers' urge to be free overwhelmed the Roman story, namely that a slave should remain a slave until the Roman state decreed otherwise, or woe betide the consequences. Although his and similar uprisings were crushed and slavery continues into modern times, such challenges to stories that embody coercion remind those who benefit from them that there are limits.

When the Soviets crushed the Hungarian uprising in 1956 it might have seemed as though the protestors had achieved less than nothing. But over the ensuing years, Hungary, while remaining communist and within the Soviet sphere, achieved a degree of independence from Soviet control. Although victorious over the rebels, the Soviet authorities were made to realize that Hungarians could only be pushed so far. By contrast, Cuba, a communist-inspired country that successfully resisted American recolonization, has been largely isolated from the West ever since. The humiliated Americans have not been forgiving.

Change, as these examples illustrate, is remarkably difficult. But this is hardly surprising as it is evolution's toughest act. Coming up with a stable structure is hard enough, even one that will only exist for as long as the energy that sustains it lasts. But allowing it to generate variations, any one of which might open up a pathway towards a new or revised structure, the rest having to be rejected, is an impressive piece of evolved design.

---

and legislature; government agencies; the business community; the medical profession; the education system; the media; universities; regulatory and oversight bodies.

Chapter 16 – Change

In biology, the change process is essentially generational. And as the life cycle of biological structures is short (compared to stars, planets and chemical compounds, for example), mutations (or variations) can become established and develop rather quickly, interacting with their general environment (sea, land and air) and each other, to form the biological system state we are familiar with and are part of.

But even biological structures tend to develop in waves, following some stimulus — some innovation or shock. This is a characteristic pattern evident in evolution within all system states. When a critical point on the temperature gradient was passed in the early expansion of the universe, this allowed a host of new sub-atomic (quantum) structures to form. Or, closer to our own time, when a critical amount of free oxygen in the Earth's atmosphere was generated by simple biological organisms this may well have triggered the Cambrian explosion of diverse biological structures to which we are heirs.

In the age of the dinosaurs, planet Earth supported a rich diversity of biological forms that remained largely stable for many millions of years. Humans were not a feature, although nascent cerebral structure was. It took a shock (a meteor, a rise in volcanic activity, climate change, or a combination of these) to stir the evolutionary pot and give new variations a chance to develop. What gained added traction was brainpower.

Brainpower seems to have been a function of social interaction. As far as we can tell, dinosaurs exhibited this characteristic. Their brains controlled their structures, telling them how to forage and fight as well as how to come together and mate and bring up their young. But having become kings of a jungle that was fully occupied and in balance, there was little advantage to be gained from variations. Like the brains of the French Bourbon kings, the dinosaurs had little reason to forget anything or to learn anything. They were doing just fine — until catastrophe struck!

The disaster, whatever it was, would certainly have offered opportunity to structures that could be flexible. Of course, in order to be flexible it helps to have an expanded brain function. Being able to adapt one's environment in small ways (using furs as clothes, tools as weapons and sounds to coordinate strategy) would have been advantageous in a hostile environment (i.e. one to which one was not naturally suited). That this evolutionary approach has managed to get two rather cumbersome biological structures onto the surface of the Moon is testament to its potential. This example also demonstrates the radical nature of cerebral structure, because no individual human brain could possibly have achieved such a feat.

Although cerebral structure relies completely on those same individual human brains, it is the tension matrix we are evolving that allows us to create what we do, and the story each of us carries in our head that makes sense of it. Take human beings out of the equation and you would have nothing — or nothing other than the remnants of a lost civilization. I dare say some machines would keep running for a while, clunking and churning and ticking and whirring, as they do in those science fiction films about the last android standing, but not for long.

* * * *

Because each of us starts within the matrix and it is the matrix that governs most of our actions, what drives us to seek change is a feeling of dissatisfaction, a feeling that things generally, or something specific, could be better. This feeling is generated by the reaction of our moral compass to actual events, mediated by any rational thoughts we might have. Now I don't want us to get hung up on the word *moral* here. It relates solely to the feeling each of us has about how things should be in relation to ourselves (and, by extension, to any others we might identify with). It is not intended to mean the outcome of some deep philosophical discourse, although I would argue that it draws on instinctive feelings that are even more profound (fundamental is perhaps a better word) than such discourse can ever be. Ultimately, all thought is an attempt to express truths about the universe that can only exist at the level of actual experience. Even pure mathematics, like music, is only relevant because it resonates within us — but I digress.

The lonely individual is up against it when it comes to change, the more so when formal mechanisms within the matrix to facilitate change are absent as has been the case during most of mankind's history. And even today we are far from immune to this problem. In a speech about the most recent economic crisis to blight humanity, the Governor of the Bank of England, Mervyn King, asked the question on everyone's lips: *Why did no one see this coming?* and then provided a succinct answer:

> In fact, most of the underlying causes of the crisis attracted attention from economists, central banks, international financial institutions and regulators. But the difficulty of overcoming coordination or collective action problems meant that nothing was done. Banks felt that they had to keep on dancing while the music was playing. Regulators could never prove that the risks they identified would crystallize, and the "top down" and "bottom up" dimensions of prudential supervision were not married. Central banks and the IMF discussed the imbalances for so long that some came to believe that they were crying wolf. And no one country could prevent the worldwide increase in asset prices.[2]

In other words (to use my language) although many individuals could see the problem, the tension matrix did not offer those individuals any means whereby they could address it. This gap in design was filled by people's biological drivers which pushed things along to a point that was bound to be self-correcting. In this instance the self-correcting contraction will be as painful for many individuals as the expansion was pleasurable, but regrettably not with equal incidence which, of course, is our ongoing moral dilemma.

For much of our history, the most consistent change agent has been death. Whatever position in the matrix an individual occupied, the only certainty was that they would not occupy it for ever. But having a different individual take over a position did not necessarily mean that its function would be altered. That said, the role of fathers and mothers, for example, as parents and even as married couples, has altered over time. Today, an increasing number of individuals are

2. From a speech the Governor of the Bank of England, Mervyn King, gave in London on March 17th 2009 to the Worshipful Company of International Bankers, whose members must have been somewhat embarrassed by the name of their fine body in light of popular opinion about them at the time.

producing children without getting married. The story that makes sense of the matrix has changed. But how does the story change?

* * * *

Not so long ago it was considered a matter of great shame for a woman to have a child outside the institution of Christian marriage. This story, at that time, was intended to strengthen a woman's resolve to avoid sex until she was in an arrangement, supported by both spiritual and secular authority, namely by the Church and the law, that would protect her and her child for the long term. This arrangement got caught up in property rights, because the hereditary transfer of the relatively few positions that existed in early society proved to be the most harmonious way of allocating power. In the absence of heredity, positions were fought over, which involved considerable disruption and loss of life.

Around the edges there was quite a degree of flexibility. The role of the harlot was vital to the smooth running of society, as it provided an outlet for male sexuality that would not undermine the social system, although it did give rise to epidemics of the pox. And for women, the protection of marriage gave them a cloak under which they could enjoy sexual congress with men other than their husbands, if they felt the need. Over time, improvements in agriculture and industrialization enabled more people to live in cities, with a corresponding increase in the diversity of positions in the matrix, and this affected the relationship between men and women.

While heredity, with the help of able advisors, can train up most individuals to exercise general power, underpinned by property, these new positions were specialized, best executed by those with particular skills. Such positions grew almost exponentially as industrialization took hold, increasing the number of people able to earn a living on the basis of their ability, and their power increased relative to those who earned a living from property. It was at this time that Karl Marx, one of the many heralds of the new story, exclaimed that all property was theft. These changes progressively undermined the hereditary system and the ecclesiastical system that had supported it, (leading, as we have already seen, to the great upheavals of the 18th, 19th and 20th centuries), a shift not lost on women.

Having been able to look forward to a career filled with babies (many of whom died), followed by children and dedicated to the management of whatever size of household their husbands could claim (a meager affair for most), the prospect of a little more independence beckoned — although they still had to struggle to get the training needed to fill the new positions that were opening up. Gradually, a few brave souls broke cover (and were often branded lesbians as a result), building independent lives for themselves.

But it was the shock of two World Wars that moved things along. The first killed so many men that countless women had to make do on their own. It was the second, however, that drew large numbers of them into the factories and onto the land while their men were away fighting, and gave them a taste for independence. With the improvements in birth control that soon followed, they never looked back.

In the face of opposition from most men, and even a few women, John Stuart Mill, the great liberal writer and politician of the 19th century, campaigned tirelessly for the rights of women. He was also fashionably opposed to the power of the landowning class. By the middle of the 20th century, the story that explained the tension matrix had changed. But like Rubik's Cube,[3] no cell in the matrix can be adjusted without it affecting other cells. Hard structure, such as the way cities were designed and people lived; formal soft structure, such as laws governing property and voting rights; and informal soft structure, such as attitudes towards women in the workplace, had to change before the story about women could move from being an aspiration of some to a reality for all.

---

3. Invented in 1974 by Hungarian sculptor and professor of architecture Erno Rubik, the surface area of the six-faced cube is made up out of either 8, 27, 64 or 125 identical mini-cubes whose faces have distinct colors (traditionally: white, yellow, orange, red, blue and green). A pivot mechanism allows each row of each surface to be turned independently. The objective is to keep turning until each face of the cube has just one color. Over 300 million cubes have been sold.

* * * *

The great virtue of the liberal story is that it has allowed a large amount of experimentation in how individuals interact with one another, but this has opened it to the charge of ideological and moral ambiguity. The problem is that there is no obvious mechanism that filters these experiments for sustainability (as there would be under the rules that govern biological evolution). Instead we are left with verbal battles (that sometimes turn bloody) about such things as abortion, gay marriage and genetic engineering. Of course the conservative-liberal divide reflects exactly the basic tension that drives our universe: energy constrained and energy unconstrained. The liberal conceit, if I can call it that, is to imagine it can exist without conservatism. The conservative fallacy is to imagine that change can be averted.

I can only imagine that these verbal battles are the way cerebral structure will evolve. But we must not lose sight of the fact that ideas are not abstractions. They are felt. If we do not design space into our matrices for individuals to live their ideas, we will have no way of ascertaining their validity and perhaps tragically we will build up frustrations that are liable to explode into open warfare. Why particular individuals fall on one side of an argument rather than another is far from clear. It may be due to no more than personal experience in the face of uncertainty. We cannot know the best way forward, because we live in a universe of trial and error. We can make our best assessment, we can act with intent, but we cannot be certain. The Protestant brotherhood may have wrapped itself inside a cloak of conviction, but doubt was its constant companion.[4]

* * * *

When Susanna Bell finally agreed to go with her husband to New England in 1634 after losing her second child, which she regarded as a providential sign in favor of the enterprise, she was one of many thousands to make the journey. Although she and her husband Thomas, a

4. And the same is likely true for Islamic Fundamentalists today.

merchant, were Protestant, they were not being unduly persecuted and economically were comfortably off. But arising out of the political tensions of the 1630s, which would lead to the execution of the Catholic-inclined Charles I, there was a feeling amongst those they associated with that Protestantism would fare better in the New World, and a belief that economic opportunity might be greater.

Although in constant anguish during the eight week voyage out to New England at the sight of so much sea and sky, as she nursed her sea-sick husband, Susanna was not immediately accepted into the Roxbury church where they settled. It was felt she had not yet experienced God's grace directly. Between the birth of children and her husband's absences on business, she lived from sermon to sermon, delivered to colonists struggling to interpret the will of God, to keep their faith pure and to survive the harsh New England winters.

As for so many others, theirs was an idea in action. Inside England, the issue came to a head in a bloody civil war, whereas in New England individuals could practice what they preached, or try to. As it happened, Susanna returned to England with her husband in 1647 and settled in Seething Lane where his business could benefit from the strength of the London merchants. She survived the Great Plague of 1665 and the Great Fire a year later, all — she felt — on account of God's great mercy, and died in 1673, a year after her husband.[5]

When you think of the matrix, you need to remember that inside every cell is an individual like Susanna Bell, struggling to make sense of life. The ideas that pass between these individuals sometimes give rise to action and sometimes not. But it is this exchange of ideas and how they mature inside each person, in light of their experience, that is the lifeblood of the matrix and gradually transforms it.

* * * *

5. For a rich account of these intrepid people: *Pilgrims, new world settlers & the call of home* by Susan Hardman Moore, Yale University Press.

In the biological world, evolution leads to species differentiation: over time, adaptations successful in particular environments cause structures to become so distinct that they can no longer breed. With cerebral structure we see something of the same in the evolution of language. Why people end up inside one boundary condition rather than another is likely due to a combination of factors, which initially might be quite random.

An individual could have a bad experience at the hands of the status quo — the prevailing story. He, or she, finds that others have had a similarly unsatisfactory experience. They start comparing notes. Perhaps one amongst them articulates these dissatisfactions, just as Martin Luther did with his list of questions to the Catholic hierarchy, posted on the door of his local church at Wittenberg in 1517. Gradually an alternative story starts doing the rounds, attracting supporters and critics alike. Eventually the stories seem so different that neither side can discuss the matter with the other. Unless there is some way for the new story to detach itself from the political control of the orthodoxy, open warfare is declared.

Luther's example illustrates how a whole raft of issues within the matrix can be affected by what seems to start as a single topic. On the face of it, all Luther demanded was that the Catholic Church stop putting form before substance, the same demand Jesus had made of the Jewish priesthood. The idea that all a person had to do in order to get into heaven was meet specific tariffs laid down by the Church bureaucracy (so many Hail Marys and a hefty payment, for example), seemed to many a long way from the original idea of Christian faith. And while one was at it, why did one need the whole opulent hierarchy with the Pope at its head anyway, in order to find one's way to God's grace?

A handed-down faith with no questions asked by a Church organization that had become elaborate, rich, sophisticated and intimately entwined with the secular world of hereditary warlords (or kings, as they became) might have suited a rural world of tribal and later feudal relationships. But for many in the expanding towns, particularly of Northern Europe, containing a growing merchant class interested in the ideas of the Renaissance (the scientific and philosophical ideas from

Ancient Greece that had seeped into Europe from the retreating Islamic world), the closed Catholic orthodoxy was proving unsatisfactory. Between 1522 and 1534, Luther translated the bible into German so that it could be more accessible, a move followed in other countries. Suddenly the word of God was there for anyone to read, and one did not need a pesky priest to interpret it.

The story of modern democracy is intimately associated with the story of Protestantism, because it was through Protestantism and the institutions of city government (which functioned in parallel to the traditional order) that individuals rediscovered the habit of thinking and acting for themselves, once prevalent in the Athenian city state of Ancient Greece. And it did not stop there; just as Judaism had provided a moral framework that enabled Jewish merchants to conduct business all over Europe, so too did Protestantism. Susanna Bell's husband continued to do business with his co-religionists in New England long after he returned to London. It was no coincidence that many of the most successful companies to emerge from Britain's industrial revolution were founded by religious non-conformists. For such people, hard work, honesty and the application of knowledge were manifestations of their religious faith.

The point is that the Pilgrims, like their successors, challenged the prevailing story. They were searching for a new path to truth because they believed the old path no longer led there. They argued and analyzed and worried and could split hairs with the best of them. Most had not wanted to leave the Anglican tradition, but when William Laud, as Archbishop of Canterbury (1633–45), started enforcing rigorous Episcopal discipline, with less emphasis on the sermon and a more formal Communion, many feared a return to the unquestioning slavery of Popish ways. The bloody Catholic fightback in England under Queen Mary (1553–58) was still vivid in peoples' minds. The Book of Martyrs, depicting the horrible burnings of those priests who refused to toe the Catholic line at that time, was avidly read.

It is probably true to say that change is driven by the passionate minority, with the majority leaning this way or that, depending on the strength of the wind. Unfortunately, this process can lead as easily to a

Third Reich as to a Commonwealth, the name given to the English Republic after the execution of its king. Eleven years of Oliver Cromwell's austere rule were enough for most people, and on the Lord Protector's death (the title he eventually chose for his office), there was a collective sigh of relief when the monarchy was reinstated under Charles II, and the rather dissolute ways of the Stuarts set the country's tone once more. That said, England had changed and would never be the same again. A new level of consciousness had been created.

* * * *

Change works on both the mind and the matrix: on the story that explains the matrix and on the relationships the matrix defines. Cerebral structure is the fusion of the two. It is for this reason that attempts to impose Western-style democracy on societies with a different tradition have usually proved so spectacularly unsuccessful. For all its importance, there is still a great deal about the human mind that we do not understand. What is it, for example, that allowed Fascist bully boys in 1930s Germany to beat up opposition supporters, almost with impunity, just as Robert Mugabe's ZANU-PF supporters did in Zimbabwe in 2008? For both regimes the imprimatur of an election was important, but how it was won was irrelevant. This points to the dark side of democracy. In a crisis, our biological drivers tell us we should act collectively, like a shoal of fish. There is safety in numbers, they say, and morality extends no further than that.

The individual human mind is not a powerful thing. And how can it be? In a world where there are 6.7 billion such minds, all more similar than they are different, how could any one possibly stand out? The answer, of course, is through the matrix. By trial and error we have evolved structures that have leveraged individuals with particular characteristics. Ancient Egyptian society needed a Pharaoh, just as modern American society needs a President, because a collective worthy of the name must have a point at which decisions are resolved and towards which the priesthood of advisors needed to organize it can make its case for this or that action. That the structure should be seen as legitimate in the minds of all those who make it up is paramount.

The Egyptian solution was to endow their Pharaohs with godly properties so that the structure of their society was a seamless matrix embracing not just themselves but the underworld and the heavens too. Left-wing intellectuals invariably fail to acknowledge the importance of heredity, but in this context — quite apart from the system's advantage in choosing a successor with the minimum conflict — having elevated a Pharaoh to godliness it would have been inconsistent to send his children back to the fields. Class structure evolved for the very same reason: it was functional and made sense. Individuals absorbed the qualities needed to perform the duties associated with the strata they were brought up in.

But even for Pharaohs this arrangement was never hard and fast. If one performed poorly (or was unlucky, which is much the same thing when you are a god), there was always another family which might take over. And from amongst the laboring masses, who were generally content to live out their lives without glory, there might always be a young man of ability (or young woman of outstanding charms) whom the hierarchy could draw into its ranks, as others slipped quietly back into obscurity.

The matrix of modern society is more complex than the one developed by the ancient Egyptians. There are many more clusters of hierarchies, each pertaining to some function valued by individuals. These clusters have their own selection criteria and individuals meeting them can gain leverage in their particular field. As societies have increased in size, clusters of functional hierarchies have multiplied both geographically and by type. Individuals can occupy positions in several different hierarchies (such as a trade body, a company, a church, a sailing club, etc.), but, like the Ancient Egyptians, we are still inclined to give extraordinarily high status to just a few positions. I would guess that the Office of the United States' President is as elevated in people's minds as was that of the Pharaoh.

We may laugh now about the idea of a Pharaoh being an hereditary god. Will we one day scratch our heads at the thought of an individual, even one elected by *we the people*, aloft in Air Force One, with the power to unleash so much destruction that it would mean the end of the human race as we know it? And if we looked at how many presidents were related to past presidents (or senior politicians), we would surely find a statistical relationship that suggested heredity was not entirely dead.

Free-market capitalism, with its ability to channel resources into organizations meeting individual needs, and equally importantly, its ability to remove resources from organizations no longer meeting them, is undoubtedly one of mankind's greatest innovations (with no apology to Karl Marx). By their nature, markets operate on the basis of trial and error, but at least free-market capitalism punishes error quite quickly. Political error can remain unpunished for far longer.

Probably the greatest difficulty we face today is that globalization, which has brought benefits to many people, has largely been a function of free-market capitalism, and our political organization has lagged badly behind. This has happened once before, in the late eighteenth, nineteenth and early twentieth centuries with the most heart-rending consequences. As was the case then, leaders — by and large — simply do not know how to adapt the political systems they are part of. In the following chapter I will discuss why this might be, but for now, I want to remain focused a little longer on the process of change itself.

* * * *

In thinking about change we need to have an idea about what changes and how. If we start with the matrix we can see that its broad dimensions are physical structure, hierarchical structure, formal rules, informal relationships, products, art and language. On the whole, these dimensions are functional, in that they facilitate certain outcomes. What makes people respond to the matrix is the story that they carry in their heads explaining its purpose and underpinning its legitimacy.

Physical structure. For man, physical structure started with the natural world, but progressively became the man-made world of towns, cities, roads, bridges, ships and the like. Although some physical structures have been remarkably long-lasting (the Egyptian pyramids are between 5,000 and 6,000 years old) most everyday objects do not last particularly long, which makes it easier for them to evolve. By contrast, such structures as cities, roads and fortifications, built to reflect the circumstances of their age and facilitate the rhythm of life, have often come to inhibit change due to their permanence. But the story behind a structure may be as important as its physicality. The Greek Parthenon (447–432 BC) and Colosseum in Rome (70–80 AD), were not only for day-to-day use, but were intended to demonstrate the permanence of the stories they symbolized and, like the pyramids, they still resonate today.

Hierarchical structure. Although hierarchy evolved as a system for organizing and focusing behavior in many animal species, humans have developed its use enormously. What it does is turn a large number of individuals into a proto-organism able to perform a specific function, such as manufacture cars, provide hospital care, or coordinate political action. Its beauty is that it can form, adapt and even dissipate in ways no biological structure is able to do. More than that, it can draw on the brainpower and diverse skills of its constituent parts (the individuals who make it up), and yet still be coordinated by a controlling brain — that of its chief executive. In early human history, this innovation was used primarily by warlords who discovered that by integrating individual men into a fighting force they could project their lustful ambitions to an extraordinary degree. Although still an instrument for magnifying power, hierarchical structures have evolved to meet a large number of human needs. Like the matrix they form part of, each has its own story that helps bind people to it.

Formal & informal rules. Formal rules are those enacted into law and enforced by a political entity embracing all the individuals within its boundary condition. Informal relationships are those that have no formal legal authority but which can powerfully influence behavior, such as membership of a family, guild or party. Often these informal relationships gain quasi-legal status, as trades unions and guilds eventually did. Unlike formal rules, informal relationships need not be constrained within a political boundary condition. As such, they have often been the scourge of political dictatorships anxious to preserve their ideology (their story). Groupings of the like-minded have been responsible for disseminating new knowledge and culture throughout the human family.

Products. Products embody knowledge and have had a similarly subversive effect on established structures, empowering individuals in subtle ways and frequently undermining the efficacy of existing arrangements. Until quite recently competition was dominated by warfare and the products that facilitated it. But as the human matrix has changed from serving the needs of the warlord and his attendants to serving those of the individual consumer, products have evolved that meet a wide and growing range of human needs.

Art. In all its forms, art is of the greatest importance because it reflects a people back to itself, and although it is likely to be in broad harmony with their story, it often challenges it in subtle ways. As a window into the soul of individuals in a matrix, it can capture growing feelings even before these have been expressed in more concrete terms.[6] The evolution of Negro music in the United States, for example, revealed a people captive at one level, reaching for freedom at another, creating an alternative story to the one given to them, which would eventually be taken up by white singers expressing their support for civil rights and their opposition to the Vietnam War.

Language. If we think of language not just as words and grammar but as the full array of devices we use to communicate with one another, it should become apparent that we *can* only communicate if we share a common story at some basic level, and of course that story is that we are human.[7] And this ability to communicate is not just restricted to humans. We can communicate with the animals we evolved from and

6. Wolfgang Amadeus Mozart's opera, *The Marriage of Figaro*, (based on the farce by Pierre Beaumarchais) was wonderfully subversive. A count, intent on using his power to deflower one of his servants who is about to marry his valet, Figaro, is eventually forced to apologize to his wife in front of the entire household. Three years after its premiere, before an anxious Hapsburg Emperor, Joseph II, the French mob stormed the Bastille and the French Revolution began.

7. Communist countries were highly suspicious of Western rock groups, because although their young might not understand a word being sung, the emotional force being communicated was very potent and quite outside the state's control. In this their leaders were not so different from America's gerontocracy in the 1950s!

they with us. Indeed much of the biological world carries meaning for us. While a language, in its pure sense, is exclusive (it can only be used by those who know it and thereby sets up a particular boundary condition), even individuals from completely different cultures are able to communicate. As I have already remarked, the proposition that all humans have evolved a basic language grammar, which enables the young to learn their own language quickly, is very likely true.

These six dimensions — physical structure, hierarchical structure, formal and informal rules, products, art and language — all impact the process of change.

* * * *

It should already be becoming clear how change works. The physical environment, mostly man-made now, is the first constraint against change although it may start out as an agent for change. When Dwight Eisenhower, as President, championed the start of the Interstate Highway system in 1956, he began a process that would speed the movement of people and commerce throughout the United States. By 2004 it covered some 46,937 miles of roadway, and is probably one of the world's largest public works programs.

In spite of the fact that it was a government initiative, it fitted perfectly into the American story of individual liberty and free enterprise. Just imagine Communist countries tying themselves into knots about how to control the movements of people such a scheme might unleash! Europe, too, began a road-building program after the Second World War, but it was not as extensive, was built up country by country, and had to contend with more existing infrastructure. Also, the European mindset was more wedded to the railways. I have always felt this was a consequence of Europe's collectivist mentality (its story) — better to herd people onto state-controlled transport than enable them to go where and when they want.

When I was growing up in California, I fell in love, like everyone else, with those great chrome-clad, gas-guzzling giants that came out every year, each model more adorned than the last. General Motors,

Ford and Chrysler tooled up for this annual fashion show, and shareholders, managers and employees grew prosperous in consequence. What was good for General Motors *was* good for America. However, when the first oil shock struck in the 1970s, all hell broke loose. Suddenly those little cars the Japanese had been perfecting and selling to an audience that didn't mind being mildly ridiculed became very popular. The American automobile industry went into a tailspin from which it has never recovered. Not only was it tooled up to make the wrong sort of vehicles, but its workers had extracted generous medical and retirement benefits from their companies in the good times that management was stuck with.

We have now (in 2009) experienced a second oil shock and America's dependence on road transport is looking like a disadvantage. Even her remaining privately-run railroads are, once again, doing good business (at least they were until the current recession struck). Europeans, though, are crowing silently as their extensive network of heavily-subsidized passenger-carrying railways is making more sense. And if the price of petrol was not enough, the poor car user in Europe is coming under a sustained barrage of propaganda from the green lobby, who accuse drivers of selfishly destroying the planet. In rapidly-industrializing India and China, however, car use is expanding massively and with joyous abandon, as it did in Eisenhower's America. The automobile remains one of mankind's great liberating innovations.

* * * *

Change must operate at many different levels, and across many different dimensions (think of Rubik's cube again), each with its own time profile, as well as against a background of uncertainty. It is, therefore, often messy and prone to go in bursts. One analogy that might be helpful to think of is an estuary. When the tide is going out, the flows of fresh water and sea water are moving in concert. But when the tide turns and begins to move in, the water becomes confused and dangerous as the sea water and salt water struggle for dominance. Change invariably affects many different kinds of relationship as well as the story that underpins the relationships in a matrix, and so until all the pieces start aligning, the new direction may not be apparent.

Because change is a constant and multidimensional,[8] and because we can never know the precise form it will take, it must surely make sense to build structures that *can* change in response to individual needs. Capitalism, regulated to operate transparently within free markets, has achieved this very effectively. Government, that term we use to describe everything from the Office of the President to a small town official, is far harder to budge. In the following chapter we will consider why.

8. Work carried out in 1994 & 1996 by Terence Mitchell and Thomas Lee at the Foster School of Business revealed that the reason individuals accept jobs or leave jobs was rarely a simple question of job satisfaction, as had been commonly assumed. Life-plan considerations, an unexpected opportunity, or even an extraneous shock, might trigger a change. In general, people have a network of relationships outside work that tie them to the job they have.

17

Politics

THE OXFORD DICTIONARY defines politics as 'the activities associated with the governance of a country or area, especially the debate or conflict between individuals or parties having or hoping to achieve power.' This definition seems to me to encapsulate everything that is wrong about what we call politics. It has a sinister ring to it with the words conflict and power. It almost implies that if you are on the losing side, you are in trouble, chum. Now, I do not deny that this can be the way politics operates, but I believe it throws us right back onto our biological drivers, and it is these, I am arguing, that we should supplant with cerebral structure — remembering always that cerebral structure must be grounded in human feeling.

So what do I think politics is? And why do leaders find it so hard to adapt the political systems they are part of, the question I raised in the previous chapter? From my perspective, politics is the process whereby the story is built, maintained and amended. And this goes some way to answering the second question because *the story* only sets the context within which the tension matrix operates. Changing the tension matrix itself requires technical skills politicians rarely possess, as well as the cooperation of many groups whose members' raison d'être is likely to depend upon the matrix as it is.

Politics is best thought of as the on-going conversation we have with ourselves about what we are, where we are going and how we plan to get there. It happens all the time, every day and at every level. To think of politics only as the process that takes place within those structures we have evolved to govern ourselves is both limiting and misleading. Concentrating on the process as it takes place within that part of the tension matrix devoted to 'government' blinds us to the adequacy of the structure itself. The Ancien Régime simply could not see another way of organizing itself other than on the basis of an hereditary monarch, divinely anointed and supported by a universal church, advised by able ministers of his or her own choosing. The adequacy of this structure, given the circumstances of the age, was entirely outside its vocabulary. Or to put it another way, it is pointless asking a peacock if it is right to be a peacock.

When the Founding Fathers constructed America's Constitution, they had the work of the best thinkers to refer to and, more importantly, a wealth of experience to draw on. Just as the law recognizes that truth is rarely one-sided, a party political system was adopted which has tended to operate with two main parties. They opted for a Congress of two legislative chambers, possibly because there were two in Britain. One, the House of Representatives, was expected to be a little rumbustious, containing elected members perhaps longer on passion than experience. The other, the Senate, was supposed to contain members whose experience had moderated their passion. Before becoming law, a piece of legislation had to secure the support of a majority in both houses and be signed by an elected President. This President was granted substantial executive power under a Constitution which enshrined the principle of individual liberty and sovereignty in law, and was upheld by a Supreme Court of eminent jurists, appointed for life by a President and confirmed by Congress.

Certain functions were reserved to the national congress, but others were left for the individual states to deal with. The congressional arrangements in the states functioned in a similar way to those at the national level. All of this was a masterpiece of political engineering. To have created a structure capable of integrating what now amount to some 300 million diverse individuals into one of the most effective political entities of modern times was a mighty achievement, whatever way you care to look at it. But is it logical to think that a structure, once established, however good it may be at the time, will remain appropriate for ever after? Surely not.

* * * *

I want to pick on just two areas, one international and one domestic, that I believe hint at problems within the American structure, and then go on to discuss the problem with politics generally. And I use America as an example because it has evolved the most successful tension matrix of the last two hundred years, on a range of measures. First, then, to the international dimension.

President Eisenhower's 1961 speech about America's military industrial complex (quoted in part on page 166) adds eloquent weight to my earlier suggestion that the present structure of the United States is such as to lead her into foreign entanglements that are likely to do her little good, and to do those she tangles with considerable harm. It may seem strange (to Americans, at least) to say that the United States was constructed to be an imperial power. But this should not surprise us. She was born in an imperial age. Her model, to a large extent, was Great Britain, hub of an immense empire of which she was once part.

While Europeans were colonizing land in Africa, the Middle East and Asia, the young United States was doing the very same thing, but within the continent of North America. The rather holier-than-thou attitude adopted by President Woodrow Wilson at the end of the First World War about the evils of colonialism was less than convincing. Teddy Roosevelt had no such qualms: *The white settlers were unflinchingly bent on seizing the land over which the Indians roamed but which they did not in any true sense own or occupy.*[1] Try telling that to the Apache, Blackfoot, Cherokee or Sioux. Sir Wilfred Laurier, Canada's seventh prime minister between 1896 and 1911 knew his neighbors well: "Our American friends have very many qualities, but what they have they keep and what they have not they want."[2]

---

1. *The Winning of the West*, by Theodore Roosevelt, Vol.3.
2. In *Lord Minto* by John Buchan, p167, 1924 edition.

My purpose is not to throw stones, because every country that could grow colonial flowers at that time was in a similar greenhouse, but to point out that, in spite of her protestations to the contrary, America always has been an imperial power. When the Second World War ended and Europe had destroyed itself, the United States controlled one half of the world — most of that part once controlled by the European powers, as well as Japan, and the Soviet Union controlled a fair part of the remainder. Britain, although nominally a co-victor, became a relatively contented junior partner on account of her greatly reduced circumstances, and dressed up this new role by calling it her *Special Relationship*. I wonder if Ancient Greece felt the same about Rome?

It seems to me that the Office of the President reflects the imperial aspiration that has always been part of the American story. Foreign adventures are more or less nodded through by Congress, on the assumption that an extension of America's influence, so long as not too much human treasure is spent, will be good for business and good for the world. Once it was the cross that accompanied business around the globe, now it is *democracy*.

As I have already said, my purpose here is not to judge these things — empires have been a fact of history — but to point out that America's political structure has been built with an imperial dimension. Ask an American in the street if this is so, and he would almost certainly deny it, which demonstrates the power of cerebral structure (the matrix and its prevailing story) to think — and so to act — for us. And here is the problem. It is almost impossible to change what you cannot see. This is why change so often only comes after one's nose has been well and truly rubbed in it. The Korean War, the Vietnam War and now the Iraq War constitute a fair degree of nose rubbing, but as Adam Smith said: there is an awful lot of ruin in a nation.

* * * *

The domestic issue I want to pick, which hints strongly at a structural problem within America's polity (and which applies to many other nations as well), is drugs. What we know is that drug use is increasing and that all efforts to prevent the habit are failing. In Brazil and Thailand the police have even adopted a zero-tolerance policy in some areas, which amounts to shooting suspected drug dealers on sight. But in spite of such extreme tactics, the practice continues. America, the most powerful country in the world, has found it impossible to stop drug-taking. What gives?

The use of drugs is demand-driven. This means governments are fighting against their own people. If the problem could be isolated to a small minority, it could be demonized and the support of the majority — perhaps — secured. But drug-taking is so widespread, covering all ages and income groups, that the authorities have to concentrate on the dealers. What this ensures, however, is that the trade is extraordinarily lucrative: occasional disruptions in supply, when the authorities secure a much-publicized victory, simply push up the price. And now designer drugs, like methamphetamine, which produces a more prolonged high than cocaine, can be made in anyone's kitchen from easily available materials. As everyone knows, but the political system seems incapable of handling, the problem is demand.

So why, in our wonderful world, awash with material and sensual pleasures, do so many people take drugs? Well, the first thing to acknowledge is that humans have been taking drugs since the dawn of human time. Altering our perception of reality for a while — the daily grind of life is not always an unalloyed pleasure — is simply fun! Methamphetamine, for example, stimulates the release of dopamine, the chemical in the brain that causes us to enjoy food and sex. It also gives a person a feeling of boundless energy and a diminished appetite. Unfortunately, the desire to experience pleasure and energy can become addictive. Over time, larger doses of the drug are needed to achieve the same feelings and this progressively damages the body.

We have all been treated to harrowing tales of addicts, but still the custom persists. One can only assume that for every drug-taker who comes a cropper, there are an awful lot more who don't. More people get killed on the roads each year than die from drugs, but only the *Greens* have tried to stop driving and their reasons for doing so have nothing to do with fatalities. We spend hundreds of millions of dollars every year on making the roads safer. But with regard to drugs, we spend hundreds of millions of dollars every year trying to prevent their use. The argument that drugs are a special class of consumer product fails the logic test, unless you say that they are special because governments have made them so, but then you would be in George Orwell or Joseph Heller territory.

Cigarette smoking, which we have known for decades can seriously damage a person's health, has finally been relegated to the margins. It is not illegal. Anyone over a certain age can do it, so long as they do not affect anyone else. People will continue to die as a result of smoking-induced cancer, but those who take the risk are gradually coming to realize that they will be on their own. Insurance companies now penalize smokers, and taxpayer-funded health services have higher priorities than treating self-inflicted illnesses. While smoking is addictive, it is an addiction that can be broken. The choice is the individual's. Government agencies do not spend millions of dollars every year attacking the channels through which cigarettes are made available. Instead, governments make millions of dollars each year from taxes on a habit many seem to enjoy.

Acknowledging that there are undoubtedly people who have something of a death wish, doubtless because their lives are so wretched, either due to the circumstances they are in or because of their particular mental makeup (or both), most who take drugs simply want to experience their mind-altering effect. Doubtless many get an extra buzz from the fact that it is illegal, but making it so seems a perverse way of giving them that pleasure. Better, surely, that individuals and companies be licensed to make products that do as little damage as possible while providing the 'lift' that people so obviously seek. Civil proceedings are available against individuals and companies whose products produce unexpected side-effects (of a negative kind), and criminal proceedings are available against these companies if their managers should reasonably have anticipated them.

* * * *

Unfortunately, the illegal drugs issue poses an even more fundamental question that is disguised by the frantic and high profile attempts to crack down on the trade. Large numbers of people, both outside and inside the consuming nations, depend on it for their way of life. Indeed, the very illegality of the trade has created that way of life. If we ignore, for the moment, the Colombian coca growers or Afghan poppy farmers, and think only of the thousands of street dealers in the cities of America and elsewhere currently dependent on drug sales, one has to ask what sort of society is it that can only function in this way? And turning to the farmers who supply many of the narcotics, what chance do their governments have of building a civil society, when so much of their country's revenues are controlled by villains?

In the case of Presidential power and drugs policy, the tension matrix in America is calling the shots because the stories that underpin its functioning in these two areas go unchallenged. The military industrial complex in the United States is vast, far outstripping that of any other nation. As its Commander-in-Chief, the President rules over a boundary condition that supplies jobs and prestige to his electorate, but which exerts its destructive influence abroad over people to whom his office is not remotely accountable. The various agencies involved in trying to stop the trade in drugs may be less glamorous than the military, but they are no less imbued with missionary zeal. And, like the military, they are deeply embedded within their communities.

* * * *

Now let us consider the politics of these two dimensions. The projection of US power overseas plays to the very heart of the nation's story. According to this story, America's boundary condition is good and should be extended as far and as wide as possible, by force if necessary. The sub-text is the military industrial complex Eisenhower alluded to. If you have it, flaunt it, biology's oldest driver. As head of the armed forces (or America's warlord if you would prefer) a president is hard pressed to resist this logic, especially when it is infused with commercial self-interest. And then there is the simple fact that exercising power is immense fun. Dress this pleasure up with lofty-sounding motives — defending the homeland, spreading freedom — and you have a concoction as stimulating as any narcotic.

US drugs policy starts with a very simple story: *drug-taking is bad.* Like the anti-liquor laws of Prohibition, it is driven by an ideology to which the majority are indifferent (save when they find junkies in their backyard), a minority espouse and a much larger minority actively flaunt. It runs hand in hand with prostitution, made illegal throughout most of America on moral grounds, but certainly not absent. The upshot is that substantial resources are deployed to prevent something that cannot be prevented. The whole edifice is built into the matrix, becoming as addicted to interdiction as the supply chain is to the money it makes. A happy symbiosis!

At the moment, the stories about Presidential power and the evils of drug-taking are articles of faith that the tension matrix is designed to uphold. In theory, the American Constitution affords the American public the opportunity to change both the stories and the matrix that underpin America's drugs policy as well as the manner in which she projects her military power overseas. However it is hard to see a candidate being elected president on a platform that calls for a diminution of America's international power anymore than it is to imagine a candidate being elected to the presidency who argues that the drugs trade should be put on a normal commercial footing.

The grammar of political argument — that is to say the fusion between America's story and her tension matrix — simply does not allow it at present.[3] When a child will call out from the crowd *but the emperor has no clothes!* is anyone's guess.[4] But it is unlikely to be before

3. Drug-takers probably prefer using their back door suppliers more than they would a local pharmacy anyway, as there is almost certainly an element of pleasurable rebelliousness in their activity. This is no doubt matched by the rush the abolitionists secure from the certainty of their mission. And when it comes to that other kind of drug - one's country's international prestige - why give it up if the costs are borne predominantly by others? Add to this mix the fact that the matrix, as currently constructed, supplies a large number of people with their livelihood and it is easy to see why the grammar of political argument is hard to change.

4. Hans Christian Anderson's charming story, *The Emperor's New Clothes* (1837), was one of the lighter challenges to the power of Emperors and Kings being made at the time.

both policies become even more ruinously expensive and even more obviously counterproductive than they already are.

* * * *

It is always risky using contentious examples, as these two certainly are, but unless a theory can handle the tough nuts it is not of much use. Of the two, the projection of power beyond a boundary condition is the more obvious expression of a biological driver. If you accept my contention that national organizations function like protospecies, then one must accept that nations will run with any advantage they secure until they are blocked. Contrary to what one might assume however, there is nothing in biological logic which says that this has to be in their best interests, only that it should be in biology's best interest. It will be through the growing awareness of outcomes that we are able to act with conscious intent and moderate what our biology dictates.

Drug-taking, on the scale that exists today, is an altogether different phenomenon. My hunch is that it reflects, in part at least, tensions that exist within the matrix. Like dreaming, it is a form of release. We are all constrained by the matrix and are aware that the story we nurture in our heads about what life amounts to is often seriously challenged by the functioning of the matrix in practice. Like sex, drug-taking can be a wonderful escape from the conflicted tensions that characterize much of modern life. If this is even half right, excessive drug-taking is a symptom of a deeper malaise that costly and brutal interdiction will only serve to reinforce.

* * * *

It is easy to smirk at the *just say no* campaign of some religious groups in America (which I'm sure applies to drugs as well as to premarital sex), the more so when one or other of their pastors gets caught in flagrante delicto with a wife other than his own, but they must surely be on the right track. In its rush to disassemble the moral authority of the church (and I confess, I would not have wanted to live in a theocracy) the Liberati threw the moral baby out with the dirty ecclesiastical bath water.

The idea that the tension matrix of a state could somehow be designed to orchestrate all relationships between individuals in a more or less satisfactory manner, without any overt reference to morality, was simply wrong. A tension matrix cannot function without a story and all stories necessarily contain moral content. Even Fascism and Communism spoke to a moral dimension within us, although overall (because each was exclusive and not inclusive) both were deeply flawed.

Because of the interlocking nature of the matrix, shifts in cerebral structure impact a range of dimensions which make it hard to bring about change, as we have shown. This leads to frustration and makes it hard for political dialogue to be measured — issues get mired in emotional gridlock. Cerebral structure plays such an integral part in the way humans function, to the extent of defining people's identity in large measure, that we find it incredibly hard to conceive of a structure different from the one we are part of.

Changes to the story that shape a polity's debate are invariably traumatic. When General Charles de Gaulle reluctantly concluded in 1960 that France should abandon Algeria (technically part of France at the time), he had to face down fierce opposition and several assassination attempts from his own countrymen. In the same year, Britain's Prime Minister Harold Macmillan, in his now famous *Winds of Change* speech, signaled that the process of decolonization, begun under the previous Labour administration, would continue, and was savagely criticized by the right wing of his own Conservative party. I don't believe that any of its members attempted assassination, however.

* * * *

So how can we make it easier for the political process to embrace change? The story empowers the matrix, the matrix reflects the story, and the story is the picture which individuals within a polity carry in their heads that enables them to function in an integrated manner. Without a fairly high degree of coherence throughout the system — the matrix has to deliver on the story and the story has to be believed by at least the great majority of people — you would have anarchy and the system would collapse.

Free-market capitalism has solved this problem by enabling new companies with a new story gradually to displace established companies whose story has been overtaken by events. Think of the transition from the mainframe computer to the microcomputer, or of the change from horse-drawn power to the horsepower of the internal-combustion engine. We are now in the early stages of a shift from a carbon-based economy to an alternative we have not yet fully identified. Free-market capitalism has managed to engineer a sort of controlled anarchy, held together by countless individuals' desire to make money on their money and driven by their consumer preferences.

Democracy, in the form of one-man-one-vote and political parties (invariably two that matter), has proved to be a much more blunt instrument. In the case of America, it is clear that the voter has no means of expressing his or her opinion about Presidential power. In fact the way the system is set up, in America and most other democracies, the voter does not get to pass judgment on the system at all, only on who should be in charge of it. And making a system *more democratic* may not be the answer either. In countries like Israel, with multi-party systems and coalition governments, national policy is frequently held hostage to the shibboleths of a minor party. Unless a candidate decides to make some part of the system an issue and wins, the system gets off scot-free! And this is in spite of the fact that systems do a great deal of our thinking for us, as they are intended to do.

In evolutionary terms, this puts us at risk of ending up in an evolutionary cul-de-sac, from which the only escape is a complete collapse of the system, followed by the resurrection of our biological drivers. We have seen what misery this has caused in the past and must surely wish to avoid its recurrence.

The only solution I can see is that we confront the matter head-on by inventing a new institution whose task it will be to consider structural issues. To be effective it will need to be local, national, regional and global, staffed by people with both theoretical knowledge and practical experience of how the systems our human family is evolving work — or don't. Its brief would be simple: to find ways of making the lives of individual men and women better. In ***Part 4*** I will outline some of the issues this body will have to address.

Part 4

IN PART 4 I LOOK AHEAD. Not very far ahead, admittedly, because the creative nature of the universe defies prediction. Having said that, much of what will happen in the future can be deduced from what has happened in the past. But what can't be predicted arises out of the capacity of the universe to create new matter, the equivalent to us, in many ways, of new meaning. I submit that we face a choice. Very roughly, this boils down to improving our collective intelligence (our cerebral structure), which is embedded within the tension matrices and stories that regulate our lives, so that the outcomes of our actions are intended, or continuing along the rather haphazard path we have followed to date, allowing biology to sort things out in its customary and often brutal fashion.

I pick out three areas for attention: our metastory, our international structures and our systems of government. But first, let me summarize, briefly, the argument that has brought us to where we are.

I started with the universe because I wanted to emphasize the common whole of which each of us is a part. Although, in one sense, it does appear as if this whole is being driven apart in a violent manner towards a cold lifeless end, in another something far more remarkable is taking place. The tension between energy constrained as matter and energy unconstrained is producing an elaboration of structures that seem to me to have developed through distinct system states, each dependent on the existence of the prior state but bound by its own particular rules. This allowed me to propose an evolving state beyond the biological which I am calling the cerebral and is intimately associated with consciousness. It is almost as if, in scattering itself to the winds, what we are part of is being driven to create an awareness of what it is.

While it is hard to escape the conclusion that we humans are a rather weak vessel within which to brew something so significant — a dilemma which lay at the heart of much religious theology — our difficulty, according to my analysis, is that we are being driven by the rules of biology (biological morality) as well as by the morality of the cerebral system state whose rules we have yet to master.

In the past, much of our moral focus has been on individual behavior and only gradually have we come to realize the importance of the structures we have created in directing it. These structures, or tension matrices as I prefer to call them, regulate individual behavior within a boundary condition defined by a story that explains and justifies a matrix to the individuals within it. The character of these matrices (their hierarchical configuration) has evolved in response to competition between them, as if they were protospecies subject to the rules of biology. The ability of human organizations to adapt in order to improve their productive and competitive potential, one with another, has resulted in great numerical success to the extent that humans now dominate their environment.

This dynamic has largely been driven by biology, although turbocharged by our increasing cerebral ability. The challenge now is to wrest control of this process from our biological drivers so that we are not subjected to biology's often fierce corrective methods of which destructive warfare is a prime example. Economic exploitation, which has been highly beneficial for many of us, has frequently been pursued without a clear understanding of its consequences, either for those individuals adversely affected or, more recently, for the biological environment. Beyond its boundary condition, economic activity has tended to follow a blind biological script: secure an advantage and run with it for as long as it lasts.

While it is tempting to think that the solution lies in central planning, state control has proved to be extraordinarily ineffective (save for short bursts in times of war when all the resources of a nation have been directed towards a single end). The reason for this is simple: collective intelligence is a function of individual input. While individual input is greatly magnified by functional hierarchies designed to pursue specific functional objectives, when these are the objectives of the few (such as planners) rather than of the many (such as all those affected by a function), the adaptive capability of a matrix becomes seriously impaired. Ideally, the design of a tension matrix should enable as many individuals as possible to express their preferences and allow for multiple approaches to meeting them.

Because the tension matrix and its story are designed to do much of our thinking for us (they in fact embody our collective intelligence), a matrix must be large enough and open enough to accommodate and encourage diverse approaches, while remaining sufficiently structured to function coherently overall. A shared morality at the individual level, that is reflected in how the semi-autonomous structures within a matrix are designed and called to account, offers the best prospect for cerebral structure to evolve with intent. Not only must individuals be educated as to the grammar that underpins this structure — from how their brains work to how change takes place, but the ability to challenge and retire embedded structure needs to be placed firmly in their hands. Free-market capitalism, which in recent years has driven structural (and technological) change, overtaking competitive warfare in this regard, has done much to empower individuals, but that part of the matrix which falls loosely under the term 'government' remains stubbornly impervious to individual influence.

I argued that institutions reflect core elements of our individual morality, but that these had frequently become servants not of individuals but of boundary conditions such as the nation state, or even themselves (as when a criminal justice system becomes dependent upon criminality or an anti-poverty program becomes dependent upon the impoverished). It seemed to me that what we call politics is really the process whereby the story gets developed, reinforced and amended and that we are inclined to confuse it with the process of government. This confusion, I suggested, has served to undermine both. While we can never be certain of outcomes — and should never pretend that we can be, or should be — we can at least build our structures with integrity and be open to the creative possibility that we can do things in a better, more life-enhancing way.

Without a shared framework of meaning (a metastory), human beings will naturally find themselves resorting to warfare in order to resolve their differences. This is the language of biology. To be effective (which means to be accepted) a metastory must recognize the dynamic nature of differences, while endorsing the need to accommodate them in an ordered way that accords with individual perceptions of morality (how we should behave towards one another). An ideal metastory is one that nurtures differences, not as ends in themselves but as the means by which conscious life is continuously enhanced through their fusion.

The second area that needs urgent attention is that relating to our international structures. Almost everyone admits these are either not working or are working less well than they might. The underlying problem is that the United Nations is a remnant of the post-war era and does not reflect today's reality. I suggest a simplified structure based upon just eight regional blocks that possess a degree of physical and cultural coherence. I also argue that our attitude towards globalization must change.

Finally, I propose that we rethink our approach to government and in particular to what we mean by democracy. The nation state, it seems to me, no longer constitutes a useful boundary condition. Not only is its scale too big for most of the functions we ascribe to government to be performed adequately, but there is much that affects an individual which falls outside its scope. I propose that a majority of collective functions be carried out at the community level (where a community consists of about half a million people) so that individuals can more readily identify with them, and that broad policy coordination takes place at a regional level (in one of the eight regions I identify).

I argue that new technologies (such as the internet) should allow individuals to set the policy agenda (the story), leaving government functions to be professionally run and monitored. I question whether there is now a need for elected representatives and suggest that we would be better off with professionally-trained legislators who understand the tension matrices which regulate our lives. Community mayors and regional presidents would still be elected, however, but they would have their power restricted to that of the pulpit.

18

The Road Ahead

IT IS HARD TO ESCAPE the conclusion that much of human society, at least over the last several thousand years, has been built around the redundancy model of biology. That is to say a goodly percentage of each population is there to be sacrificed, in one way or another, for the collective good. Competition between populations has proved highly stimulative, and in spite of substantial individual loss, our aggregate population is higher than ever.

However, to keep working, the biological model will firstly need individuals to be sacrificed on a prodigious scale and I don't think people will be willing to accept that. Secondly, modern warfare has become too dangerous. Thirdly, our existing numbers are already straining the earth's resources. And fourthly, the blind morality of biology (which, if left to its own devices, will cancel the previous two out) is surely not that to which we should aspire.

Before writing a chapter entitled *The Road Ahead*, a sane person might wish that they were not starting from here. Global dialogue is colored more by conflict than cooperation. Warfare rages. And national governments are becoming increasingly dysfunctional. But the great thing about cerebral structure is that all this *can* be changed.

Mindful of the mistake many of my predecessors made in trumpeting the unalloyed benefits that science would bring to the human condition, only to see their theories degenerate into worldwide revolution, followed by two world wars and untold misery, I intend to be circumspect about what I propose and acknowledge that what we have achieved has been won at great cost and so should not be ridiculed. That said, I believe there are three areas we need to work on with some urgency: our metastory, our international structures and our systems of government. Naturally, all three are interlinked.

1. Our Metastory.

The reason we need a metastory should be obvious by now. Without a common reference point or framework at the level of consciousness, our biological drivers will continue to rule the roost. Can we develop a metastory that will be accepted by all of us? In chapter one I laid out, as best I could, what we know about the universe. This knowledge does not change just because a person is European, Russian, African or Chinese, even though how the members of each group relate to it may. By the same token we should be able to construct a grammar that captures the human dynamic in a way that is universally applicable. Such a grammar cannot tell us whether the Chinese story is better than the American story. That is not its purpose, any more than the purpose of physics is to tell us whether matter is 'better' than antimatter.

Such qualitative judgments are a unique facet of individual consciousness. Our metastory should do two things. It should describe, as accurately as it can, the dynamics of man. This is the first thing it must do and what ***Notes*** has primarily been about. The second thing it must do is express, in clear language, the aspirations of universal man. This is the [*we hold these truths to be self-evident,*] statement, the [*that all men are created equal, that they are endowed by their Creator with certain unalienable Rights, that among these are Life, Liberty and the pursuit of Happiness*] baseline.

If every individual were asked, before being thrown into the melting pot of life without any foreknowledge of their status, to outline the metastory that should govern it, would they come up with a statement along these lines? Not necessarily. I think they might want to say something about the stability of the environment they were being thrown into and about the availability of food and shelter.

That wonderful American declaration, quoted above, assumes a lot. It was endorsed by men confident in their position, if not entirely confident in the outcome of their actions at the time. They were, after all, rebelling against the most powerful empire of their age. But many were lawyers and most were property owners of one sort or another, engaged in business, and they had a pretty clear idea of the sort of world they wanted. It was largely the world they already had, but without the overhang of a 'foreign' power.

An Amazonian Indian, by contrast, would not understand the meaning of *equality*, would have no concept of *rights*, and would take *life*, *liberty* and *happiness* for granted. These would not be things he needed to pursue, but would be facts of his everyday existence. His chosen metastory would probably be encapsulated in the wish that the forest he inhabited should remain munificent (and more recently might include the added wish that Europeans leave him alone). The American declaration is, as much as anything, a reflection of how far our evolved tension matrix has driven individuals away from their natural relationship with one another.

To mean anything, a metastory must be actionable. It took Rosa Parks in Alabama in 1955 to trigger an application to America's Supreme Court before segregation on busses was put under the spotlight of the Constitution and found wanting. In spite of America's metastory, that all men are created equal, the systematic indignities meted out to African Americans persisted for 168 years after its constitution was adopted before being challenged. If it is to be more than a myth, a metastory must be grounded in the facts of everyday life and be accessible to an individual on that basis.

If you are an unemployed auto-worker in America today, whose unemployment insurance has run out, whose home has been repossessed, whose health insurance has been terminated and who is unable to find work, what good does it do you to know that your country's metastory asserts your right to life, liberty and the pursuit of happiness? When will one of these unfortunate individuals take his government to the Supreme Court for gross mismanagement? My point is that if a metastory is to be more than saccharine words it must give the ordinary individual the power to call the matrix to account. I will outline some aspects of the cerebral grammar we are going to have to address if we are to construct a credible, acceptable and dynamic metastory.

The evolution of our metastory. The basis of any metastory has to be expressed in terms of the individual, even though it is the interaction between us that gives rise to our collective intelligence and expanding consciousness. Biological morality is only interested in the individual as a means to the end of a particular species' survival. Certainly there is a difference between a grain of corn and a mammal in that the latter possesses greater individual variation. Consequently, the characteristics of an individual mammal will play a larger role in reproduction, tending to accentuate its species' particular advantage.

In the world of deer, for example, the finest male specimen will drive off his competitors and mate with the most females. But while the competition between males will ensure that the best example of deer maleness will be transmitted to the next generation, it does nothing to protect the deer species from a change in the environment that will make the deer structure ineffective. The biological system state as a whole protects itself against a threat to its existence by diversifying into multiple structures, such that if some cannot cope with a change there are likely to be others that can.

As we have moved away from the biological system state, we have had to construct our own morality. The great religions have tended to emphasize the sanctity of individual life, and for good reason. With consciousness came the ability to choose (as opposed to react) and one of the choices open to us was to eliminate those who stood in our way. The anarchy that would ensue if we all resorted to such an option gave rise to formalized ways of exercising this option such as warfare and judicial murder. But these were only small steps away from biological morality, not a severing of our connection to it.

What is becoming clearer, as our collective consciousness expands, is that the evolution of cerebral structure depends absolutely on the individual and that as more individuals are drawn into the process, the richer and more adaptively capable cerebral structure becomes. Just as biology protects itself by evolving into many structures and assuming a high degree of redundancy (at the individual level and even the species one), so we have come to realize that organizational diversification is a potent evolutionary tool. We have struggled, however, to marry the need for organizational redundancy (the creative process requires that not all approaches will prove sustainable) with our self-belief in the sanctity of individual life.

Various mechanisms have evolved to deal with this. Our war dead are eulogized. Our criminals are demonized. And more recently we have come to accept that when a company fails (as companies in a competitive environment are bound to), it is in all our interests to help those made redundant. Many in our liberal democracies are currently very exercised by discrimination against individuals on the basis of such criteria as race, age, sexual orientation and economic background. All of these initiatives spring from the fact of individual consciousness and our personal belief that we matter. The fact that this belief itself springs from the drive of structure to exist, a fundamental characteristic of our universe (the interplay between energy and matter), is largely invisible to us.

All of these things are being fed into our metastory but are being waylaid within boundary conditions, such as the nation state or a particular religious orientation, that are far from being universal and so color its character. Also invisible to us, I think, is that mere existence does not appear to be what the universe is about. Evolution has displayed a clear trajectory through successive layers of structure — the system states I talk about — with the second building on the first and so on, culminating in consciousness. To be consistent with this pattern our metastory should surely embrace the expansion of consciousness as a level of existence distinct from the biological system state out of which it is evolving. This means that acknowledging the sanctity of individual life is not enough. Our metastory needs to be concerned with its quality.

Developing a universal grammar. If I am right and it is the story that enables people to function effectively inside a matrix, the grammar of these stories across different cultures and backgrounds may be quite similar, even when the words are completely different. What we do know with certainty is that people can behave extraordinarily badly towards one another when their story encourages it and the tension matrix within which they function facilitates it. When a boy pokes a frog with a stick he is driven by an irresistible urge. Whatever motive he has lies deep within him, the product of survival scripts his biology has evolved over hundreds of thousands of years.

When that boy becomes a man and we send him to war, the excitement he feels before his first 'kill' is overlaid with a cerebral motive — that of fighting for his country. If that young man, back in Civvy Street, kills a member of an opposing gang in the heat of conflict we call it murder. The cerebral structure we have evolved can draw on a biological impulse to produce a desired outcome and yet condemn another outcome that owes its genesis to that same impulse. In other words, cerebral structure (a tension matrix and its story) works on an individual's conscious mind, which is informed by that person's deep biological instincts.

And it is not a purely logical association of the type if A, then B. What cerebral structure seeks to do is to evoke a positive feeling about killing in war and a negative feeling about killing in peacetime. This is achieved by implanting into the brains of individuals images of heroism and collective congratulation to encourage the first act, and images of punishment and condemnation to deter the second. While it may be tempting to regard cerebral structure in purely functional terms (as a behaviorist would do) it is a temptation we should resist because I don't believe it works that way.

Having said that, it does *almost* work that way. A tension matrix and its story work on the assumption that it does, and for much of the time we act as the matrix and its story suggest. But here's the rub — or the grain of sand that gets into the oyster and causes it to create a pearl — that pesky thing inside each of us called the 'self' is not one hundred percent trapped within the matrix or its story.

There is something about the way in which we are connected to the universe as a whole — and could this be the point at which quantum decision-making comes into play (see page 176) — that allows our conscious mind sufficient space to judge whether what we are doing is appropriate, even as we are doing it. If we judge that it is not we become sensitive to signals from others who are reaching a similar conclusion, and open to changing both the story and the matrix.

Now we know that change comes in fits and starts, with boundary conditions forming around competing ideas which often lead, as the Historical Perspective chapter laid depressingly bare, to out-and-out conflict and great loss of life. What I believe this demonstrates is that we need a metastory that embraces the process of change, without prejudging what that change should be. At the same time it must acknowledge the absolute need for orderly change, because in its absence our biological drivers will always provide.

Imagine. It is easy to dismiss John Lennon's 1971 lyrics, especially if you are world-weary:

Imagine there's no heaven
It's easy if you try
No hell below us
Above us only sky
Imagine all the people
Living for today. . . .

Imagine there's no countries
It isn't hard to do
Nothing to kill or die for
And no religion too
Imagine all the people
Living life in peace . . .

You may say I'm a dreamer
But I'm not the only one
I hope someday you'll join us
And the world will be as one.

The immense popularity of the song suggests that it reflects an aspiration many of us share. And although he might not have thanked me for pointing it out, another individual who lived over 2,000 years ago and who also suffered an untimely end at the hands of his fellow man, was saying much the same thing. Our problem has never been an inability to imagine heaven. It has been how to create the darn thing here on earth. That said, creative artists like Lennon do help to prepare our minds for a new story. And although religion has repeatedly soiled its nest, the founders of Judaism, Christianity and Islam also did just that.

The Cleft. Doris Lessing's 2007 novel, *The Cleft*, is about a tribe of women who reproduce asexually until, to their great surprise, they start giving birth to some male children, which they call monsters. These they throw away, but the little creatures are carried off by eagles to a valley where a kindly deer suckles them and they grow up. After many years a lone woman wanders into the valley and is duly raped by the now adult males. To cut a good story short, the two fractious tribes eventually merge and the foundations of our human race are laid.

When she was interviewed about the book, I remember Doris Lessing saying that if it had been left to women, we would probably still be sitting around on rocks! What she was alluding to, of course, was the dynamic tension between the sexes that has been at least partly responsible for our evolutionary trajectory. Men's warlike proclivities, which in a biological sense are clearly sexual, have infused human organization and contributed to the productive progression I have described. Although we have increasingly managed to justify our actions using fine cerebral words, it has all too often been our biological drivers that have called the shots.

The dilemma of consciousness. The evolution of awareness within the biological system state was certainly a precursor of cerebral structure, but when human awareness evolved the capacity to reason (*if this, then that — subject, verb, object*) and to project outcomes, the tension matrix that regulated human existence (which was predominantly biological at first) had to be reinterpreted within this new consciousness and given meaning. The stories that we built sought to reinterpret the nature of our existence (which previously we had taken for granted) at the level of consciousness. The dilemma of consciousness, of course, is that we are obliged to attribute meaning to things, whether we understand their true nature or not.

The continuing evolution of cerebral structure. As we have seen, the tension matrix and its story embody meaning. Meaning is not abstract but felt. The same person can embody the heartfelt yearnings expressed in John Lennon's *Imagine* as well as the impulse found in Doris Lessing's male monsters. What we have to do, in designing the structures that regulate our lives, is to marry our understanding of the human condition with our goals, recognizing always that those same structures embody meaning at the deepest levels of our evolved experience. This requires that we engineer boundary conditions that are both robust and allow for change in response to individual aspirations.

Fusion. Several years ago there was much excitement at the prospect of cold fusion — the idea that nuclear fusion at low temperatures was possible and would provide an abundant source of cheap energy. Sadly, nothing has come of it to date. But within the cerebral system state fusion occurs all the time. Indeed, it is how cerebral structure evolves. In the Western world a concerted effort has been made to equalize the power of men and women within the matrix. This represents a break from the traditional relationship between the sexes which consigned females to an essentially domestic, passive role and males to a political, active one which frequently expressed itself in flamboyant displays of competitive warfare.

With the growth of consumerism, which gave individuals from all backgrounds an opportunity to shape their lives, and the redirection of at least some of our exploitative impulses away from warfare and into competitive free-market capitalism, a fusion has taken place that amongst other things has enhanced the lives of women without in any way diminishing the lives of men. This net gain is not just a function of increased productivity, but represents a genuine expansion of human consciousness which our conversation with one another, through all branches of the media, has done much to enhance.

The overriding need for structural integrity. Because the matrix does a great deal of our thinking for us (it is an embodiment of meaning), it goes without saying that structures should do what it is claimed they do. A program that professes to eradicate poverty, for example, but does no more than ameliorate it, is clearly immoral, unless you believe in an embedded class system (which may have been moral when our productive capacity was much less than it is). Similarly a military structure justified on the basis of defense is clearly immoral if its reach goes well beyond that.

In our contemporary world it is likely that some structures (especially in the government arena which is not subject to the discipline of the market place) exist more to benefit those within them than the wider interest the story assumes they support.[1] Over time this disconnect will merely serve to distort meaning and undermine the tension matrix.

Incomplete logic. We will always be prisoners of incomplete logic. This is because meaning is an evolving construct, a consequence of the creative nature of the universe. Take globalization. It is regularly claimed to be in mankind's long-term interest because it utilizes resources efficiently (by directing the factors of production from where they exist, such as in 'poor' regions, to where they can generate the highest return, such as in 'wealthy' regions) and raises living standards worldwide (by drawing all regions into the same advanced economic system).

In fact most of the time globalization is simply a form of economic imperialism in which a social structure that has developed an organizational advantage over other structures exploits that advantage. As happened to our fictional Shona's village, a settled matrix and its story can be completely destroyed by outsiders in possession of an advantage (such as firearms and a jeep). Having destroyed settled communities by introducing such innovations as monoculture to satisfy global markets and advanced weaponry that undermines consensual leadership and replaces it with that of warlords, the theoretical *leveling up* process is only likely to occur when the exploited communities learn how not to be exploited.

It took the people of Western Europe many centuries to recover from the Roman Empire's tender embrace. And the people of Africa

1. The French sociologist, Pierre Bourdieu (1930–2002), has gone much further showing how those within the boundary conditions that make up a matrix unconsciously use many devices (including language, eating habits and education) to maintain their position, regardless of that boundary condition's overall efficacy.

have shown few signs of having reaped a particularly rich harvest as a result of their involvement with Europe's later empires. That said, a fusion often does occur that produces something more than existed previously, but only after a long time and much suffering — intermediate steps our incomplete logic tends to ignore.

The residue of personal rivalries. At one level, it is hard to escape the conclusion that civilization is the residue of personal rivalries. All a tension matrix does is provide the framework within which people act. All the story does is provide a broad moral justification for those actions. Individuals are driven (to the extent they are) by a desire to express their identity. It is this energy that a tension matrix and its story serve to channel. An ambitious Roman could secure wealth through trade, recognition on account of his military prowess and power if he possessed the necessary political skills.

The great buildings whose ruins we admire today were both expressions of individual success (in the power-getting, money-getting game) as well as expressions of Roman civilization. In a physical sense, they are manifestations of her cerebral structure, but they are also the residue of personal rivalries and individual ambition. How individual energy is channeled — by the matrix and its story — will determine the nature of our cerebral structure.

Ebb and flow. Much is made of cycles but when it comes to predicting the future they have proved to be a fickle concept. Mostly this is because people want to get a handle on the immediate future and cycles tend to be long-drawn-out, elastic and often layered affairs. But they undoubtedly exist and we need to have a rough idea why. The simplest way of thinking about it is to recognize that a tension matrix consists of hard and soft structures (from buildings, to systems of communication, to organizations — such as how the soldiers in armies are trained — on to laws and customs). When a new story is building, the matrix is not static but dynamic and seeks to facilitate the story.

In England, in the 18th century, the idea of progress through applied knowledge was growing and sat comfortably within the idea of an expanding empire based upon maritime power and trade. The Industrial Revolution, as it came to be called, transformed British society (her tension matrix) at every level. But by the end of the 19th century, the story was becoming far less clear. Other parts of the world were industrializing and social upheaval caused by the mass migration of people from the country into the new industrial towns was fomenting a desire for political change. Factories that had once been symbols of pride and progress became symbols of exploitation and class oppression instead.

By the middle of the 20th century, having fought two world wars, Britain was effectively bankrupt. In contrast, the American story and matrix, which had been building over that previous 200 years within its large, under-populated and commodity-rich continent, into which many of Europe's most energetic individuals had flocked, seemed to possess an unstoppable momentum. With its story and matrix perfectly in tune, the world became its oyster. But all things must pass. Stories change and when they do, change faster than an embedded matrix ever can.

The glue of relationships. It is easy for us to see how those hard parts of a tension matrix, such as city layouts and transportation networks, might initially move a matrix towards the fulfillment of its story, but then act as a drag when that story begins to change. England's early push to industrialize led to the construction of canals until these were superceded by the railways. America followed a similar path with water transport, such as the Mississippi trade Mark Twain was so familiar with, being superceded by the great railroads. But President Eisenhower's interstate highway system trumped the lot, giving America an advantage that overbuilt and divided Europe could hardly match — at least until oil proved hard to come by.

Less easy to imagine, perhaps, is that every wave of change that impacts a matrix, in response to an evolving story, is accompanied by a whole new set of relationships. People with particular skills and educational backgrounds, for instance, might find themselves levered up into the top slots of those hierarchies that drive the matrix. For change to occur they must displace at least some of those individuals who owed their positions to a previous story. Relationships (that is to say 'knowing' the people you deal with) are natural, often a pleasure, and certainly help the wheels of life to go round, simply because people who have an affinity with one another are usually pursuing compatible objectives — they are operating within the same story.

But like an outdated city center or an old-fashioned transportation system, relationships that are built around an old story (as those were that once characterized the Ancien Régime) must inevitably act as a drag against change. Some drag may be no bad thing. What is new rarely arrives fully-formed and without shortcomings. The trick must surely be to encourage what is good about relationships and discourage what is bad. Competition laws attempt to do just that.

Morality. I have talked about morality frequently in these ***Notes***, and I hope I have made clear what I mean by it. But as it is such an important part of our Metastory I will summarize its essence again. There are three parts to my definition. The first holds that the universe is not illogical but is defined by rules, so that objective reality is a fact of our existence. Moral relativism won't do. The second part is that the universe is also a creative enterprise. What this means is that we can't just formulate laws — such as the ten commandments — and be done with it.

The dynamic nature of the universe will keep throwing curved balls at us. Instructions that we should keep the Sabbath holy, or that we should honor our fathers and mothers (the 4th and 5th Commandments) might have to be reinterpreted. Even the obvious *do not kill* has been blithely ignored in respect of our enemies, but perhaps it is the concept of an enemy that we should reappraise.

The third part of my definition is a function of the other two. If there are absolutes but these absolutes are dynamic (i.e. cannot be reduced to simple dos and don'ts, regardless of circumstance), then we are stuck with a continuing process of discovery as to where exactly truth lies in every new situation we encounter. It seems to me that the only proper way for this process to be conducted is if all those affected are involved.

I am skeptical about leaving it to elites to decide upon complex moral issues, but accept that the general public must be both informed and educated in order to play that role. For morality to mean anything it must be felt. Only if people at large are forced to think about moral issues, in the context of situations they can identify with, will they do so. In this, religion, art and the media can be a great help.

Education. The extent to which education avoids addressing the process of change is remarkable. If we have a metastory that embodies certain fundamental aspirations it should be a legitimate part of the education process to examine the structural impediments in the way of their fulfillment. Most of our young start their working life with the sketchiest notion of how the human world works. Consequently, they have little idea how to change it.

Most young people have an acute sense of justice but little idea how to express it in terms of the grammar that describes what I am calling the dynamics of man. They can be told about slavery and be disgusted with the comfortable indignation that distance from an event provides. But when it comes to contemporary issues, the best most education can do is to touch on these obliquely by referring to men and women who have struggled with issues in the past. The status quo is assumed. It is not the job of education to radicalize or politicize the young, it is claimed. Well why in heavens name not? After getting them to master counting and writing shouldn't the young be focused entirely on how to make life better — more efficient, more inclusive, more just, more fun — for themselves and everyone else, in whatever fields that intrigue them most.

Accessing the matrix. A recurring theme throughout ***Notes*** has been the assertion that the tension matrix and its story do much of our thinking for us. There is nothing wrong with this. Indeed it is how we have overcome the limitations of the individual human brain and pooled our resources so as to achieve what we have. But this fact makes two things imperative. The first is that we must build our structures with moral intent. We need to be clear as to their purpose and ruthless in assessing whether they are meeting it. The second thing is that education has to embrace, in a way that it does not at present, the universal dynamics I have tried to explain. Only by learning what drives us will we be able to break free from the biological treadmill.

Because our feelings are often conflicted and because absolute truth can only be approached, never fully grasped, it is to the tension matrix we must look both to guide us and give us the freedom to express whatever potential we have. Although our metastory needs only to be a simple summary of those aspirations each of us share, these must ultimately be enshrined in law, within a boundary condition that embraces us all.

A metastory can only be of use if we are able to access and change the matrix. To be able to do this we must first understand how it works. The matrix must then be designed to be responsive to those individual aspirations the metastory reflects. In the following two sections I will suggest some changes that should help push this process along.

2. Our International Structures.

It will be clear to anyone, who gives it a moment's thought, that our international structures are pitifully inadequate. As always, the problem is how to get from here to there, even when we have a fairly good idea where *there* should be. From an evolutionary standpoint, it is a little like saying to the peacock, now Mr. Peacock, can I ask you to become a chicken instead. The logic of the boundary condition that has evolved to define a nation runs counter to any logic that calls upon nations to pool their sovereignty and become something else.

Attempts to build an international structure have always followed periods of extreme conflict. It is as if the horrors of war are sometimes sufficient to push people out of their biological sandbox, at least for a while. The first such attempt, in modern times, was the Congress of Vienna.

The Congress of Vienna. By May 1814 when France surrendered (but before Napoleon's 100 days of freedom after escaping from the island of Elba, that ended in his final defeat at Waterloo in June of the following year), Europe had been at war for the best part of 25 years. There had been the French Revolutionary Wars, the Napoleonic Wars and the dissolution of the Holy Roman Empire. Europe's ambassadors assembled in Vienna to thrash out a new political order for the continent. The leading players were Lord Castlereagh of Britain, Prince Metternich of Austria, Prince Talleyrand of France (who brought along his beautiful and socially accomplished niece, the Duchess of Dino, to help him augment France's standing at the proceedings) and Count Nesselrode of Russia.

The outcome was a set of agreements that kept the continent free of armed conflict for the next 100 years. Amongst these was that Russia was granted most of the Duchy of Warsaw (modern Poland); Prussia was granted some of Saxony, the remainder of the Warsaw duchy, Danzig, and the Rhineland (Westphalia); a German confederation of 38 states was created from the previous 360 of the Holy Roman Empire under the presidency of Austria; and the Netherlands and Southern Netherlands (Belgium) were united by a constitutional monarchy. Some have criticized the Congress for not giving more consideration to the economic and social tensions that were building beneath the surface. But I doubt if its members even had a language that would have allowed them to address these. They did, at least, condemn the slave trade.

The League of Nations. The League of Nations was founded after the carnage of the First World War and at its greatest extent had 35 members. Its mission was to uphold the rights of man, disarmament, preventing war through collective security, settling disputes between countries through negotiation, diplomacy and improving the global quality of life. As an example of moral aims supported by an immoral structure, the League was hard to beat. Let me explain.

Conceived largely in private by the high-minded Woodrow Wilson, America's 28th President, it became part of the Versailles Peace Treaty in 1919. Germany, as the aggressor in the war that had just ended, was initially excluded (but joined later) and the United States did not join because Congress would not ratify its participation. Members of the League failed to agree on either a language or a symbol. Hitler withdrew Germany in 1933, the same year as Japan withdrew and the Soviet Union joined the following year to gain international standing at the expense of Germany. Appeasement of aggression was widespread within the League and almost everyone acted in ignorance of von Clausewitz's warning that war was a continuation of politics.[2] The League was finally abandoned after the Second World War[3] and

2. In his famous book, *On War*, Clausewitz (1780–1831) sees armed conflict as being a dynamic, inherently unstable interaction of the forces of violent emotion, chance and rational calculation. For a fuller understanding of von Clausewitz's ideas, refer to Christopher Bassford, professor of strategy at the National War College of the United States.

3. The League of Nations was formally wound up in Geneva in April 1946.

the United Nations, whose charter was signed in San Francisco in 1945, took its place.

The United Nations. When it comes to the prevention of war, there is no logical reason why the United Nations should be any more successful than the League of Nations. What little success it has had in the military sphere owes almost everything to American military power, and without the support of the United States, which covers some 22% of its running costs, it probably would not exist at all. There is sense in the assertion that since its inception the United Nations has largely been an arm of *Pax Americana*, with the Soviet Union (now Russia) and China both blocking any moves that strayed into their perceived areas of interest. World government the United Nations is not.

Interestingly, the World Health Organization, an organ of the United Nations and originally part of the League of Nations (as the tripartite Health Organization[4]), has been very successful. The reason for this seems simple enough: disease knows no politics and as the Black Death of the Middle Ages demonstrated, it is blind to the boundary conditions (such as ethnicity, religion or class) that we humans have erected around ourselves (save for that established by inoculation). When it comes to cooperating for our own good, our problem is not one of cooperation but of knowing what our own good is. And as I am arguing in ***Notes***, our perception about what is good for us is heavily influenced by the tension matrices we are part of and the stories that sustain them.

If you are an American or a Russian, an Argentinean or a Briton, a Hutu or a Tutsi,[5] an Israeli or a Palestinian — where does one stop? —

4. Comprising a Health Bureau of permanent officials, a General Advisory Council of medical experts and a Health Committee.

5. At the start of 1994, a force of some 2,500 United Nations peacekeepers had been deployed to maintain a fragile peace between Hutus and Tutsis in Rwanda. Under Belgian colonial rule, the minority Tutsis had been treated as an aristocracy (in the manner of colonialism's standard strategy of divide and rule). Following independence in 1962, the Hutu majority seized power and began a campaign of systematic discrimination against the Tutsi minority. Over 200,000 Tutsis fled to

your biological drivers will be telling you that you must defend your boundary condition, no matter what. And lest we become overly self-righteous about the raw brutality that has erupted recently in parts of Africa, dropping bombs on towns has much the same effect, even if it seems more civilized from an aggressor's point of view.

Now we cannot do without boundary conditions and it would be naïve to assume that we could do without a defense capability like the city fathers who rather charmingly declared their Scottish town[6] to be a nuclear-free zone, but we should be able to manage our boundary conditions better than we do. In this, the European Union is pointing the way. Nations that have been embroiled in conflict for centuries have created a new boundary condition around themselves, defined by those things they have in common. It is not perfect. It is work in progress (as, of course, evolution always is). But it is surely the right idea.

A new world order. As I have argued in ***Notes***, boundary conditions are not just figments of our imagination or something that a well-meaning bureaucrat can create by drawing lines on a map (as was attempted by the European powers in the Middle East and much of Africa). They are expressions of our long-term memory, of our history, and give meaning to the very nature of who we are. As the United States of America demonstrated, people with different histories can forge a new identity, but they must be eager for this to happen and the story and matrix they join must be robust and to their liking. So the importance of boundary conditions is one principle we should pay attention to. Another is that we should only build structures that work.

---

neighboring countries and formed the Rwanda Patriotic Front. In 1990 this rebel army invaded Rwanda and forced the elected Hutu President, Juveanl Habyalimana, to share power. In April 1994 a plane carrying Habyalimana was shot down. Over the following 100 days up to 800,000 Tutsis (men, women and children) were slaughtered in a bloodbath of ferocious savagery. In the face of this escalating violence, the United Nations withdrew its forces.

6. Dundee.

The United Nations, as presently constructed, is almost designed not to work. The Security Council (charged with maintaining international peace and security) has five permanent members: China (eventually given a place in 1971 as successor to the Republic of China which had been confined to the Island of Taiwan by China's communist forces since 1949), France, the Russian Federation (following the dissolution of the Soviet Union), the United Kingdom and the United States. Such logic as there is to this membership owed everything to the imagination of the United States and to the political landscape that existed at the end of the Second World War. These five members are also the only nations recognized as having nuclear weapons under the Nuclear Non-Proliferation Treaty of 1968. Someone writing a farce could hardly make this up.

We need to start again. All conflicts in the world begin as regional conflicts. More often than not it has been our global structures that have turned these regional conflicts into global conflagrations. Sad to say, but such lofty concepts as *maintaining international peace and security* have generally meant protecting some superpower's global interests (which they almost certainly acquired through aggression in the first place).

If our objective is to eliminate global conflict and to restrict regional conflict, then the obvious thing to do is to keep regional conflicts regional. This requires that we divide the world into a coherent number of large regions, each with responsibility for managing the conflicts inside its boundary. The Iran-Iraq War between 1980 and 1988 (started by Iraq) cost the lives of around 1 million Iranians and between 250,000 and 500,000 Iraqis. This sorry affair would have been much less bloody had the West and its regional allies not granted some $70 billion in loans to the Iraqi state.

There is a charming picture on file of Donald Rumsfeld in 1983, as America's special envoy in the Middle East, offering his country's fraternal greetings and support to Iraq's leader, Saddam Hussein.[7]

[7] My novel, *Like No Other* — the words used by the then US secretary of defense, Donald Rumsfeld, to describe the war he was about to prosecute — offers a different perspective on America's invasion of Iraq in 2003.

And we glow with self-righteous pride when we finally manage to haul the Bosnian Serb leader, Radovan Karadzic, in front of the International Criminal Tribunal in the Hague, another organ of the United Nations.

A reasonable basis for the regions I have in mind would be geographic proximity, ethnicity and history. Here are my eight: (1) North America, to include Australia, New Zealand and the Pacific Islands; (2) South America, to include the people of the Caribbean; (3) the European Union; (4) Russia, to include its former satellites in the Caucasus; (5) the Middle East including North Africa; (6) Sub-Saharan Africa; (7) the Indian subcontinent; (8) the Far East.

This division is not perfect. There would doubtless need to be wiggle room around the edges. But it has to be a better basis for a global structure than what exists at present. In reality there are not that many things that need to be decided at a global level, but a council of eight, with a rotating presidency, would surely attend to them better than the pantomime we are operating at present.

It follows from this that the basis of what we call economic globalization will have to be rethought. In the main, each region would run its own economic policy. Armament sales between regions should be banned and regions would need to aim for food and energy self-sufficiency. Such an adjustment would undoubtedly lead to a decline in world trade over the medium term, but world trade at present is so wholly unbalanced (as between exporters and importers) as to be unsustainable anyway. My hunch is that if regions concentrated their efforts internally they would more than make up for this loss.

At this point I can almost hear the mantra, but what about human rights, what about the starving and the dispossessed? To that I would simply say this: we must learn to stop wearing our hearts on our sleeves. I don't doubt that many in the West are appalled by the scenes of human misery that all too often flash across our television screens. But magic wands only work in fairy stories. Societies have to be built from the ground up, brick by brick. Throwing aid at people and occasional peacekeepers merely continues a pattern of intervention that has been destabilizing communities for centuries and is largely responsible for the misery that now upsets us so.

Unless we are willing to march in and run people's lives for them, as the old empire-builders once did, we must give them the space to do it for themselves. Without order, in the first instance, no level of civilized life is possible. How order is first established is rarely a pretty sight. And it is made worse by the arms we sell to warlords, whose flimsy structures could not possibly have manufactured them, in return for commodities that make our own lives a little easier.

There will be times when we have to look on in disgust, for sure. However we will do more for our fellow man if we get our own houses in order than we will if we pursue what are often self-interested interventions in theirs. Harsh as it may sound to say it, there is a sense in which aid is the price we have to pay in order to justify our own lives, just as alms to the poor once were. It is not charity that sets men free, but the opportunity to live by their own efforts.

3. Our structures of government.

We are inclined to think of government as we once thought of God: as being a kindly or angry old gentleman who is out there somewhere, ready to run our lives ragged or to give us a helping hand, depending on his whim. But as I have tried to show in ***Notes***, this characterization of government (and God) is wide of the mark.

Government is actually the tension matrix that we have constructed to regulate how we interact with one another. In a very real sense it 'governs' our lives. The story is the moral justification that persuades us to do its bidding. The tension matrix is imbued with an array of positive and negative stimuli intended to reinforce the story and ensure the potency of the matrix. Positive messages are designed to make us feel good, such as those about driving slowly through towns (the *Thank you for driving carefully* signs you sometimes see when leaving city limits). The prospect of a speeding ticket is meant to make us fearful of what will happen if we transgress.

The elaborate, expensive and not very effective thing that we call government is largely a charade. It is in trouble on two counts. The first is because the boundary condition it is associated with has become too big. The second is because, too big as it is, much of what takes place in the world falls outside its boundary condition. Both problems can be traced to our fixation with the nation state.

The nation state. The nation state is a comparatively new phenomenon. Its precise definition is argued over, but in general terms it means a modern political entity in which its people think of themselves as 'one', as opposed to an empire, for example, that is made up of many groups of people with separate identities. But I would go further and define the nation state as a modern political structure (and by modern I merely mean an integrated entity in possession of certain technologies, such as systems of communication, a bureaucracy, transport and finance) able to control a large number of people.

This kind of tension matrix crept up on us. Sovereigns struggled to assert their authority over powerful individuals whose basis of power (control over land) was similar to their own. But bit by bit the mechanisms of state control (a secret police, law courts, taxation, an army, a council of ministers) grew behind the sovereign, so that even when an hereditary monarch was eventually disposed of, a mechanism of control was in place that any new leader could take over.

The way this new kind of leader came to power was by 'popular acclaim' frequently expressed through the technological innovation of elections, which were rigged to a greater or lesser extent. The new tension matrix, which was industrial and commercial, tied larger numbers of people together, more tightly, than had ever been possible before. The nation was its story. The individual was now a wage earner and a consumer. To exist at all he had to be part of some great enterprise and the idea of *The State*, as the hierarchy that contained all other hierarchies — Jean-Jacques Rousseau's *enfant terrible* — gave people the illusory sense that they were in control of their lives. In reality, what populism did, fired up by state communication, was to sucker the masses into handing their lives over to monsters.

In spite of the appalling failure of government in the 20th century, which we can attribute directly to the limitation of national boundary conditions (the economic collapse of the 1930s was global), we have retained a touching attachment to our national structures. Only the members of the European Union appear aware of the need to move on. The nation state is, frankly, an immoral structure. Or, to put it more fairly, the morality of the nation state is biological. Internally it can exercise an excessive degree of crude control over large numbers of people, but in doing so runs the risk of turning them into unthinking automatons. Externally, its level of effective control is largely limited to warfare.

The global tension matrix. I think there is an uneasy feeling in the West that we are on the cusp of change and that it might not be for the better — a feeling, really, that things are running out of control. In developing countries, by contrast, the sense is one of optimism that at last their economies are about to start showering their citizens with all those consumer goods that have so far eluded them. While developed countries are becoming obsessed with climate change — the now inevitable alterations to our planet's sea levels and weather patterns that will come as a consequence of our use of fossil fuels — the first priority of developing countries is to industrialize, and to hell with the extra carbon their exertions will spew into the atmosphere.

Behind the West's feeling of unease, I think, lies globalization. When it was a question of the developed regions of the world using their technological advantage to exploit the remainder, from the West's perspective, all seemed well. A wave of prosperity developed after the Second World War around American hegemony, technological innovation and a rising population. To be popular, governments strove for growth because growth was associated with rising living standards. The gradual expansion of credit accelerated this growth because it allowed people to purchase today what they would otherwise have had to wait until tomorrow to buy. Sometimes this growth ran ahead of itself, pushing up inflation which had to be reined in, forcing people and companies to retrench.

These pleasant upswings (that had an uncanny knack of following the electoral cycle) and usually short but uncomfortable retrenchments (together known as the business cycle) followed a generally upward path. But beneath the surface something fundamental was happening: larger doses of credit (both on the government side and individual one) were needed to prime the pump each time. And this is where globalization comes in. Developing countries became adept at producing products consumers in the developed world wanted, at the same time as their counterpart manufacturers in the developed world were falling in hock to special interests — *see note 12 on page 163.*

What this meant was that an ever larger portion of the credit used to finance consumption in the developed world was ending up paying for goods produced by the developing world, who promptly lent the money back to the developed world because their own economies were insufficiently developed to absorb it. The American and British governments, in particular, were entirely complicit in this, even though it was obvious that such a trend was unsustainable — yet another example of our biological drivers at work because the structures of government lacked integrity (i.e. they were not designed to ensure intelligent action).

Almost to a man, economists are arguing that protectionist pressures should be resisted. But I am afraid this falls squarely into the category of the *well one wouldn't want to be starting from here* kind of problem. Their model assumes a global boundary condition that does not exist. As occurred in the 1920s, global trade has simply run ahead of global structures. To imagine that developing countries can go on exporting and developed ones go on importing on the back of debt run up by the latter in favor of the former, is not economics but the logic of Voltaire's Dr. Pangloss.[8] Whether the protectionist impulse is resisted or not, debt-fueled consumption in the developed world is going to fall back significantly and world trade will contract as a result.

The protectionist sentiment is not illogical. It draws from a boundary condition's inbuilt dynamic to protect itself. In the absence of an adequate global structure or boundary condition, what the process of

8. The tutor in *Candide* (1759) who remained optimistic regardless of the circumstances.

globalization does is undermine national boundary conditions to the point that those inside them experience an acute loss of control. This loss is real. Globalization shifts power away from nations to a structure beyond them that is not fully formed. To manage this process with intent, rather than merely react to it, we must improve the intelligence of our structures. I have already described how I believe our global architecture can be strengthened (the eight blocks I described earlier in *Our International Structures*) but our national architectures need an equally radical overhaul.

Regaining control over government. What we have to do is realign our boundary conditions with our objectives and ensure that the structures that make them up will perform as we intend they should. The thinking behind the eight blocks is that they are big enough to ensure economic security for those inside them and coherent enough to work, with there being little likelihood of any one block wishing to go to war with any other. Nationalist tensions are most likely to occur within blocks, and it will be for these to learn how to manage them. The suggestion that each block should aim to be economically self-sufficient, particularly in energy and food, is an important part of regaining control over government, so let me elaborate.

If we start thinking of government not as the men and women in white coats who pretend to run the asylum, but as the entire tension matrix that affects an individual's life, then we need to embed this matrix within a boundary condition we can get our minds around and whose story we can identify with. If our well-being is reliant upon resources that are outside our boundary condition we will end up in either an exploitative relationship or a dependent one. The first exposes those we exploit to abuse, the second exposes us to it, and both are best avoided.

The eight blocks should be quite large enough for vibrant economic activity to take place within them, regulated by a policy framework that is broadly agreed, while at the same time limiting systemic risk that is global and to which we are presently vulnerable. It will also make it easier to address such issues as climate change because each block will be more likely to develop structural tools which have some impact, instead of trying to rely on global structures that sit better with one block than another.

It is inevitable that each block will develop rather differently, but this will be a reflection of their underlying differences anyway. And besides, multiple approaches to the evolution of cerebral structure must be welcome as we have no means of knowing which approaches will be most fruitful. Having said that, I think we do know that it is the fusion between different approaches that leads to creative breakthroughs, so I am not advocating that each block soldiers forward in determined isolation. Cross-cultural interaction through tourism, education, the arts and non-strategic trade should make the fusion of ideas possible.

One would expect each block to adopt at least the outline of a bill of rights applicable to each of its citizens and to constitute a court in which cases can be brought. There will doubtless be reluctance within some blocks for this to occur, but all one can hope is that the best practice in blocks will spur the citizens in those that are laggards to call for change. The need to develop trade and cooperation between blocks will stimulate the evolution of compatible legal systems, and some of this will filter into the continuing development of our global architecture.

* * * *

I want to turn now to what should go on inside these blocks, concentrating on three areas in particular: community, democracy and competence. But before I do, cast your mind back to the tribe living in the Australian outback or Amazon rainforest and remind yourself what these people's tension matrix consists of. In part it is their interpersonal relations, but in the main their tension matrix is the outback itself or the rainforest they live in, given meaning by their stories, built up over generations. Power disparities between individuals are very limited and the freedom they enjoy is due to the sustaining quality of the environment each person has learned to master.

Now remind yourself that the environment (the tension matrix) we live in today is largely of our own making. Our freedom should be derived in just the same manner. And when it comes to power disparities, a distinction needs to be drawn between those that relate to the functional hierarchies that go to make up our tension matrix, and which exist solely for the purpose of levering up individual competencies for the benefit of us all, and our moral status as individuals. The former are not only legitimate, but essential. The latter are illegitimate and should be eliminated.

What this means in practice is that the environment we have constructed should be no less accessible and no less life-enhancing than the rainforest or outback is to its aboriginal inhabitants. This has to be derived from our metastory as an expression of our morality. To achieve this, education and income levels need to be sustained at a high level and the collective provision of essential services considered on its merits. So as to give people a sense of ownership in the matrix that sustains them and an understanding of its costs versus its benefits, communities need to be rebuilt as the essential building blocks of our governmental structures.

Squeezed between eight blocks at the top and hundreds of communities at the bottom, the nation state will wither, although as a sensible level of aggregation for a number of functions it might not actually die. If the average size of a community were 500,000 (a size sufficient to carry out most of the functions that an individual requires to access within a matrix) a country like England would need 100, the United States 600, Sweden 18 and China 2,660. The European Union would need about 1,000.

* * * *

Now this brings me to the vexed question of democracy. We know how our system of elected representatives came about, but is it really the most effective system we could devise if we were starting today? I recently listened to the treasurer of the state of Illinois interviewed about his state's $9 billion deficit. He hardly had a kind word to say about the elected legislators he was obliged to report to, as it seemed they had taken every opportunity over the decades to pay out money to their pet projects (doubtless those that got them elected) regardless of the money coming in, putting aside nothing in the good times for the inevitable bad ones that had now come along. In California, the governor, faced with a 2009 deficit of some $26 billion, had to push his state towards bankruptcy in order to force the legislature to deal with it. And in the Mother of Parliaments a large number of British legislators were recently caught fiddling their expenses.

As I have previously argued, it is virtually impossible to make the case that the majority of our elected officials actually govern. Even those that become part of the executive are faced with a tension matrix that does most of the governing for them. So what on earth do we need this class of people for? In theory, they represent us but as the programs they put forward in order to get elected are so bland (usually managing to combine a pledge of lower taxes with a commitment to increase government programs) that we are generally left to decide on the basis either of party affiliation (with its vague attachment to this or that general story — such as more government or less), or whether they appeal to us personally. Rarely is the issue one of competence. If our objective is to select Everyman (or Everywoman) then we might as well save ourselves the bother and expense and select individuals at random as we do for jury service.

As I outlined in the chapter on politics (chapter 17), we need to differentiate between story-building, legislating, the functions of government and oversight. We also badly need some mechanism that allows us to look at the structure of the matrix itself, particularly that bit which sits under the heading of 'government'. Paul McCulley[9] coined the phrase *the shadow banking system* in 2007 to describe the unregulated credit instruments that banks had invented to exploit the abundance of debt Western governments had allowed to build up inside their economies (and which has since come crashing down). Well we have been living with a *shadow government* for a hundred years or more, tucked discreetly behind our elected officials, doing the actual work, more often than not in spite of them. If we are serious about democracy, this too must be exposed to public scrutiny.

So the first part of gaining control (over our lives as much as over government) is to reinvigorate the idea of community as the entity that

9. Managing Director of the fund management company PIMCO.

expresses our morality and from which we cannot be ejected. This is the unit that must support us as whole human beings. Even prison time, if needed, should be spent within our own communities. The ethos would be one of reverence towards that which sustains us, in the way aboriginals revere the physical environment that sustains them, with an abhorrence of waste. The dynamic commercial world (the capitalist free-market economy) would continue to exist in parallel, evolving in response to personal needs expressed through investment decisions and individual purchasing power. However, the undue influence it can have at present would be less, because individuals would expect to be supported by their communities, and not by their corporations.

I have said that each of the eight blocks should be largely self-sustaining, but I would go further and suggest that we should build our communities with a similar end in mind. There are various reasons for this but all, in the end, come down to the idea of being able to feel responsible. We know that to moderate climate change we must wean ourselves off a carbon-based economy, but as individuals we feel powerless. Even our national leaders seem condemned to gesture politics as they attend one international meeting after another, putting their names to a succession of communiqués that are long on general intentions and short on specific actions. The problem, of course, is that no global boundary condition exists with a tension matrix capable of regulating individual action. A community structure, which individuals felt they owned, would stand a far better chance.

* * * *

So how, exactly, do I think the process of government should work? Taking the legislative process first, it is clear that to be a good legislator requires particular skills, experience and the absence of political (that is to say, partisan) pressure. Legislating is about building and changing the tension matrix. Legislators, it seems to me, should be part of a body (why not a college of legislators?) that is able to look at the matrix overall. Like lawyers, legislators should surely be properly trained to recognize the interrelationships within a matrix and to understand how these work. This is no longer a function that should be dominated by amateurs.

The departments of government — the organizations charged with delivering specific programs, should function in much the same way as organizations in the private sector. But in place of the discipline of the market place (the market place for capital and the market place for goods), there has to be transparency and accountability. Part of the legislative process needs to include the drawing up of contracts with departments, establishing that department's objectives, its budget, and the timescale over which its activities will be reviewed. In all cases a departmental head should assume responsibility for his or her department's performance in respect of these contracts. Contracts would always be time-limited and only renewable by agreement.

An essential department would be the budget office, or treasury, whose job it would be to ensure that all departmental programs were properly funded. The overarching responsibility of this department would be to ensure that tax receipts and government expenditure balanced in the medium term with a judicious use of borrowing in any downturn, to be redeemed when things were better. Some permanent level of government debt would be appropriate, but to fund capital projects, not expenditure.

Oversight of government programs is clearly essential and my inclination would be to include on oversight committees at least one of the legislators involved in establishing the contract, as well as any citizen who had a particular interest in the program. Naturally all oversight meetings would be open to the public and so to the media.

So far I have not resorted to 'elected representatives' and I have not discussed how priorities would be set. When you think about it, establishing priorities is exactly what the story-building process is about. Priorities define what the matrix is supposed to be achieving. They feed into the moral framework that underpins the matrix and imbues it with whatever potency it has. The way the priority-setting process has evolved is through interested individuals vying with one another to gain the ear of those with the power to set the legislative agenda. The idea of parties is far older than we might imagine. Individuals have always formed groups around shared interests for the purpose of exerting pressure on government policy, and ultimately on government action. There has been a king's party, a queen's party, the parties representing Catholicism versus Protestantism, and parties promoting the interests of landowners, factory owners, workers and gays — wherever there has been a shared interest there has been the basis of a party.

The idea behind democracy was that all those subject to a particular government should have a say in its composition. In this way, it was hoped, its actions would carry moral authority. Eventually adult individuals won the right to vote for a candidate of their own choosing to sit in the legislative body. But just as anyone, in theory, can come up with a perfectly wholesome breakfast cereal, only to find it impossible to get their cereal onto a supermarket shelf, so candidates quickly discovered that they needed to be part of an electoral machine if they were to stand a chance. These electoral machines formed within boundary conditions, defined by some general story — such as more or less government — and marched forth like any branded product.

So the choice the voter has is really between two pre-selected candidates (democracies often end up with two major parties) and two rather vague programs (so as to garner most votes parties attempt to move to the middle ground on issues, while at the same time trying not to alienate their core supporters). In effect, millions of votes (very expensively purchased) largely cancel each other out and the special interest groups, that every part of the matrix employs to get its message to the legislators, are left to influence the general direction that government takes. At best what this system does is detect a shift of opinion in respect of the burning issue of the day, but by and large the matrix and the prevailing story are the winners and things go on largely as before.

We can surely do better. If we stick with two chambers, I see no reason why the upper chamber shouldn't be appointed on the basis of professional legislative competence and the lower chamber be 'open house'. By that I mean it should be open to anyone to champion legislation. Now here's the twist. Internet technology is becoming increasingly sophisticated and it should be perfectly possible to devise a system that allows all of us to put forward changes that we think will help us. These could be aggregated and split into special interest issues and general interest issues. Almost certainly they would be echoed by individuals in the open house.

A system would have to be devised whereby issues were worked up into draft legislation (and costed). If they were of general interest, they would be thrown back for a general vote, or if only of special interest, voted on by those who had registered an interest. It would be the task of the legislative body to keep improving the tension matrix in response to the concerns of the public. Of course there is a legion of technical issues to be addressed here, but the purpose of the exercise is to empower people and make the tension matrix as a whole the object of their attention. This would facilitate change, help individuals to understand the process they are part of far better than they do at present, and greatly improve — I think — the effectiveness of government.

As for elected legislators, my inclination is to do without them. The 'open house' would be just that, a place where those with a strong competent interest in an issue came to garner public support. The evolution of the story would become more interactive in this way and if legislation was put in the hands of professionals who had an obligation to bend the matrix to the public will, the alignment of the matrix to the story would surely be much improved. I think we would still need to be represented by individuals at some level, however, because each of us is an individual and it is as individuals that we make sense of the world. So let every community elect a mayor and each block a president, and give these office-holders the authority to appoint advisors, but otherwise restrict their power to that of the pulpit. This, doubtless, sounds radical, but may be less so than it appears.

* * * *

In large part, ***Notes*** has been about how the matrix makes decisions for us. If you have bought into my argument, then it follows that leaders are not the independent operators we imagine them to be. When the Kennedy administration made the fateful decision to increase America's military involvement in Vietnam, this had little to do with the personal preferences of the President and everything to do with the State Department's collective belief that Communism would spread like a line of falling dominoes and its officials' view that the North Vietnamese were communists before they were nationalists. The tension matrix and its story made the decision and the President endorsed it.

By the same token, I must accept that even a president whose power was restricted to that of the pulpit would be vulnerable to the logic embedded within the tension matrix and prevailing story. But as the elected president of a block (one of the eight), drawn (as seems most likely) from amongst one of the elected community leaders, such a president would be oriented more towards community values (and their morality) than towards the biological values of the thrusting nation state. It would have been interesting to have had from the defense establishment at the time a detailed analysis of why the United States should involve itself in such a faraway place, and how it intended to impose American ideology on the Vietnamese people using bombers and as few ground troops as its advanced weapons of war would allow. And America and her allies are still at it, in Iraq and now Afghanistan.

* * * *

Although only formed as a modern state in 1747, Afghanistan has a rich history. Probably home to Indo-Europeans as long ago as 2000 BC, it has been a centre of Zoroastrianism (1800-800 BC), was a patron of Buddhist culture in 1st century AD and had become the eastern frontier of the Islamic Caliphate by 750. It has been part of Persia, the Greco-Bactrian Kingdom, as well as the Ghaznavid (977-1187), Mogul (1225-1335) and Timurid (1370-1506) Empires. During the 19th century it came under British influence, was invaded by Russia in 1979 and is currently occupied by the United States with Britain as a junior partner. It has experienced every form of government known to man.

Why has this land-locked country (the world's 41st largest), with few natural resources, attracted so much attention? Because it has had the misfortune of being the nexus between numerous competing cultures. To the north, Tajikistan, Turkmenistan and Uzbekistan; to the west, Iran; to the south, Pakistan; and to the east, China. At the height of their empire, British officials incurred sleepless nights worrying that Russia would invade India through it. Now it is American planners who lose sleepless nights and American (and still British) soldiers who lose their lives because this country of 32 million souls, only some 11 million of whom function outside the tribal system, is seen as a hotbed of terrorism and their arch-enemy. If ever there was an example of intersecting boundary conditions of the mind blighting a people, this must be it.[10]

Our tension matrix and its story are leading us badly astray because we have no effective mechanism for changing either, until humiliating and costly defeat — the biological way — does it for us. If we are to build cerebral structure with intent we need to understand its grammar, and then work tirelessly to escape its embedded preconceptions.

* * * *

Thought is the tool by which one makes a choice.[11]

This journey is almost at an end, but I want to leave you with a question. I wonder whether we accept that the biological world which exists on Earth will one day die? As it is with our own individual lives, it is tempting to argue that because the event is so far off it is not worth worrying about, and to conclude that as there is nothing we can do about it anyway, it makes sense to live life to the full regardless of the consequences. That is until consciousness whispers into our ear and tells us, no, that won't quite do.

Conscious life is imbued with a will to survive, a fact to which this book and others like it bear witness. I have argued that up to now we have been in thrall to our biological drivers. It is not that biology is pathologically suicidal, only that biology is not a blind watchmaker but a blind opportunist. Allied to our as yet poorly-formed intelligence, its human form has run rampant. But biology self-corrects according to its own rules. The Maya of the Yucatán Peninsula were forced to abandon their great cities in the 8th century when the farming technologies they

10. *Warlord*, a novel I wrote in 2007, highlights some of the cross-currents that afflict a country in this position. The book was dedicated to Anna Politkovskaya, a contemporary martyr who possessed great courage.

11. From *Atlas Shrugged*, by Ayn Rand (1905–1982). Penguin Books, 2007, p214.

had so skillfully evolved started to suck more from the ground than the ground could consistently produce. Does the same fate await modern man? Certainly, unless we start acting with conscious intent, instead of chasing every opportunity that crosses our path like enthusiastic hounds bamboozled by rabbits.

If we are ever to cut the umbilical cord that ties us to Earth, the first step will probably be a city of 500,000 that orbits it. Please God, not in my lifetime, will be the response of many to such a prospect! A wholly man-made world in which the sole purpose of every individual is to sustain and enhance conscious life. But there would be no walks in the forest. No running down hills and plunging into lakes. No morning birdsong. No deer to come upon, moist-nosed and ears a-twitch, alert to every danger. No wind in our faces nor rain to take shelter from. No moss to stretch out on under the sky. No leaves to catch in October or look forward to in March. No fruits to pick from hedgerows. No trout to catch in streams. No snowflakes. Just each other, our memories and the technological marvel we will have built to sustain us.

Our cities have taken us further along this path than we realize, but we are still a long way from being ready to abandon the biological world. And yet we are engaged in a full-frontal attack against it. It is as if our biological selves and our cerebral selves are locked in a frenzied dance of self-destruction. We need to disengage. If we shift our emphasis towards the construction of self-sustaining communities we will move closer to a kind of future that may come upon us sooner than we expect, while at the same time easing the pressure we have put on the biosphere. This mid-course correction will help to reorient structural morality away from the biological and towards the evolution of the cerebral system state, in which the wonders of our shared consciousness continue to unfold.

Index

C

T

U